THE HOLINESS MANIFESTO

THE HOLINESS MANIFESTO

Edited by

Kevin W. Mannoia and Don Thorsen

WILLIAM B. EERDMANS PUBLISHING COMPANY
GRAND RAPIDS, MICHIGAN / CAMBRIDGE, U.K.

© 2008 Wm. B. Eerdmans Publishing Co.

All rights reserved

Published 2008 by

Wm. B. Eerdmans Publishing Co.

2140 Oak Industrial Drive N.E., Grand Rapids, Michigan 49505 /

P.O. Box 163, Cambridge CB3 9PU U.K.

Printed in the United States of America

12 11 10 09 08   7 6 5 4 3 2 1

Library of Congress Cataloging-in-Publication Data

The holiness manifesto / edited by Kevin W. Mannoia and Don Thorsen.

p.   cm.

ISBN 978-0-8028-6336-2 (pbk.: alk. paper)

1. Holiness — Christianity.   2. Wesleyan Church — Doctrines.

I. Mannoia, Kevin W.   II. Thorsen, Donald A. D.

BT767.H63   2008

270.8′3 — dc22

2008003710

www.eerdmans.com

Contents

v

Contents

Holiness in Historical and Theological Perspective

Holiness in Ministry

Appendixes: Descriptions of Holiness

Contents

HOLINESS IN THE TWENTY-FIRST CENTURY

A Guiding Vision for the Future

KEVIN W. MANNOIA

Many years ago while attending a theological conference on holiness, I heard a statement made at the lunch table that "the Holiness movement has lost its ability to renew itself, and its churches have become merely a repository of historical information." I bristled but did not speak, since I was still a student and overwhelmed by the scholars around me. I did not agree, nor do I today.

A few years ago, in response to a reporter's question, I told a press conference that evangelicals are being called to reintegrate social holiness and personal holiness. Our task is the transformation of hearts and of culture; we are not so much to define the perimeter as to define the center from which our identity proceeds. The block walls of division must give way to picket fences of collaboration in a new day of missional growth toward impacting culture.

Perhaps these comments sound defiant or even arrogant. They are not intended to be. They may not be precise, surgical statements, but at closer inspection of the moves of God across the church they remain accurate. In recent years, we have seen broad discussions seeking truth beyond the "*solas*" of the Protestant Reformation: *sola gratia* (grace alone), *sola fide* (faith alone), *sola scriptura* (Scripture alone).

During the twentieth century the predominant evangelical tactic for public influence proceeded from an enclave attitude, involving political and social efforts to take over and dominate the culture. Yet this propositional strategy of influence by precept has proven ineffective if not counterproductive to Kingdom purposes.

In forming new spiritual leaders for the church in the future, defending the rational side of the gospel by intellectual arguments has given way to a rise in the relational, personal dimensions of truth. This shift is exemplified in a new generation of pastors and upstart churches for whom doctrinal purity is second to the relational nature of faith in Christian community. However, this does not mean there is equivocation at the point of orthodoxy. It is secured in the fact that truth is understood to be a Person. Three pillars sustain the curiosity and the Kingdom thinking of these leaders: the Lordship of Jesus Christ, the authority of Scripture, and the transformation of life. Against this backdrop, conversations are springing up where they never existed before among groups and people who seldom engaged in dialogue.

The principles of integrating social and personal transformation are no longer merely the rhetoric of councils and denominations engaged in turf wars. The old battle lines have become blurred and groups who historically would never have conceded to one or the other are talking similar languages and calling for authentic engagement. People who attacked each other are now humbly learning from one another.

Throughout denominations and new networks of churches alike there is interest in generous, "centered-set" theology. Allowances for grace in context are growing; and a call for the "convertive piety" described by Donald Dayton is coming from unexpected pulpits, as is the message of social responsibility. In truth, the diverse streams of the church are finding common confession that "we believe in right practice along with right belief," in the words of Donald Thorsen.

Those who have adamantly interpreted the church as a force for social influence are coming to a new appreciation for those who have focused their energy on the personal nature of the faith, and vice versa. In the middle of these factions, the Holiness movement, including its Pentecostal stream, has carried in its heritage the commitment to a personal transformation of life that has social and public impact around Kingdom principles consistent with the nature of God.

Before us is a new door requiring a compelling, guiding vision that is theologically rooted and outwardly directed on transformation that is not sectarian, not isolationist, not enclavish, not dogmatic, but integrative, personal, social, apostolic, and missional. That vision is coming as a result of a greater desire for holiness. It requires new terms, new constructs, new voices, new alliances, but old, very old principles. It cannot involve fighting

4

artificial enemies along shadow lines that puff up our institutional existence at another's expense.

This is a discussion regarding the identity and mission of the church for the next generation and beyond. The Wesleyan-Holiness tradition is well equipped to speak into this context and provide a guiding framework for the mission that lies ahead of the church. This is a time for those within that tradition to generously give their heritage, and confidently rise to clear articulation in perfect harmony with the call of God upon the church for the coming decades.

The future of the church will be much more defined by missional and theological streams of thought than it will by the institutional and structural lines often manifested in sectarian or organizational competition. Organizations will morph into networks. Contracts will become partnerships. Negotiated statements will become relationships. In this dynamic and messy environment, the clear voice of God's call to holiness can serve in unprecedented ways for unity and direction.

To that end, the Wesleyan Holiness Study Project was begun in the spring of 2004 after two years of work bringing the initial groups together in commitment to the project. The topic to be explored by the project participants was the mission of the church. In order to achieve the outcomes of the project, academics and church leaders secured the partnership of a number of churches:

Church of the Nazarene
Free Methodist Church
The Salvation Army
Church of God, Anderson
Shield of Faith
Brethren in Christ
Evangelical Friends
Church of God in Christ
International Church of the Foursquare Gospel
Christian and Missionary Alliance
International Pentecostal Holiness

The Wesleyan Holiness Study Project was not intended to be a project centered in an academic institution, but rather one belonging to the church. The desire was to work across denominational lines with theological compatibility in the Wesleyan Holiness tradition in order to learn from one another and to collectively offer the work to the broader church. It provided a way for ecclesiastical support to empower a common issue, rather than simply relegating the matter to an academic effort. The dynamic force of the project is centered in the church, not the academy.

It is the denominations listed above, along with a number of others, that have been most representative of the Wesleyan Holiness movement. Through their participation in the project, they are expressing their interest in and focus on a re-articulation of the Holiness impact on the church. The fastest-growing segments of the church worldwide have roots in this tradition. This book represents the recognition of our collective stewardship of this unique message that has significantly influenced the church and will increasingly impact its global mission.

In the commitment of the various ecclesial leaders of these denominations is the synergy not only of compatibility in a common heritage, but unity in a future mission. At the end of three years, the "Holiness Manifesto" was completed and released as an outcome of the participants' work. This document has become a useful tool for pastors, lay leaders, and denominations in training and development. Likewise the subsequent "Fresh Eyes on Holiness" is a document that gives pastors and church leaders seminal thinking on the issues that lie ahead as we walk together into a future of unity around this message.

Many of the papers written for the project served as the foundation for this edited book, which provides a source for re-elevating the importance of the Holiness message for a new century of mission in the church. It is intended to be a theologically sound and cooperative compilation focused on a timeless message. Although holiness is particularly important for the churches represented in the project, it is relevant and applicable to the broader church. Pastors, priests, and leaders from mainline Protestant, Catholic, Orthodox, evangelical, and new upstart churches will find insight and understanding in these chapters. As the Holiness voice is considered, we hope to be responsible in faithfully carrying our heritage forward in the larger mosaic of the church.

Students and leaders alike will profit greatly from this thoughtful call to holiness given by a diverse group of authors from many denominational backgrounds. In that fact there is also a clear message of unity in mission that is centered in our common heritage and commitment to holiness of life.

It is my hope that this book will assist church leaders and laity with helpful material that meets an increasingly felt need in churches from all traditions.

May God's grace guide us all to deeper intimacy and greater effect in reflecting God's holiness.

The Context: Past and Present

BARRY CALLEN

"Holiness" is a quintessential attribute of God. Its central meaning is separateness from all that is evil, unclean, ordinary; therefore, holiness transcends all that belongs to the finiteness of this passing world. For us humans, holiness is being separate from evil, cleansed from fallenness, elevated to true Christ-likeness and oneness with God. Addressing seriously the subject of biblical holiness is not to be dismissed as merely the preoccupation of emotional revivalists, religious individualists, or narrow-minded legalists. It is the heart of biblical revelation and essential for disciples who desire to be God's faithful and effective people in this world.

Christian holiness is intended by God to be universal in scope and missionary in nature. The point is *participation*. God wants *all people* to be in wholesome relationship with the divine and also to be active citizens of a holy church for the sake of the salvation of a lost world. Those committed to holiness are to conduct themselves in a way that commends faith in the Holy One. The point is to encourage others to see a real-life difference in Christian believers and to be drawn to God's holy grace. 1 Peter 2:12 makes the task clear: "Conduct yourselves honorably among the Gentiles, so that, though they malign you as evildoers, they may see your honorable deeds and glorify God when he comes to judge."

Periodic renewal of a holiness emphasis has been at the heart of numerous Christian movements over the centuries. Doctrinal apostasy, excessive church institutionalization, and/or compromise with prevailing cultures have plagued the Jesus people, and in response, reform movements have sought to reverse such negative trends. They have been influential on the established churches — by either renewing them or finally moving beyond them with something new. Given the centrality of the concern biblically and in all of church history, holiness should be appreciated for its rich past and its potential for meeting the great spiritual needs of the present.

The Biblical Base

The Bible is central in one way or another to all of the numerous traditions of Christianity. Directly or indirectly, the entire Bible addresses the subject of holiness. Basic to all of its witness is the revealed fact that God is holy. Isaiah 6 begins with the seraphs calling to others in heaven, crying out about God: "Holy, holy, holy is the LORD of hosts; the whole earth is full of his glory." We then are told something startling and most demanding. Just as God is holy, so *the people of God are to be holy:* "Like obedient children, do not be conformed to the desires that you formerly had in ignorance. Instead, as he who called you is holy, be holy yourselves in all your conduct; for it is written, 'You shall be holy, for I am holy'" (1 Peter 1:14-16). Biblically speaking, the ultimate goal of a believer's spiritual life is to be holy — separate from the world, cleansed from sin, and elevated to Christ-likeness in being and action.

Holiness, according to the Bible, is defined by the very nature of God as that is understood best in Jesus Christ. Further, the scope of holiness is not restricted to spiritual elites, believers who are especially emotional, or those who hope to escape this world by being radically different and safely disconnected. To the contrary, according to the Bible, holiness is for *all who believe* in the biblical God made known through Jesus Christ and who are willing to be part of what God intends, the redemption of this present world.

The biblical narrative, from its Genesis beginning to its Revelation ending, is about holiness granted, holiness lost, and holiness recovered. This long biblical journey toward a renewed holiness started with a creation in perfect relation to God, and God's intent that it stay that way. The actual circumstance soon changed by human choice and the struggle was on for the elect people of God to somehow again be a cleansed and whole people, holy in relation to a holy God and holy in the midst of a fallen world. God called a people to be his very own, to be like him, to be an instrument of holiness restoration, to be a set-apart people who would bring light to the nations — not more darkness in shallow religious dress.

Sadly, so the biblical story says, this liberated people of God, this people who were no people until God miraculously brought them out of Egyptian slavery, chose to be "like the nations" (1 Sam. 8:20). And how were they like the nations? They had become unholy, i.e., they lived by their own values of strength and self-reliance, not by God's grace and law. God had said that his people "will be a people holy to the Lord your God" (Deut. 26:19). But the people decided to do their own thing like everybody else. By being like the nations in attitudes, in social practices, and even in political organization and military reliance, God's people no longer were being like God, thus not holy.

The sad results of holiness rejected are seen in God's typical accusation against his people. They no longer were available for God's mission in this world. According to the biblical prophets, lack of holiness is usually evidenced in three ways by those supposed to be God's own: (1) there is social injustice quietly sanctioned; (2) there is inordinate trust in the sword — their own money, traditions, talents, and influence; and (3) the people hide behind a life of worship in which God takes no delight, no matter how good it looks, sounds, and even smells.

The earliest Christian movement was successful in its establishment and expansion primarily because the risen Christ pulsated with divine life among the believers, and they chose holiness, i.e., living "in him" (Col. 2:16). Being the holy people of God did not center in formulas of spiritual experience or codebooks of precise dos and don'ts; instead, it centered in *the Spirit of God being present and active through their willing hearts.* Nothing is more likely to draw the unbelieving nations to God than openly living lives that look like Jesus' and are empowered by the Spirit of Jesus.

"Behold, how they love one another!" was an early observation by the world about a holy church that could not be ignored. The dynamic of the church's success was taking seriously Paul's appeal to believers "to present your bodies as a living sacrifice, holy and acceptable to God, which is your spiritual worship" (Rom. 12:1). The goal of the Christian spiritual pilgrimage was and still should be gaining and living in the mind that was in Christ Jesus (Phil. 2:1-11).

Across the Centuries

How are disciples of Jesus to be God's holy people? Answers have varied across the centuries as Christians have sought to be transformed by and represent the Christ in a troubled and constantly changing world. There is no precise holiness prescription affirmed universally by the Christian community. There are, however, certain patterns of conviction and commitment that often have appeared. They are worthy of careful note.

The Roman Catholic Church has a long tradition of emphasis on holiness. Much focus on the subject has come out of this church's monastic tradition, very influential on Christianity as a whole. However, from the time of the earliest martyrs and apologists, Catholic Christians have embodied as well as preached and taught holiness. Almost every manifestation of Catholicism emphasized holiness in its many expressions. Franciscans and Dominicans emphasize holiness through mendicant vows; Carmelites emphasize holiness through contemplative prayer; Jesuits emphasize holiness through missionary and educational work; Marianists emphasize holiness by emulating Mary; and so on. Roman Catholic history is rich with exemplar Christians, whose holiness garnered the honor of being called Saints of the Church.

Also ancient in its Christian roots is the Orthodox Church. Bishop Kallistos Ware represents this long tradition by underlining the Christian's need for *living experience*. For the Orthodox, he observes, "loyalty to Tradition means not primarily the acceptance of formulae or customs from past generations, but rather the ever-new, personal and direct experience of the Holy Spirit *in the present*, here and now."[1] The "mystical" tradition of Christianity would certainly affirm this focus as its own. Directness, immediacy, and life transformation are holiness essentials.

The Anabaptist or "radical" reformation[2] had its roots in sixteenth-century Europe and stressed the following four points as central for the proper, the holy Christian life:

1. Jesus is the norm;
2. The Bible dependably informs believers about Jesus;

1. Bishop Kallistos Ware, *The Orthodox Way*, rev. ed. (Crestwood, N.Y.: St. Vladimir's Seminary Press, 1999), p. 8.

2. For a full treatment of the Anabaptist or Believers Church tradition of Christianity, see Barry L. Callen, *Radical Christianity: The Believers Church Tradition in Christianity's History and Future* (Nappanee, Ind.: Evangel Publishing House, 1999).

3. Commitment to Jesus Christ brings into being a distinctive new community, the church of the Spirit of the Christ;
4. This church is to be in the world in a distinctive, a holy, cross-like way, the Jesus way marked by grace, the life of the Spirit, peace, and self-giving servanthood.

References to "distinctive," "life in the Spirit," and a "self-giving servant-hood" are typical of the Anabaptists and of holiness traditions generally. In the case of the Anabaptist or "Believers Church" tradition, only truly transformed and disciplined believers are considered members of the church. Holiness is viewed as more than individual spiritual experience. The body of Christ itself, the church community, is to be holy. Other Christian renewal movements like the Pietists, who reacted to the formalization of the sixteenth-century Lutheran reformation, have tended to highlight the more individual focus seen in John Bunyan's Puritan classic *The Pilgrim's Progress.* A spiritual plateau finally was reached by the Christian pilgrim. It lay beyond the Valley of the Shadow, out of the reach of the Giant Despair, and out of sight of Doubting Castle. It was a vision of the highland of holiness.

The goal of "going on to perfection" is a persistent stream of prominent concern in all holiness traditions of Christianity. A new creation in Christ "can and clearly should, by God's grace, attain to a holiness that involves having the mind of Christ, with love reigning as the habitual state of the soul because of humble openness to the abiding presence of the Holy Spirit."[3] The claim is that a genuine holiness of heart and life is available to every believer, even in this present life, by way of the sanctifying grace of God.

The taproot of the early Methodist spiritual formation of the eighteenth century lay in the dialectic of salvation by divine grace and disciplined growth of one's spiritual life through faithful participation in the "means of grace" resident in the church. God graciously provides personal and moral transformation and the power to develop "holy habits." The increasingly ingrained holiness (virtue) of Jesus focuses on the "royal law of love," a law that is "governed by the maturity of love rather than the imma-

3. Barry L. Callen, *Authentic Spirituality: Moving Beyond Mere Religion* (Lexington, Ky.: Emeth Press, 2006), p. 148.

turity of binding legalism." It provides "the internal resources to live in that way, instinctively and without reservation."[4]

The holiness tradition greatly impacted the social and religious landscape of Great Britain in the eighteenth century. John Wesley (1703-1791), fountainhead of this particular holiness revival, came to embody key elements of the ancient Orthodox and the more recent mystical, as well as the Roman Catholic and Protestant Reformation traditions combined in his immediate Anglican context. The goal was not to create a new church body or build a new theological system. It was to reintroduce an "optimism of grace" that can transform lives into agents of divine love. Wesley saw God's providence at work in the way Deism was undermining traditional Christianity in his day. He saw a disregard for all religion as paving the way "for the revival of the only religion which was worthy of God!"[5] What is worthy centers in a holy people worshiping a holy God and living holy lives through the power and grace of God's Holy Spirit.

Typical of the many leaders of the Holiness movement in America during the nineteenth century was Phoebe Palmer (1807-1874), who longed for "entire sanctification." A chief mentor of all these leaders was the earlier John Wesley in eighteenth-century England who had called Christians to go on to "Christian perfection." The mainstream of this American Holiness movement emphasized inner cleansing and sinless living by the power of God's Spirit — being "sanctified," "filled with the Spirit," and dominated by the intentions (if not perfections) of love. This movement had its seeds in the 1830s, drew support from persons of many ecclesiastical traditions and denominations, particularly Methodist, and impacted a wide range of social and economic institutions. It took various forms after the Civil War and spawned numerous new church bodies, especially beginning in the 1880s. Without doubt, it altered the religious and social landscapes of the United States.

The active promotion of holiness moved from America back to Great Britain with the founding of the Keswick Convention in 1876. This ongoing "deeper life" movement took on a more Reformed (Calvinistic) coloring than the Arminian-Wesleyan-dominated American movement. Theo-

4. Richard Foster, *Streams of Living Water: Celebrating the Great Traditions of Christian Faith* (San Francisco: HarperSanFrancisco, 1998), p. 7.

5. John Wesley, "Of Former Times," in *The Works of John Wesley*, ed. Thomas Jackson (London: John Mason, 1829-1831), vol. VII, p. 165.

logical coloring aside, many of the central concerns were the same. Soon the Holiness movement spread well beyond North America and Great Britain. Sampling significant books on this subject reviewed by David Bundy and appearing in the *Wesleyan Theological Journal*, one sees a significant Holiness movement in Angola, Barbados, Chile, Colombia, Germany, Japan, Korea, Sweden, and elsewhere. The human heart has cried out for the deeper life in God's Spirit, regardless of century or nation.

By promoting entire sanctification, the Holiness movement of the nineteenth century in the United States helped make possible the rise of Pentecostalism in the early twentieth century. Later in the nineteenth century, various holiness advocates began using the phrase "baptism of [or with] the Holy Spirit" to describe the deeper work of grace or the "second blessing" of "entire sanctification." Some also began to identify "speaking in tongues" as the outward sign of receiving this baptism. This new teaching led to a fracture in the larger Holiness movement and the emergence of still more new churches in the years following the 1906 Azusa Street Revival in Los Angeles, an event generally regarded as the beginning of the modern Pentecostal movement.

Historian Melvin Dieter judges that the nineteenth century "saw the greatest outburst of evangelism and missions activity within Christianity since apostolic times," and also "witnessed an equally unparalleled quest for Christian holiness and a fuller understanding of the work of the Holy Spirit in the individual, the church, and the world."[6] This activity and quest proceeded vigorously into and throughout the twentieth century, as recounted well by Vinson Synan.[7] In fact, the "Pentecostalization" of world Christianity in the twentieth century joins the ecumenical movement as the most significant worldwide trends of this century.

The Pentecostal movement was, in large part, a fresh search for a fuller integrity of life in God's Spirit, a search for a credible holiness that truly transforms lives and advances the Kingdom of God on earth. The number of Pentecostal/charismatic Christians in the world at the end of the twentieth century was about 470,000,000, or about 24 percent of all Christians worldwide. They were present in all established churches, in their own de-

6. Melvin Dieter, *The 19th-Century Holiness Movement* (Kansas City, Mo.: Beacon Hill, 1998), p. 23.

7. Vinson Synan, *The Holiness-Pentecostal Tradition: Charismatic Movements in the Twentieth Century*, 2d ed. (Grand Rapids: Eerdmans, 1997).

nominations, and in nearly every nation, especially in the Americas, Asia, and Africa. This indeed may be a new "Age of the Spirit."

The Holiness Challenge Today

Holiness is about life being transformed by and in God's Spirit. It is about serious believers in Jesus Christ, who they are, who they are intended to be, who they have actually become, and who they might yet be by the grace of God. It is about forming communities of faith that reflect the Spirit of the Christ and are actively about Christ's agenda in the world. God still wants a people who will dare to be his own, trust him, love him, and risk for him, in short, who will be *like God* in character and *with God* as God works redemptively in this world.

Thinking institutionally, there now are several million Holiness adherents in North America, some one hundred colleges and universities with holiness as part of their missions, at least three holiness-oriented seminaries, and two interdenominational and holiness-oriented missionary societies, along with innumerable local associations, camp meetings, and denominational agencies. The numbers are large and the influence very significant in the larger Christian community.

There has never been a time in greater need for a compelling articulation of the message of holiness than today. Christian pastors and other leaders at every level of church life have come to new heights of frustration in seeking ways to revitalize congregations and denominations. Much of what has been going on is not working adequately. Membership in churches of many traditions has flat-lined or declined. The power and health of churches have been drained by the incessant search for a better method, a more effective fad, a newer and bigger program to yield growth. In the process of trying to lead growing, vibrant churches, many pastors have been largely ineffective and fallen prey to a generic Christianity that results in congregations that are indistinguishable from the culture around them. Churches need a clear, compelling message that will replace the "holy grail" of methods as the focus of Christian mission.

Many church leaders are ready to abandon dramatic ministry "success stories" that seem to borrow much from the capitalistic culture around them. What the church needs are humble, broken Isaiahs of God (see Isaiah 6). We do not need more "great" men and women of God, but men and women who really know a great God! No one gets into the Kingdom of God by standing tall, but by the "woe is me" humility that comes when one is face to face with the holy God. The initial and primary preparation for effective Christian ministry is not going to another workshop on new ideas for effective ministry. Believers are to become holy by being filled with a radical amazement about the loving God and God's transforming grace. As Jesus said, we are holy when we humbly pray, "Hallowed be Thy name," and then live in a distinctive way that actually blesses God's name. We can walk with a difference because we have encountered the different God and received his renewing grace.

God's future is today. The Kingdom of God yet to come already has come in Jesus Christ! Today is the day of salvation! The call is less to dream of future utopia, a millennium on earth by and by, and more to exhibit now the fruit of the Spirit, the reign of God made visible in us together as the church. And it is happening! Harvey Cox reported the phenomenon in his book *Fire from Heaven,* announcing

> Nearly three decades ago I wrote a book, *The Secular City,* in which
> I tried to work out a theology for the "post-religious" age that many
> sociologists had confidently assured us was coming. Since then,
> however, religion — or at least some religions — seems to have
> gained a new lease on life. Today it is secularity, not spirituality, that
> may be headed for extinction.[8]

The new lease on life has appeared especially among those seeking the deeper life in God, Christians known variously as holiness, Wesleyans, Pentecostals, and charismatics. Reports Richard Foster: "Today a mighty river of the Spirit is bursting forth from the hearts of women and men, boys and girls. It is a deep river of divine intimacy, a powerful river of holy living, a dancing river of jubilation in the Spirit, and a broad river of un-conditional love for all peoples."[9] Holiness brings life and unity to God's people.

Not only is it happening, but such deeper-life Christians are seeking to overcome classic divisions among them. At the academic level, the Wes-leyan Theological Society and the Society for Pentecostal Studies chose to

8. Harvey Cox, *Fire from Heaven: The Rise of Pentecostal Spirituality and the Reshaping of Religion in the Twentieth-first Century* (Reading, Mass.: Addison-Wesley, 1995), p. xv.
9. Foster, *Streams of Living Water,* p. xv.

meet in joint annual sessions in 1998, 2003, and 2008. The 1998 meeting convened at the Church of God Theological Seminary in Cleveland, Tennessee, around the theme "Purity and Power: Revisioning the Holiness and Pentecostal/Charismatic Movements for the Twenty-First Century." At a more denominational level, the Wesleyan Holiness Study Project met from 2004 to 2007. It consisted of scholars and denominational leaders from a range of Wesleyan and Pentecostal churches who were seeking to reconceive and promote biblical holiness in today's churches. There also has now arisen the Wesleyan Holiness Consortium and a Steering Committee that is guiding a series of programs that arose from the 2004-2007 meetings of the Study Project. These programs are assisting pastors and congregations to newly grasp and creatively implement the holiness vision. The "Holiness Manifesto" emerged from these meetings and highlights for larger audiences the heart of the concern.[10]

People today are hungry for a faith community with a difference, a people who really care, love, and serve, a congregation that is clearly different because it knows and walks with a holy God. As Howard A. Snyder has boldly said, "Perhaps Western culture is nearing a point where the Christian faith can be successfully reintroduced. Maybe the collapse of the present order will lead to a new outbreak of revolutionary [holiness-oriented] Christianity."[11] May it be so!

---

10. See Don Thorsen, "The Holiness Manifesto: An Ecumenical Document," *Wesleyan Theological Journal* 42:2 (Fall 2007).

11. Howard A. Snyder, *The Radical Wesley & Patterns for Church Renewal* (Downers Grove: InterVarsity Press, 1980), preface.

The Holiness Manifesto

WESLEYAN HOLINESS STUDY PROJECT,
AZUSA, CALIFORNIA, FEBRUARY 2006

The Crisis We Face

There has never been a time in greater need of a compelling articulation of the message of holiness. Pastors and church leaders at every level of the church have come to new heights of frustration in seeking ways to revitalize their congregations and denominations. What we are doing is not working. Membership in churches of all traditions has flat-lined. In many cases, churches are declining. We are not even keeping pace with the biological growth rate in North America. The power and health of churches has also been drained by the incessant search for a better method, a more effective fad, a newer and bigger program to yield growth. In the process of trying to lead growing, vibrant churches, our people have become largely ineffective and fallen prey to a generic Christianity that results in congregations that are indistinguishable from the culture around them. Churches need a clear, compelling message that will replace the "holy grail" of methods as the focus of our mission!

Many church leaders have become hostages to the success mentality of numeric and programmatic influence. They have become so concerned about "how" they do church that they have neglected the weightier matter of "what" the church declares. We have inundated the "market" with methodological efforts to grow the church. In the process, many of our leaders have lost the ability to lead. They cannot lead because they have no compelling message to give, no compelling vision of God, no transformational understanding of God's otherness. They know it and long to find the centering power of a message that makes a difference. Now more than ever, they long to soak up a deep understanding of God's call to holiness — transformed living. They want a mission. They want a message!

People all around are looking for a future without possessing a spiritual memory. They beg for a generous and integrative word from Christians that makes sense and makes a difference. If God is going to be relevant to people, we have a responsibility to make it clear to them. We have to shed our obsession with cumbersome language, awkward expectations, and intransigent patterns. What is the core, the center, the essence of God's call? That is our message, and that is our mission!

People in churches are tired of our petty lines of demarcation that artificially create compartments, denominations, and divisions. They are tired of building institutions. They long for a clear, articulate message that transcends institutionalism and in-fighting among followers of Jesus Christ. They are embarrassed by the corporate mentality of churches that defend parts of the gospel as if it were their own. They want to know the unifying power of God that transforms. They want to see the awesomeness of God's holiness that compels us to oneness in which there is a testimony of power. They accept the fact that not all of us will look alike; there will be diversity. But they want to know that churches and leaders believe that we are one — bound by the holy character of God who gives us all life and love. They want a message that is unifying. The only message that can do that comes from the nature of God, who is unity in diversity.

Therefore, in this critical time, we set forth for the church's well being a fresh focus on holiness. In our view, this focus is the heart of Scripture concerning Christian existence for all times — and clearly for our time.

The Message We Have

God is holy and calls us to be a holy people.

God, who is holy, has abundant and steadfast love for us. God's holy love is revealed to us in the life and teachings, death and resurrection of Jesus Christ, our Savior and Lord. God continues to work, giving life, hope, and salvation through the indwelling of the Holy Spirit, drawing us into God's own holy, loving life. God transforms us, delivering us from sin, idolatry, bondage, and self-centeredness to love and serve God, others, and to be stewards of creation. Thus, we are renewed in the image of God as revealed in Jesus Christ.

Apart from God, no one is holy. Holy people are set apart for God's purpose in the world. Empowered by the Holy Spirit, holy people live and love like Jesus Christ. Holiness is both gift and response, renewing and transforming, personal and communal, ethical and missional. The holy people of God follow Jesus Christ in engaging all the cultures of the world and drawing all peoples to God.

Holy people are not legalistic or judgmental. They do not pursue an exclusive, private state of being better than others. Holiness is not flawlessness but the fulfillment of God's intention for us. The pursuit of holiness can never cease because love can never be exhausted.

God wants us to be, think, speak, and act in the world in a Christ-like manner. We invite all to embrace God's call to:

- be filled with all the fullness of God in Jesus Christ — Holy Spirit-endowed co-workers for the reign of God;
- live lives that are devout, pure, and reconciled, thereby being Jesus Christ's agents of transformation in the world;
- live as a faithful covenant people, building accountable community, growing up into Jesus Christ, embodying the spirit of God's law in holy love;
- exercise for the common good an effective array of ministries and callings, according to the diversity of the gifts of the Holy Spirit;
- practice compassionate ministries, solidarity with the poor, advocacy for equality, justice, reconciliation, and peace; and
- care for the earth, God's gift in trust to us, working in faith, hope, and confidence for the healing and care of all creation.

By the grace of God, let us covenant together to be a holy people.

The Action We Take

May this call impel us to rise to this biblical vision of Christian mission:

- Preach the transforming message of holiness;
- Teach the principles of Christ-like love and forgiveness;

- Embody lives that reflect Jesus Christ;
- Lead in engaging with the cultures of the world; and
- Partner with others to multiply its effect for the reconciliation of all things.

For this we live and labor to the glory of God.

Fresh Eyes on Holiness:
Living Out the Holiness Manifesto

WESLEYAN HOLINESS STUDY PROJECT,
28 MARCH 2007

As leaders press forward in living out holiness in their ministry, the following represents themes they will need to consider carefully in future years. We offer this as an invitation to engage together in unity around the transforming message entrusted to our care.

1. Dimensions of Holiness

Holiness has several dimensions. Within each dimension there are contrasting realities. It is important to embrace both elements of each contrast in order to experience and practice holiness in its completeness.

a. *Individual and Corporate:* We are called to be holy persons individually and to be a holy people corporately. The corporate aspect of holiness which is prominent in Scripture needs to be emphasized again in this time and culture.
b. *Christ-centered and Holy Spirit-centered:* The Holy Spirit's work within us leads to conformity to the person of Jesus Christ. Neither should be expressed without the other.
c. *Development and End:* God has an ultimate purpose for each person, which is to be like Jesus Christ. Teaching on development in the Christian life should keep the end of Christ-likeness in view.

d. *Crisis and Process:* A definite work of God's grace in our hearts and our ongoing cooperation to his grace are to be equally emphasized.

e. *Blessings and Suffering:* Full union with Jesus Christ brings many blessings but also a sharing of his sufferings.

f. *Separation and Incarnation:* Holy people are in but not of the world. Holiness requires both separation and redemptive, reconciling, and restorative engagement.

g. *Forms and Essence:* Holiness always expresses itself in particular forms, which are the ways in which it is translated into life and action. But the forms must not be confused with the essence of holiness itself.

How do you balance these contrasting realities in your personal life and ministry? Where do you see the need for greater balance?

2. Essence of Holiness

The essence of holiness is that God is holy and calls us to be a holy people. The challenge is reflecting Jesus Christ in a relevant and contextual way that transcends social location and diversity. Indwelled and empowered by the Holy Spirit, holy people live and love like Jesus Christ. Walking intimately with him overflows in compassion and advocacy for those whom God loves.

How can you effectively embody holiness in the context where you are now, personally and in ministry?

3. Catholicity of Holiness

Although differences have led to fragmentation in churches, holiness invites unity. God wants to heal — to make whole — the brokenness of people, churches, and society. The impact of holiness goes beyond boundaries of tradition, theology, gender, ethnicity, and time to affect people and institutional structures. The resulting healing unites all Christians in wholeness, growing up into Christ-likeness. The message of holiness involves conversation and engagement with others.

What conversations and actions do you need to engage in to bring healing to people, churches, and society?

4. Holiness and Culture

Holiness people, while themselves influenced by culture, must convey the holiness message within multiple cultures. Culture affects the holiness message and churches because we are socially shaped human beings. Culture challenges us to mediate holiness in ways that are relevant and transforming without losing the integrity of the message.

How do we exegete culture and subculture in order to achieve transformation? How might you embody the holiness message in your immediate pastoral setting?

5. Holiness and Community

Individual and corporate holiness require that faith communities pursue organizational structures, processes, and content that promote radical obedience to Jesus Christ. Holiness does not develop in isolation from other believers and faith communities that provide spiritual support and accountability.

What communal structures, processes, and content would help promote radical obedience to Jesus Christ, personally and in ministry?

6. Holiness and Social Concern

Social engagement is an essential incarnational expression of personal and social holiness. It includes ministry among the poor, disenfranchised, and marginalized. Holiness requires a response to the world's deepest and starkest needs. Social engagement is the continuing work of Jesus Christ in and through the church by the Holy Spirit for the world.

Since proclamation of the gospel of Jesus Christ to the poor is essential, how do you embody the continuing personal and social engagement with the disenfranchised and marginalized?

7. Communicating Holiness

Christians live in environments of changing language. They must communicate a holiness message in ways that are clear, relevant, and winsome.

The message of holiness often has been communicated with terms and paradigms that are not understood today.

What terms and paradigms could you use to communicate the holiness message in a compelling way?

HOLINESS IN SCRIPTURE

CHAPTER 1

Goodness and Worship:
A Perspective on Old Testament Holiness

JON HUNTZINGER

The Ubiquity of Holiness

Holiness is ubiquitous in the Old Testament. So common are the references to this divine perfection[1] that the theology of the Old Testament has been described as one of holiness.[2] This ubiquity is evident in the large number of occurrences of the root *qdš* (קדשׁ) in the Pentateuch, prophets, and worship literature. The root occurs almost 850 times and is most common in the first five books of Moses, especially Leviticus (152 times), Exodus (102), and Numbers (80), as well as in the prophets Ezekiel (105) and Isaiah (73). Of the remaining books of the Old Testament, the book of Psalms uses the noun form of the root sixty-five times.[3]

Of course, each of these books gives special attention to the worship of the people at various times in their history: the Pentateuch describes the means by which a covenantal relationship with God is established and

---

1. Colin Gunton believes the term "perfection" is preferable to "attribute" for describing aspects of God's character (even though he himself uses "attribute") because it better connotes the revelatory dimension of what may be known about God by people. See *Act and Being: Towards a Theology of the Divine Attributes* (Grand Rapids: Eerdmans, 2003), p. 9.

2. See Walther Eichrodt, *Theology of the Old Testament,* trans. John Baker (Philadelphia: Westminster Press, 1961), vol. 1, p. 270.

3. Information gathered from Francis Anderson and Dean Forbes, *The Vocabulary of the Old Testament* (Rome: Editrice Pontificio Istituto Biblico, 1992) and from the *Theological Dictionary of the Old Testament.*

maintained by Israel — Exodus not only describes the deliverance of the people from servitude, but it records the building of the tabernacle and its furnishings and the preparation of the priests for service there (chapters 26–40); Leviticus describes the nature of sacrificial worship in the tabernacle and the priesthood that will perform this worship, and clearly shows that all of life is defined in terms of holiness[4] — and the prophets like Isaiah and Ezekiel urge the people to return to a covenantal relationship with God as they anticipate a future in which they will worship him and enjoy his abundance.

Ezekiel is a priest in exile who understands more poignantly than others the link between incompetent worship and judgment as he sees in a vision the glory of God leave the temple (Ezekiel 8), and Isaiah is a prophet for whom worship becomes a transformative event that leads to recognition of God's holy nature and his own neediness: "Woe is me! For I am lost; for I am a man of unclean lips, and I dwell in the midst of a people of unclean lips; for my eyes have seen the King, the LORD of hosts!" (Isa. 6:5).[5] This Lord of hosts is thrice holy and fills the earth with his glory (6:3). Much of the Old Testament story is about holiness and this holiness is often linked to the notion of worship.

Holiness in the Beginning

The first chapter of Genesis presents God's creation as good. Seven times the biblical writer uses the word *ṭôḇ* (טוֹב) to describe the result of God's word (vv. 4, 10, 12, 18, 21, 25, 31). The seventh time the writer gives emphasis to the goodness of the whole work of creation by declaring it to be *ṭôḇ mě'ōḏ* (very good). The creation is good in that it is (1) necessarily what is beneficial to humanity and (2) representative of God's nature.

That the world is perfectly designed to support and maintain human life is apparent to most people. The scientific community recognizes this fact and refers to it as the anthropic principle. This principle asserts that the physical universe is exactly what it must be for human life to exist.[6]

---

4. See Gordon Wenham, *The Book of Leviticus*, NICOT (Grand Rapids: Eerdmans, 1979), pp. 18-25.

5. English translations are taken from the ESV.

6. There are various permutations of this principle, some of which distinctly discount any divine origin for the universe. See Hugh Ross's discussion in his chapter, "A 'Just Right'

That the creation reveals God to be good and moral in his activities also is apparent. This is not all that it reveals about him, however. This goodness speaks of God's holiness. As Abraham Heschel has observed, "To the Bible the idea of the good is penultimate; it cannot exist without the holy. The holy is the essence, the good is its expression."[7] From this perspective, the good creation of God reveals his holiness. A holy God created in the beginning, forming with his word a world perfectly designed to sustain the life of the man who was made in his image and perfectly designed to reveal his holy nature.

Interestingly, it is in the midst of this *good* creation that God plants a garden *(gan)* where he sets the man after making him a living being. What is the significance of the garden? First, since *gan* (גַּן) is elsewhere used of an enclosed area where flowers and vegetables are grown, its planting indicates a place of peace and provision. For example, it is used in Isaiah to describe a future place that will resemble Eden where all people will know God and experience his provision (51:3). Second, it also refers to the royal garden of the king; a special place reserved for him and his family (2 Kings 21:18, 26; 25:24; Jer. 39:5; 52:7; Neh. 3:15).

Finally, according to Genesis 2–3, the garden is where the man will exercise responsibility before God, find fulfillment in another, and experience God's presence. The cultivation of a garden within the creation is evidence that God has a specific purpose for the man. What is this purpose? The language of 2:15 suggests that it is to worship in the manner of a priest. Though most English translations describe the man's responsibilities as involving "work," the Hebrew roots *'bd* (עבד) and *šmr* (שמר) speak of service and devotion.[8] God's holy ambition, then, is for the man to live in the garden, worship him, and enjoy his divine provision.[9]

The man and woman are forced from the garden for disregarding

---

Universe," in *The Creator and the Cosmos: How the Latest Scientific Discoveries Reveal God,* 3d ed. (Colorado Springs: NavPress, 2001), pp. 145-67.

7. *God in Search of Man: A Philosophy of Judaism* (New York: Farrar, Straus and Giroux, 1955), p. 16. This recalls John Wesley's observation that "holiness is covered glory, and glory is uncovered holiness" (*Explanatory Notes on the New Testament,* Rev. 4:8).

8. In particular, the verb *'ābad* most often means "serve" when found in the Qal stem in the books of Genesis and Exodus.

9. John Sailhamer writes, "The man is put in the Garden to worship God and obey him. The man's life in the Garden was to be characterized by worship and obedience; he was to be a priest, not merely a worker and keeper of the Garden." *The Pentateuch as Narrative* (Grand Rapids: Zondervan, 1992), p. 101.

God's command and, according to the structure of the biblical narrative, undertake a journey eastward away from there. Throughout the early chapters of Genesis people move eastward *(miqedem)*, farther and farther away from the garden (3:24; 11:2; 13:11). This journey represents a move away from the place of God's purpose, provision, and presence. It is a move away from the place of a holy God. In that God is the absolute subject of his own creation, the movement of the man in the Genesis passages from the garden is a move away from God himself.

This story of beginnings, then, speaks of a holy God's particular intention for humanity to worship him within historical time and space, and the separation of humanity from God's holiness. It serves as a definitive introduction for the Old Testament story of the holy God who is active in bringing humanity back to an original place of worship of him.

A Definition of Holiness

At this point it is appropriate to ask: what is the Old Testament conception of holiness? Different answers have been given to this question. Most agree that holiness is separation from everything that is common or mundane: "The holy is that which is separate from the profane, the impure, the ordinary."[10]

Anthropologist Mary Douglas, in her study of the dietary laws of Leviticus, says that holiness is separation and wholeness: "We conclude that holiness is exemplified by completeness. Holiness requires that individuals shall conform to the class to which they belong. . . . Holiness means keeping distinct the categories of creation."[11] Another answer is given by theologian Rudolph Otto, who says that Old Testament holiness is otherness or mystery that engenders a profound sense of awe. It is the numinous that elicits emotional, non-rational response from people.[12] So holiness is variously viewed as separation, wholeness, and otherness.[13]

---

10. Michael D. Coogan, *The Old Testament: A Historical and Literary Introduction to the Hebrew Scriptures* (Oxford: Oxford University Press, 2006), p. 146.

11. *Purity and Danger* (London: Routledge Classics, 2002), p. 67.

12. *The Idea of the Holy* (Oxford: Oxford University Press, 1950), pp. 5-24, 72-80. Jürgen Moltmann says, along this line, "Before the Holy we stand before something Wholly Other, something alien to us which alienates us from the world. The holy is the inviolable." See *The Source of Life: The Holy Spirit and the Theology of Life* (Minneapolis: Fortress Press, 1997), p. 44.

13. Another way to conceive biblical holiness is in terms of fairness. For John Wesley the

A complementary view of Old Testament holiness that draws upon the discussion of Genesis above understands it in terms of divine goodness. In this approach, holiness is *that state or relationship of goodness that is in equipoise with the purpose of God and is reflective of his presence.* All things are good in the beginning in that they reflect the personal will of the Creator. Within this good creation a garden is planted where the man participates in the Creator's purpose and lives in his presence. Douglas's remark quoted above deserves to be repeated: "Holiness means keeping distinct the categories of creation."[14] This original state of divine purpose and relationship should be seen as a primary aspect of the Old Testament's conception of holiness.

Deliverance and Holiness

In that the man moves eastward of the place of God's purpose, provision, and presence, the Old Testament story is largely a recounting of the return of humanity to God. This return centers on God, who is consistently seen by the biblical writers as holy because of his works.[15]

God's works, beginning with the creation of heaven and earth and continuing through the deliverance of the Hebrew people from Egypt and later from exile, as well as the making of a covenant and the giving of the law, are described by the biblical writers as good. It is through these works that God manifests his holiness to Israel as well as to the nations. Colin Gunton writes, "Holiness . . . is both action and attribute, both relative and absolute. . . ."[16] Deliverance signifies a return to the good and holy place of

---

notion of justice most accurately describes God's holiness and is displayed in the fair manner in which he engages sinful humanity. See Randy Maddox, *Responsible Grace: John Wesley's Practical Theology* (Nashville: Kingswood Books, 1994), p. 53.

14. Douglas, *Purity and Danger*, p. 67.

15. Of course, the biblical writers regard God as holy by nature. As Gordon Wenham says, "Holiness characterizes God himself and all that belongs to him. . . . Holiness is intrinsic to his character" (p. 22).

16. *Act and Being*, pp. 24-25. The notion of being and doing is central to John Wesley's moral theology, according to D. Stephen Long, and is especially developed in his teachings on the Sermon on the Mount. Long summarizes, "The life of virtue and the life of Jesus collapse into one in Wesley's moral theology. Ethics and doctrine, goodness and God cannot be finally divided. Jesus himself is 'the new law of the Gospel.'" *John Wesley's Moral Theology: The Quest for God and Goodness* (Nashville: Kingswood Books, 2005), p. 170.

original relationship with God and the covenant the means by which this relationship will be experienced. Since the creation account has already been discussed above, examples of God's holiness in deliverance and covenant-making will be discussed below.

God shows his holiness in the story of the Exodus and the return from Babylonian exile. With respect to the Exodus, God takes the initiative when he appears to Moses in the wilderness and through a dramatic series of events liberates the people from the rule of Pharaoh.[17] A summary of the Sea of Reeds deliverance is found in the Song of Moses (Exod. 15:1-18), in which God is praised for his power. Specifically, God's act of deliverance is "majestic in holiness" *(ne'dār baqōdeš)*. It is a phrase that is parallel in the song to "glorious deeds" and to "doing wonders." God's holiness is manifested in the deeds and wonders that he has done as he leads the people to his holy dwelling *(nĕwēh qoḏšekā)* to plant them on his holy mountain (vv. 13, 17). It is an act without analogy and reveals him to be the holy God.

Before the people enter the land of promise, however, Moses exhorts them to keep God's commands because he has delivered them from Egypt and, in doing so, has revealed his intention "to do you good *(lĕhêtiḇka)* to the end" (8:16). Moreover, it is God's intention to establish the people in a *ṭôḇ* land (Exod. 3:8; Deut. 1:25; 3:25; 4:21-22; 6:18; Ps. 85:12; Ezek. 34:14, 18). Doing good for the people by leading them to a good land reflects the holy nature of God.

In the same way that God manifests his holiness in the Exodus, so he reveals it when he leads the people back to the land from Babylon. Ezekiel prophesies that God will manifest his holiness in Zion among the people once they are in the land where they will worship him and provide a witness to the nations:

> For on my holy mountain . . . there all the house of Israel, all of them, shall serve me in the land. There I will accept them, and there I will require your contributions and the choicest of your gifts, with all your sacred offerings. As a pleasing aroma I will accept you, when I bring you out from the peoples and gather you out of the

17. Brevard Childs writes, "The God of the Old Testament consistently takes the initiative in his pursuit of mankind" for the purpose of revealing his nature. *Old Testament Theology in a Canonical Context* (Philadelphia: Fortress Press, 1985), p. 41.

countries where you have been scattered. And I will manifest my holiness *(niqdaštî)* among you in the sight of the nations. (20:40-41)

Finally, in the well-known psalm of God's word, Psalm 119, the psalmist declares, "Your rules are good" and represent an alternative to a life of reproach (v. 39). God's commandments provide good judgment and knowledge (v. 66) and his statutes reveal the goodness of God's being and that of his works (v. 68). God's word — rules, commandments, and statutes *(mišpāṭim, miẓwôṯ, ḥōqim)* — is good, allows for good judgment, and reveals the good nature of God. It is this good word that serves as the divine design for the people to live a holy life before God.

Worship and Holiness

Not only does God reveal his holiness through creation and acts of deliverance, but he makes his people holy as a result of such acts. Jürgen Moltmann remarks, "God sanctifies the people of Israel by freeing it from its enslavement in the country of the Pharaohs, with its many gods, and by accompanying Israel into the promised land of liberty."[18]

God's efforts to make his people holy give rise to the command of holiness: "Be holy because I am holy" (Lev. 11:45; 19:2; 20:26; 21:8, 15, 23). Here holiness is expressed as a requirement both in response to what God has done as well as in anticipation of what he plans to do through his people. What is this plan? The answer is found at Sinai.

The biblical narrative in Exodus 19-20 describes the appearance of God to Moses and a *prepared* people *(qidaštām)* to speak the words of his covenant *(kol-haḏebarîm hā'ēleh)*, known as the Ten Commandments (20:1-17), so they may serve as a kingdom of priests *(mamleḵeṯ kōhănîm)* and be a holy nation *(gôy qāḏôš)*. (See 19:5-6.) The words that God gives to Moses are given not only that they may live in a covenant relationship with him, but that they may also lead the nations in the worship of him as a kingdom of priests just as he intended the man to be a priest in the garden in the beginning.[19]

---

18. Moltmann, *The Source of Life*, p. 46.

19. Heschel says that the idea of a holy people, and not simply holy individuals, is unique. "The idea of the holiness of an entire people, Israel as a holy people, is without parallel in human history. . . . Only extraordinary, supernatural events in the life of all of Israel would have made the usage of the term 'a holy people' possible." *God in Search of Man*, p. 245.

Thus, fidelity to these words in the rituals of the tabernacle (and temple) as well as in daily life (outlined in passages such as the Holiness Code in Leviticus 17–26) was the essential manner in which the people lived in the presence of God in worship and, too, led others in worship of him.[20] Heschel is helpful once again when he says that the people of God obeyed the commandments of the covenant in "the conviction that acts of goodness reflect the hidden light of His holiness."[21] Living according to these words of God constituted "acts of goodness" by the people and represented the way by which God's holiness was made known in the community as well as displayed to those outside of it.

A World of Holiness

Throughout the biblical period, the people conceived their world of time and space in terms of holiness. Time was viewed as holy as people gave uninterrupted attention to God (Exod. 20:8-9; Deut. 5:12-13; see Gen. 2:3; Exod. 20:11). The Sabbath and special festivals (Passover, Pentecost, and Tabernacles) were distinguished from other days and times as the people fulfilled his purpose through worship and enjoyed his provision.

Space also was viewed as holy as people believed the holy of holies in the tabernacle, and later the temple, to be the center of God's creation. From this axis, specific areas were designated as more or less holy from others where people could experience God's presence and participate in his purpose in greater or lesser ways.[22]

This conception of the world is linked to the story of creation and the original good work of God described above. By viewing one place as more special than another, for example, the people simply recalled the delineation of space when God planted a garden in his good creation.

By dividing time into days of work and the Sabbath the people drew upon the differentiation of time when the man participated in God's purpose in the garden (by naming the animals; Gen. 2:19-20) and seemingly

20. The most important aspect of worship among the ancient Hebrews was sacrifice. See Raymond B. Dillard and Tremper Longman III, *An Introduction to the Old Testament* (Grand Rapids: Zondervan, 1994), p. 76.

21. Heschel, *God in Search of Man*, p. 290.

22. For a pictorial depiction of degrees of holiness in relation to time and space, see Coogan, *The Old Testament*, p. 147.

enjoyed his personal presence (3:7). The spheres of holiness which the Hebrew people conceived for their everyday lives thus recalled the creation account when God stood the man in a place of purpose, provision, and presence to worship.

Conclusion

The passages above show that the biblical writers did not think that God had removed himself from the realm of humanity. He was not distant in holiness. Rather, he was near in his holiness through deliverance as well as in the giving of the law of the covenant. The Old Testament view of God's holiness is found in his work as Creator, Deliverer, and Covenant-maker. As Creator, God provides a revelation of his holiness through his good creation; as Deliverer, God shows his holiness by leading the people out of a hard land of slavery into a good land of provision ("flowing with milk and honey"; Exod. 3:8, 17); as Covenant-maker, he gives his words to the people so they may live as a holy community and fulfill their calling as priests through worship. In other words, throughout the Old Testament God is depicted as bringing his people into a relationship of goodness with himself so that they might fulfill his purpose for them. This is Old Testament holiness.

Such an understanding of holiness anticipates the ministry of Jesus recorded in the New Testament. As one endowed with the Spirit of God, Jesus goes about doing good (Acts 10:38) and initiates a return to God through word and deed. In this way he leads people into the sphere of God's purpose, provision, and presence, which he names the kingdom of God. The prayer he teaches the disciples underscores the importance of Old Testament holiness in his own thinking: "Our Father in heaven, hallowed be your name. Your kingdom come, your will be done . . ." (Matt. 6:9-10).

CHAPTER 2

Holiness in New Testament Perspective

KENNETH L. WATERS SR.

Purity of Heart and Mind

If we may speak first in accordance with common English practice and use the metaphors "heart" for the emotional or affective self and "mind" for the rational or cognitive self, then "purity of heart and mind" would be a straightforward and familiar way of describing human holiness in the New Testament. In this case, "purity" would mean the absence of base impulses or emotions — such as lust, greed, anger, hate, envy, and jealousy — that drive human beings toward egotism, arrogance, dishonesty, excessive indulgence in bodily pleasure, depravity, and violence; but purity would also mean the *presence* of summit attitudes and aspirations, such as love, generosity, kindness, self-control, humility, and mercy that propel human beings toward justice, service, self-sacrifice, heroism, and peace-making.[1] Holiness understood as this kind of inward purity is central in the thought of Paul the Apostle and other New Testament authors.

When Paul, for instance, addresses one congregation he states that his reason for being in mission to them is "to establish your hearts blameless in holiness before our God and Father" (1 Thess. 3:13). Paul moreover de-

---

1. David A. deSilva, *New Testament Themes* (St. Louis: Chalice Press, 2001), p. 44. deSilva calls attention to a "wholly ethical view of pollution and purity" in the teachings of Jesus in which "mirroring God's holiness as purity of heart" and separation from corrupting attitudes and behaviors replace the rules governing ethnic separation in the Old Testament.

clares to this same congregation that God did not call us to impurity, but to holiness (1 Thess. 4:7). Here we see the emergence of themes that fix holiness in the heart, and justify "purity of heart" as an equivalent term. It is clear that in this part of Paul's discourse holiness also means the exercise of self-control, rejection of carnality, and fairness to others (1 Thess. 4:3-6). In other writing, Paul equates "perfecting holiness in the fear of God" to "cleansing ourselves of defilement of the flesh and spirit" (2 Cor. 7:1). In a Pastoral Epistle, "a pure heart" or "a clean heart" is the fount of love, righteousness, faith, peace, and a good conscience (1 Tim. 1:5; 2:22).[2] On this point we can compare another apostolic tradition that assigns the origin of "brotherly love" to a "pure heart" (1 Peter 1:22), and yet another that charges the "double-minded" with the words "purify your hearts" (James 4:8). Concerning those who are saved regardless of ethnic origin, it is said that the Holy Spirit "cleansed their hearts by faith" (Acts 15:9). In the Gospels we learn that the "purity of heart" theme originates in Christian tradition with Jesus who said, "Blessed are the pure in heart for they shall see God" (Matt. 5:8).[3]

We return to Paul the Apostle for themes that fix holiness in the mind. In his most weighty treatise he gives us a contrast between the mind set on the flesh and the mind set on the spirit (Rom. 8:6-7), and then finally urges his hearers with the words, "be transformed by the renewing of your mind" (Rom. 12:2).[4] In another letter the theme of holiness as "purity of mind" is strongly expressed in the words, "whatever is true, whatever is honorable, whatever is just, whatever is pure, whatever is lovely, whatever is reputable, if there is any virtue and praise, think upon these things" (Phil. 4:8-9).

We must acknowledge, however, that Paul and other New Testament authors may not be strict in their use of the metaphors "heart" and "mind." Either word could refer to the affective or cognitive self, or to both

---

2. The state of debate prevents us from casually assuming actual Pauline authorship for the Pastorals and other disputed Pauline Epistles. I will therefore hold this issue in suspense until space can be devoted to its discussion.

3. Cf. W. T. Purkiser, *The Biblical Foundations,* Exploring Christian Holiness 1 (Kansas City, Mo.: Beacon Hill, 1983), pp. 81-82. Purkiser refuses to restrict the possibility of "heart purity" to "a future Kingdom Age." He sees this and all the other qualities of the beatitudes as obtainable in the "here and now."

4. Purkiser, *Biblical Foundations,* pp. 146-48, 153. Purkiser refers to Romans 12:2 as "the positive outcome of consecration" which is "deep inner renewal."

at the same time. When Paul declares that the peace of God which surpasses all understanding will guard our "hearts and minds" in Christ Jesus (Phil. 4:7), it is not clear that he is referring to altogether distinct aspects of the inner self. It is clear, however, that Paul is able to use "heart" and "mind" interchangeably as he does when he equates those whose "minds were hardened" to those who have a "veil lying on their heart" (2 Cor. 3:14-15). In the Gospel tradition, heart, mind, soul, and strength are at the very least closely related in Jesus' love command (Matt. 22:37; Mark 12:30; Luke 10:27), although appearing to denote separate aspects of the human self. Despite this ambiguity in kerygmatic and apostolic language regarding the heart and mind, the emphasis on inward purity remains in the New Testament message of holiness.

Holiness as Inward and Outward

Actually, holiness has a dual character in earliest Christianity. Although holiness is a quality of the soul, an inward quality, it is nevertheless outwardly manifested in the pattern of human response and behavior, lifestyle, relationships, missional activity and vocational commitments. Holiness and outward righteousness are parallel in the Christian Scriptures (Luke 1:75; Eph. 4:24). It is especially in Pauline tradition where we see "true righteousness and holiness" laid out in terms of human response and behavior (Eph. 4:24-32). Paul, however, draws such a close connection between holiness and lifestyle that he conceives of holiness as the fruit of righteousness (Rom. 6:19-22). Under the banner of presenting our bodies as "living sacrifices, holy and acceptable to God" (Rom. 12:1), Paul lists a number of responses that illustrate vocation and mission (Rom. 12:7-8), and lifestyle, behavior, and relationships (Rom. 19:9-21). In Paul's thought, the works of the flesh include "impurity" and other evils both inward and directed toward others; in contrast, the fruit of the Spirit includes "love," "kindness," "generosity," and other boons both inward and directed toward others (Gal. 5:19-23).

Paul's language leaves no doubt that he is contrasting "unholy" and "holy" lifestyles even though he does not use these specific terms. Our case is only strengthened when the term "holy" is nevertheless included in similar language used elsewhere in the Pauline Letters. "As God's chosen ones, holy and beloved, clothe yourselves with compassion, kindness, humility, meekness, and patience. . . . Above all clothe yourself with love" (Col. 3:12-14). Because of self-evident outwardly-active and other directed terms such as "compassion" and "kindness," it is not at all difficult to see that holiness in New Testament perspective is more than inward piety. In this case, as elsewhere, it is also clear that Paul and Pauline tradition see holiness as inseparable, or better, indistinguishable, from "love," particularly love demonstrated through outward acts of kindness, compassion, and support (Rom. 12:9; 13:8-10; 1 Cor. 13:1-8; Eph. 1:4; 5:2). When we visit other apostolic traditions we see that holiness is especially manifested as a response to the needs of others, even though the terms "holy" and "holiness" are not specifically used. As a clear expression of holiness we are told that "religion that is pure and undefiled, is this: to care for orphans and widows in their distress, and to keep oneself unstained by the world" (James 1:27, NRSV). We must therefore refer to apostolic holiness as more than a character trait or virtue. It is also human response to the needs of others. Holiness is both inward and outward.

Earlier, we noted that New Testament holiness involves not only the absence of base character traits but also the presence of summit character attributes. This calls attention to a dual aspect of New Testament holiness. Therefore, when we describe holiness as both inward and outward we are acknowledging a second duality in how holiness is understood in the New Testament.

Holiness as Holistic and Singular

A third level of duality also appears in the New Testament theme of holiness. Rather than being presented as one virtue among others, holiness is shown to be holistic, that is to say, it is attested as an overarching good, the sum and source of all other virtues, and that which describes both the body and spirit. On the other hand, holiness is singular, that is to say, one virtue among others, inseparably bound and complementary to the others, but yet distinct in its own right.

Paul speaks holistically of holiness when he exhorts believers to present their whole selves as "a living sacrifice, holy and acceptable to God" (Rom. 12:1). He implies that holiness should characterize the whole self and not just one aspect of the self. Paul continues to speak along these lines when he supports the aspirations of unmarried women and virgins to be "holy in body and spirit" (1 Cor. 7:34), which he evidently sees as an achievable goal. Paul also warns against immorality with a statement that reflects a holistic understanding of holiness. "For God's temple is holy, and you are that temple" (1 Cor. 3:17). In other Pauline tradition, God elects "us" in Christ to be "holy and blameless before him in love" (Eph. 1:4). Moreover, those who are reconciled to God through the death of Christ are presented to him "holy and blameless and irreproachable" (Col. 1:22). In each case, holiness is assigned to the whole self. When we return to an earlier reference, we see that holiness is not just one virtue beside others, but the very foundation of compassion, kindness, and other virtues (Col. 3:12-14).

Yet holiness can still be singled out as one virtue among others, such as when it is listed in a series with faith, love, and temperance as the *children* of those who will be saved (1 Tim. 2:15);[5] or listed with hospitality, uprightness, self-control, and other virtues as qualifications for bishops (Titus 1:8).

Holiness as Corporate and Individual

We can discern a fourth duality in the Christian doctrine of holiness — the corporate and individual nature of holiness. When Christian Scripture treats holiness as a corporate calling, it indicates that it is the people of God as a whole that is summoned to holiness, whether they be understood as Israel or the church. Apostolic tradition preserves the most forceful expression of this perspective with "you are a chosen race, a royal priesthood, a holy nation, God's own people" (1 Peter 2:9; cf. Exod. 19:6). Here we also see convergence between the themes of holiness and election. We have sufficient convergence of these themes to establish that to be holy is to be elect and vice versa, whether we are speaking corporately or individually (Rom. 11:5, 7, 28; Col. 3:12).

In one of his most enigmatic metaphorical pronouncements, Paul assigns holiness to a series of collectives: "and if the first-fruit is holy, so is the lump, and if the lump is holy, so are the branches" (Rom. 11:16). Close

---

5. This alludes to a new interpretation of "childbearing" in 1 Timothy 2:15. For a more detailed and extensive discussion, see Kenneth L. Waters Sr., "Saved through Childbearing: Virtues as Children in 1 Timothy 2:11-15," *Journal of Biblical Literature* 123:4 (Winter 2004): 703-35.

attention to the larger context of Paul's discourse shows us that the "first-fruit" refers to the "remnant," or more plainly, Jewish believers in Jesus Christ, while the "lump" can only be the whole of ethnic Israel. Somehow, the whole of ethnic Israel is sanctified or made holy by their relationship to those of their kin who like Paul became believers in Jesus Christ. When Paul speaks of the branches he is referring only to a segment of Israel, which he will later call the "hardened rest." By virtue of their membership in whole Israel, the hardened rest are still elect, and also still holy. This corporate view of holiness is typical of Paul's Hebrew background and heritage.

Paul also speaks of corporate holiness in reference to Gentile believers in Christ. He particularly refers to "the offering of the Gentiles" who are sanctified or made holy by the Holy Spirit (Rom. 15:16). In other places in the Pauline corpus "the household of God" is referred to as "a holy temple" (Eph. 2:19), and the church as the bride of Christ is "sanctified" by Christ and "cleansed" by "the washing of water with the word" and made "holy and without blemish" so that she may be both presented and received by Christ (Eph. 5:26-27). These are themes of corporate holiness.

Most of the New Testament is an address to a collective, the people as a whole. This is more clearly seen in the Greek text, where we find a distinctive plural form of both the second-person verb (*-esthe* stem) and the pronoun "you" *(hymas, hymon)* in most second-person expressions (e.g., Matt. 5:20; Rom. 12:1; 1 Cor. 6:11, 19; 1 Thess. 1:4; 1 Peter 1:15-16).

We therefore know that Petrine tradition speaks to the whole church as obedient children when urging them to "be holy yourselves in all your conduct," and again when evoking God's word in Leviticus 11:44-45, "you shall be holy, for I am holy" (1 Peter 1:15-16).

Individuals are said to be holy only as they share in the life of a holy people. In this way, individuals are "partakers" in the heavenly calling (Heb. 3:1). Even in the apocalypse, there will be individuals "blessed and holy" because they share in a collective called "the first resurrection" (Rev. 20:6). When the angelic messenger says let the "holy still be holy" (Rev. 22:11), the implication is that this can only be done through continued participation in that community that has washed their robes and made them white in the blood of the lamb (Rev. 7:14; 22:14).

However, there are places where the emphasis is inverted. Holiness is primarily the calling of individuals, and the church is holy because of its individual members (2 Tim. 2:20-22). In the apostolic preaching, Gentiles are "no longer strangers and sojourners." They are now "fellow citizens with the saints and members of the household of God" (Eph. 2:19-20). This is a corporate address, but the speaker has not lost sight of the individual. When he maintains that salvation is by grace through faith and not by works, "lest any man should boast" (Eph. 2:9), we have a brief overture to the individual. As individual members of the household of God, believers are "built upon the foundation of the apostles and prophets, Christ Jesus being the cornerstone, in whom the whole structure is joined together and grows into a holy temple in the Lord" (Eph. 2:20-21). We perceive that the church can grow into a holy temple only because holy members are being added to it. They are, after all, called "saints" and "fellow citizens with the saints" (Eph. 1:1; 2:19; 5:3).

Individual holiness is also in view "in a great house" where "there are not only vessels of gold and silver but also of wood and earthenware, and some for noble use, some for ignoble" (2 Tim. 2:20). Regardless of whether an individual is likened to a vessel of gold, silver, wood, or clay, "if any one purifies himself from what is ignoble, then he will be a vessel for noble use, consecrated and useful to the master of the house, ready for any good work" (2 Tim. 2:21). If "the great house" refers to the church, then its purity or holiness derives from those who individually offer themselves as purified vessels of the Lord. Holiness in earliest Christian thought is both corporate and individual.

Holiness as Process, Goal, and Possession

We are finally drawn to what appears to be a fifth complexity in New Testament holiness doctrine, but it cannot be called another duality because now it involves holiness in *three* modes — present process, future goal, and present possession. Holiness in earliest Christianity appears as a process frequently referred to as sanctification (Rom. 6:22; 1 Cor. 1:30; 1 Thess. 4:3-4; 2 Thess. 2:13; 1 Peter 1:2). Even though there are numerous occasions when sanctification appears to be a completed process or present possession for the believer (1 Cor. 1:2, 30; 6:11; 7:14; 1 Peter 1:2; Heb. 10:10, 14), there are instances where entire sanctification seems to be a process that continues until the coming of the Lord. "May the God of peace himself sanctify you entirely; and may your spirit and soul and body be kept sound and blameless at the coming of our Lord Jesus Christ. The one who calls you is faithful, and he will do this" (1 Thess. 5:23-24). Another verse is similar: "as you await the revealing of our Lord Jesus Christ who will keep you until the end blameless in the day of our Lord Jesus Christ" (1 Cor. 1:8).

These are Paul's words, but in the context of the New Testament, the idea expressed does not stand without support. In the Johannine tradition, it is acknowledged that as God's children, "what we will be has not yet been revealed. What we know is this: when he is revealed, we will be like him, for we will see him as he is" (1 John 3:2). What the elder says next has bearing on the theme of holiness as process and future goal. "And all who have this hope in him purify themselves, just as he is pure" (1 John 3:3). This suggests that there is a sense in which we can be pure like Jesus; but then there is an implied sense in which we cannot be completely like him, or completely pure, until he is revealed. This further suggests that those who "purify themselves, just as he is pure," are in actuality involved in a process that prepares them for Christ's appearance.

It is worth noting that although there are places where Paul speaks of "being like Christ in his death and resurrection" as if it were a present possession (Rom. 6:2-4, 11; 8:10; 1 Cor. 4:11; Gal. 2:19-20; cf. Eph. 2:5-6; Col. 2:12), he still acknowledges that this type of perfection is something that awaits the future, particularly for him; "not that I have already obtained this or have already reached this goal; but I press on to make it my own" (Phil. 3:12). Paul again anticipates the completion of a divine process at the day of the Lord's appearing, saying, "I am persuaded of this very thing, that he who has begun a good work in you will complete it at the day of Christ Jesus" (Phil. 1:6). Although holiness is sometimes spoken of as a present attainment, it appears in some contexts as a process of attainment, and in other contexts as a goal to be reached only at the end of the process. While we acknowledge dualities in other teaching on holiness, here we have a triplicity, holiness as present process, future goal, and present possession.

Old Testament Precedents

Whether holiness is seen as a primarily corporate or individual attribute, it is a quality of the individual human soul; and this seems to be a unique emphasis in earliest Christian teaching on holiness. We see this uniqueness in greater relief over against the holiness theme as it unfolds in the Hebrew Scriptures.

At some level of meaning, holiness belongs only to God in the Old Testament. Although other beings and even objects are said to be holy, there appears to be a primary sense in which God alone is holy.[6] We therefore hear prophetic voices say "Who is like you, O LORD, among the gods? Who is like you, majestic in holiness?" (Exod. 15:11); and again, "There is none holy like the LORD" (1 Sam. 2:2); and yet again, "To whom will you compare me, or who is my equal? says the Holy One" (Isa. 40:25). Incidentally, this theme of God's exclusive holiness will be later echoed in the New Testament in a line from the Song of the Lamb, "Lord, who will not fear and glorify your name? For you alone are holy" (Rev. 15:4). It is therefore clear that some unequaled or incomparable sense of holiness is ascribed to God in both the Hebrew and Christian Scriptures.

It is a challenge to discern both the sense in which only God is holy in the Hebrew Scriptures, and the senses in which other beings and objects can be said to be holy, because the differences are nowhere explicitly stated. We can only try to meet the challenge through inferences from the Scripture.

One strong inference is that God is incorruptible.[7] We hear this as a straightforward declaration, "The LORD exists forever; your word is firmly fixed in heaven. Your faithfulness endures to all generations" (Ps. 119:89), and "They will perish, but you endure; they will all wear out like a garment . . . but you are the same, and your years have no end" (Ps. 102:25-27). Again we hear, "he is the living God, enduring for ever; his kingdom shall never be destroyed, and his dominion shall be to the end" (Dan. 6:26). Moreover, if we take note of a typical literary maneuver in Hebrew Scriptures, and recognize "the word of our God," "my salvation," and "my deliverance" as circumlocutions or literary substitutes for God's very person, then we will also recognize the theme of divine incorruptibility in such prophetic declarations as, "The grass withers, the flower fades; but the word of our God will stand forever" (Isa. 40:8; also 1 Peter 1:24-25), and "the heavens will vanish like smoke, the earth will wear out like a garment, and those who live on it will die like gnats; but my salvation will be forever, and my deliverance will never be ended" (Isa. 51:6). When the contrast is drawn be-

---

6. Purkiser, *Biblical Foundations*, p. 119.

7. Cf. A. W. Tozer, *The Knowledge of the Holy: The Attributes of God: Their Meaning in the Christian Life* (New York: Walker and Company, 1961), p. 90. "Any deterioration within the unspeakably holy nature of God is impossible."

tween the incorruptible God and human beings the phrase "steadfast love of the LORD" stands in the place of God. "As for mortals, their days are like grass; they flourish like a flower of the field; for the wind passes over it, and it is gone and its place knows it no more. But the steadfast love of the LORD is from everlasting to everlasting on those who fear him" (Ps. 103:15-17).

However, there is more. Not only is God incorruptible, but God is also remote from and untouched by anything that is corruptible. In places, this theme is expressed through descriptions of God as "high and lifted up" (Isa. 6:1), "seated on high," (Ps. 113:5), or "in the heavens" (Pss. 2:4; 103:19; 115:3). In other places, it is expressed through reference to insulating boundaries such as "clouds and thick darkness" or "light" surrounding God (Pss. 97:2; 104:2); or through other barriers fatal to living creatures such as fire or lightning (Exod. 19:18-19; Ps. 97:3-4). Herein lies the exclusive and unique meaning of holiness when it is assigned to God in the Hebrew Scriptures. Only God is both incorruptible and untouched by anything that is corruptible; as such, God alone is holy. In this sense, holiness is the obverse to God's transcendence.

Old Testament testimony fiercely preserves and protects the transcendence of God, precisely because it fiercely preserves and protects the holiness of God. Angels, particularly the mysterious Angel of the Lord, seem to appear in the narrative of the Hebrew Scriptures for this very purpose — to allow divine interaction with the corruptible world of created beings, while at the same time preserving the distance between God and all that is corruptible (Gen. 16:7-9; 19:1; 32:24-30; Judg. 6:11-12; Num. 22:23-35; 2 Sam. 24:16-17). In time, other intermediary figures or constructs would rise alongside of and subsequent to the Angel of the Lord, namely, Moses (Exod. 4:16; 19:9; Deut. 34:10; Num. 12:6-8), the tent of meeting (Exod. 40:35-38; Num. 18:3-7), the ark of the covenant (Exod. 40:21; Judg. 20:27; 1 Sam. 4:3; 2 Sam. 6:2; 1 Chron. 15:1), the temple (1 Kings 8:29-30), the holy of holies (Exod. 26:33-34), and the high priest (Lev. 21:10-15; Num. 17:39-40). These mediators share the common function of allowing interaction with God while protecting and preserving divine transcendence and holiness. As a result of this function, these mediators are also holy — not in the same transcendent sense as God, but in a functional sense. They signify the unique, supreme holiness of God. As such access to them is denied to all that is unclean, and to all who are not consecrated for specialized services (Lev. 16:2; 21:1-15; Num. 3:4; 8:5-26; 17:12-13; 18:22). In this way, God's holiness is recognized, honored, and respected.

It should be acknowledged that there is no sense in which God can be defiled, contaminated, or in any way endangered by contact with creation. When it comes to this latter it is in fact creation that is endangered through contact with God (Exod. 19:12, 24; 20:18; 33:20; Judg. 13:22; 1 Sam. 6:19-21; 2 Sam. 6:7). By protecting and preserving God's transcendence Scripture is instead declaring the stark unworthiness of any earthly being or object to abide in God's presence, let alone make contact (1 Sam. 6:19-21). It is a way of affirming that God has no equal, an affirmation that is critical for human creatures, for it is only through this very affirmation that human creatures come to know their place under God and in the universe.

We also discern from Scripture that God alone is *all* holy, by which we mean God alone possesses both intrinsic and extrinsic holiness. God's holiness can be said to be intrinsic, insofar as we can conceive an internal aspect of God, because there is no base emotion or desire in God that is counter-posed to love and mercy. God is "not partial and takes no bribe, who executes justice for the orphan and the widow, and who loves the strangers, providing them food and clothing" (Deut. 10:17-18). God's holiness is extrinsic, insofar as we can conceive an external environment for God, because God's environment excludes corruptible beings and objects (cf. 1 Cor. 15:50). God is asked to look down from "your holy habitation, heaven" (Deut. 26:15). God resides in a "holy dwelling place in heaven" (2 Chron. 30:27). On a scriptural basis, only God can be properly said to be holy both within and without.

Old Testament Scripture nevertheless speaks of earthly beings and objects as holy, but mostly in some derivative or extrinsic sense.[8] This is because earthly beings and objects are corruptible in themselves and furthermore touched by others that are corruptible in themselves. They therefore cannot be holy like God, but only in a functional or ceremonial sense.[9]

Holiness for earthly beings and objects requires division of the world of the corruptible into two realms, the realm of the clean and the unclean, or, in other words, the realm of the holy and that which defiles (Lev. 10:10). Holiness for earthly beings and objects does not require non-contact with

---

8. Cf. John E. Hartley, "Principles of Orientation for Holy Living as Found in Genesis 1–11," in *Holiness as a Root of Morality: Essays on Wesleyan Ethics in Honor of Lane A. Scott*, ed. John S. Park (Lewiston: Edwin Mellen, 2006), p. 164. Hartley observes, "Since only God is holy, anything else that is identified as holy is holy by reason of God's presence or by its being dedicated to God's service."

9. Purkiser, *Biblical Foundations*, pp. 19, 30.

the corruptible, for that would be impossible, but rather non-contact with that which defiles. Through non-contact with that which defiles, earthly beings and objects are pointing to or signifying a higher holiness, God's holiness — a holiness which not only means non-contact with that which defiles, but non-contact with the corruptible altogether. In this way, earthly beings and objects are holy only in the sense of being a testament or memorial to God's holiness. As the Scripture declares, "be ye holy, for I am holy" (Lev. 11:44-45).

Surprisingly perhaps, the angels are also holy in a derivative sense, but still in a sense quite different from earthly beings and objects.[10] They have the advantage of holiness in a circumstantial or participatory sense, that is to say, they share an environment with God, insofar as we can speak of an environment of God (Job 1:6; 2:1; Pss. 103:19-22; 148:1-4; Isa. 6:2; cf. Luke 1:19). Angels cannot be said to be holy in the same sense as God, because, as Scripture makes clear, they come in contact with beings and objects that are in themselves corruptible (Gen. 32:24-30; Josh. 5:13-15; 1 Kings 19:7; Ps. 91:11-12; Dan. 10:18), and even that which defiles (Zech 3:1-5; 5:5-11). We also see isolated instances of moral corruption among angels in the Hebrew Scriptures (Gen. 6:2), and in the New Testament for that matter (Matt. 25:41; Luke 10:18; 2 Peter 2:4; 1 John 3:8; Jude 6).[11] Nevertheless, when acting as agents of God, angels cannot be contaminated by contact with the corruptible, not even with that which defiles. For this reason, they are able to "reenter" the presence of God without violating God's unsurpassable holiness (Judg. 13:20; Isa. 6:6-7; Luke 1:19).

When human beings are in view, holiness in the Hebrew Scriptures is primarily corporate, as it continues to be in the New Testament. It is actually the people or community that is elected for holiness. Individuals are holy through membership in the holy community. In a sense, the community sanctifies the individual. However, the converse is also true: the community is sanctified by its membership of holy individuals. Holiness, as a corporate phenomenon, is the highest order of interaction between the community and its individual members.

10. However, the term "holy angels" occurs only in the New Testament (Matt. 25:31; Mark 8:38; Luke 9:26; Acts 10:22; Rev. 14:10). Cf. "elect angels" (1 Tim. 5:21).

11. Cf. Tozer, *Knowledge of the Holy,* p. 202. "God is holy with an absolute holiness that knows no degrees, and this He cannot impart to His creatures. But there is a relative and contingent holiness which He shares with angels and seraphim in heaven and with redeemed men on earth as their preparation for heaven."

Tragically, the corporate character of the covenant community occasions a vulnerability, namely, the community can be defiled through the failure of a single individual. As in the case involving Achan, son of Carmi, the community may fail to exclude from its midst all that defiles; a failure that often goes unperceived until some traumatic event in the life of the people (Josh. 7:1-9). However, when the failure is finally perceived the community is mandated to ritualize or signify its recovery of holiness by eliminating the offending presence (Josh. 7:10-26).

Actually, the community can never achieve complete separation even from that which defiles, but this is beside the point in Old Testament perspective. Israel, the covenant community, must still ritualize or signify its attempt to separate from the defiling not to actually attain perfect separation, but to raise a testament and memorial to the holiness of God (Lev. 11:13-45; 12:2-8; 13:2-59; 14:2-57; 15:2-33). Holiness in the Old Testament is therefore an external and functional act for both the community and the individual. Holiness remains an intrinsic and thoroughgoing quality for God alone.

Christ and Holiness

These complex themes of holiness in the Old Testament as they apply to God, on the one hand, and to the covenant community and its members on the other, are carried forward and presupposed in the New Testament (Luke 2:22-24; John 11:55; Acts 10:14; 1 Cor. 7:14-15; 1 Tim. 6:16; 1 Peter 1:15-16; Rev. 4:8). It is worth emphasizing that the Old Testament ideas of God's unsurpassable holiness and the extrinsic holiness of the covenantal community and its effects are not abandoned in the New Testament. Nevertheless, it is in the New Testament where holiness for the most part becomes an intrinsic trait of the human soul, just as it is an intrinsic trait of God.

That is not to say that the theme of intrinsic holiness for the individual human being is completely absent from the Hebrew Scriptures. Clearly this theme is not absent (Pss. 24:4; 51:1-12; Prov. 20:9), but its presence is certainly marginalized by the emphasis upon external and functional holiness. In the New Testament, it is the reverse. It is the emphasis upon inward holiness that marginalizes the theme of outward and functional holiness (Matt. 9:10-11; 15:10-20; Mark 2:16; 7:1-23; Luke 5:20).

Jesus Christ is the herald and hallmark of human holiness.[12] He shows us that intrinsic holiness which pleases God and fulfills the divine calling that we each have received. We achieve Christ-like holiness when we surrender heart, mind, and body to God in faithful obedience (Rom. 6:1-19; 12:1-2; Eph. 4:20-24).

In the Synoptic Gospels holiness is an inward trait of the soul; however, it is a soul trait that is turned outward in a life of compassion and mercy (Matt. 23:23; Luke 11:42). It is in the Synoptic tradition where the Levitical mandate "be ye holy, for I am holy" (Lev. 11:44-45) develops first into "be perfect as your heavenly Father is perfect" (Matt. 5:48) and then into "be merciful, even as your Father is merciful" (Luke 6:36).[13] Here we can trace an intertextual transition in how holiness is understood, first, as an extrinsic, functional pattern; second, as an intrinsic or spiritual quality; and finally as an outwardly expressed response to others.

Holiness carries the sense of moral integrity in the Gospel of John (13:10-14, 34); however, here it is also a matter of being "sanctified in the truth" (17:17-19), or, to restate the theme, to be made holy by abiding in Christ and his word (13:8; 15:3-4). Moreover, the fourth evangelist is concerned to show that in Jesus, the holy God becomes incarnate in a corruptible world (John 1:14-18; 3:17-21). Through Christ, God is at one and the same time present in the world, yet untouched by the world (John 1:18).

In modern theology, the existence of God and the fact of evil are recurring theological problems. However, for the four Gospel writers the central theological problem was reconciling the transcendence of God with the immanence of God. How could God be removed from us and present with us at the same time?

We have already observed how the Angel of the Lord and other mediators in the Hebrew Scriptures served to answer this question for an earlier generation; however, in the Gospels, God the transcendent and holy one, has come to us in Jesus Christ. Matthew, Mark, and Luke tend to portray Jesus as the precursor of the apocalypse. Jesus is "the holy one of God" who signifies the in-breaking of the Kingdom of God (Matt. 1:23; Mark

12. Paul S. Minear, "Holy People, Holy Land, Holy City: The Genesis and Genius of Christian Attitudes," *Interpretation* 37 (January 1983): 22. Minear refers to Jesus as "the measure and standard of all holiness."

13. deSilva, *New Testament Themes*, p. 45. deSilva observes that Luke shows Jesus "rewriting" Leviticus 11:44-45 to emphasize God's mercy as the chief characteristic of the children of God.

1:24; Luke 4:34); but nevertheless preserves the transcendence of God (Matt. 3:17; 17:5; Mark 1:11; 9:7; Luke 3:22; 9:35). John, however, tends to resolve the problem of God's transcendence and immanence by emphasizing the "oneness" of God and Christ (John 10:30).

Like the angels, Christ is not contaminated by contact with the world, neither by contact with the corruptible nor that which particularly defiles. In fact, it is the world, even that which particularly defiles, that is sanctified through contact with Christ (Matt. 8:2-3; Mark 1:40-45; Luke 5:12-16).

When Scripture refers to Christ as holy it indicates both the same intrinsic quality found in God and also the ability to make holy or to sanctify (Mark 1:24; Luke 4:34; Acts 2:27; 3:14; 4:27-30; Heb. 7:26). Where contact with God once meant destruction for any earthly being or object, contact with God in Christ now means sanctification and life.

Even though Christ in his earthly sojourn enters a world kept distant from the corruption-free environment of God and the angels, Christ nevertheless extends holiness into the earthly realm. In the Hebrew Scriptures, the earthly realm is not allowed to encroach upon the heavenly realm; indeed, it is impossible. In the New Testament, this is still the case. However, this does not prevent the heavenly realm from encroaching upon the earthly realm, and in Christ this is in fact what happens. We can therefore speak of a holy environment surrounding Christ, just as for God. However, the holy environment surrounding Christ is uncontained, usurpative and invasive.[14]

In this sense we can also speak of Christ from a New Testament perspective as all holy. He is intrinsically holy insofar as there is no base impulse or emotion counter-posed to love and mercy in him; and he is extrinsically holy insofar as the environment he generates allows for no demonic nor defiling presence.

---

14. Klaus Berger, "Jesus als Pharisäer und Frühe Christen als Pharisäer," *Novum Testamentum* 30 (1988): 240-41 refers to this idea as "offensive purity" *(offensive Reinheit)* or "offensive holiness" *(offensive Heiligkeit)* as acknowledged by Mark R. Saucy, "Miracles and Jesus' Proclamation of the Kingdom of God," *Bibliotheca Sacra* 153 (July-September 1996): 294. See also Craig L. Blomberg, *Contagious Holiness: Jesus' Meals with Sinners*, New Studies in Biblical Theology 19 (Downers Grove: InterVarsity Press, 2005), who speaks of this in terms of "contagious holiness" and "pervasive purity."

Holiness and Humanity

Our observations have the following import for human beings. We cannot be holy in an external sense *like* God and the angels, but we can be holy in an external sense like Christ. In other words, we cannot remove ourselves from the realm of the corruptible, but in Christ we can expel or eliminate the demonic and defiling from our environment.

Also, we cannot be holy in an internal sense like God or Christ, but we can still be holy in an internal sense *through* Christ. That is to say, we certainly cannot claim to be eternally nor even primordially free of base emotion or impulse, but we can *become* free of such through Christ Jesus.

Holiness in this internal sense is a heart and mind shaped by love of God and neighbor. This is a consistent theme throughout the New Testament canon, with some variation in the thought of different New Testament authors (Matt. 22:37, 39; Mark 12:30-31; Luke 10:27; Rom. 13:9; 1 Peter 1:22; 1 John 4:12, 20).

We have emphasis upon the outward manifestation of this inward holiness, in the Gospel of Matthew (5:20-48; 6:1-4; 7:1-21; 25:31-46). In the Gospel of Mark, holiness is a doctrine hidden beneath the emphasis on sincere faith as the key to wholeness (5:34; 9:23; 10:21, 52; 11:22). Luke appears more concerned with how holiness is obtained through repentance and the forgiveness of sins (13:5; 19:8-10; 24:47; Acts 2:38; 10:43; 13:38; 15:8-9; 26:18).[15] John calls attention to faith and spiritual rebirth as the prerequisite for holiness (3:3, 7, 16).

Paul the Apostle expounds holiness as the outcome of dying and rising again with Christ (Rom. 6:4, 12). In Ephesians and Colossians, however, we have the added doctrinal element of holiness through mystical union with Christ (Eph. 1:20; Col. 2:12-15). In the Pastoral Epistles holiness is achieved through adherence to sound doctrine (1 Tim. 1:10; 2 Tim. 1:13; Titus 2:1).

Holiness in the book of Hebrews is a moral and spiritual discipline forged in the crucible of persecution and obtained through participation in the holiness of God. There is question whether the author of Hebrews believes that God causes this persecution or only permits it. This is because the author says, "He disciplines us for our good, that we may share his ho-

---

15. Cf. Robert W. Wall, "'Purity and Power' according to the Acts of the Apostles," *Pneuma* 21:2 (Fall 1999): 231. Wall observes, "Purity of heart in Acts results from divine forgiveness."

liness" (12:10). Holiness is exhorted as that which accompanies the response to potential enemies or persecutors, "Strive for peace with all men, and for the holiness without which no one will see the Lord" (12:14). Holiness in this case involves exclusion of the "root of bitterness" by which many become defiled, and also an immorality and irreligiousness akin to that seen in Esau who sold his birthright for a single meal (12:15-17).

A thematic comparison can be drawn between the Letter of James where "faith without works is dead" (2:26) and the Gospel of Matthew where "unless your righteousness exceeds that of the scribes and Pharisees you shall not see the kingdom of God" (5:20). These Scriptures seem to have an identical emphasis upon holiness as the outward manifestation of an inner purity.

A thematic comparison can also be drawn between the Second Letter of Peter, the three Johannine Epistles, and the Pastoral Epistles which we have already considered. In these texts, the greater concern is with adherence to orthodox teaching or sound doctrine as the key to holy living (2 Peter 2:1-3; 1 John 2:26-27; 2 John 7-11; 3 John 4).

A final thematic comparison is possible between the First Letter of Peter and the book of Revelation. Holiness in these Scriptures is the disciplined life shaped through faith and endurance in the face of persecution and death (1 Peter 1:6-9, 13-16, 22; 4:12-17; Rev. 7:14; 14:12-13; 20:6; 22:14).

Throughout the New Testament, however, holiness appears as a disposition of the soul manifested outwardly through works of love and faithful obedience to God. There is some variation in the means that are expounded for obtaining holiness; and in the contexts in which the theme of holiness is visited, but the essential nature and outward appearance of holiness remains consistent among diverse New Testament voices.

Wesley and New Testament Holiness

John Wesley favors the New Testament theme "without holiness no man shall see God" (Heb. 12:14) and proceeds to characterize holiness as an inward quality of the soul.[16] However, his distinctive emphasis is upon holiness as an outwardly manifested quality. He reflects this duality in his doc-

---

16. Albert C. Outler, ed., *John Wesley,* Library of Protestant Thought (New York: Oxford University Press, 1964), p. 378.

trine of holiness when he speaks of both "inward and outward holiness" and "holiness of life and thought."[17]

Wesley speaks of holiness as "scriptural perfection" and "salvation continued." As "scriptural perfection" holiness is "pure love filling the heart and governing all words and actions." As "salvation continued" holiness is "faith working by love." Wesley maintains that there is "no true Christian holiness without that love of God for its foundation."[18]

Holiness is also "the goal of Christian life" and "the fullness of faith." For Wesley, the relationship between "faith and true holiness" constituted a "holy and spiritual law."[19] Wesley attacks the teaching that holiness is made unnecessary by faith. He sees such teaching as a perversion of biblical truth concerning grace and justification by faith apart from works. Drawing upon Romans 3:31, Wesley upholds the life of holiness as the way we "establish the law," by which he means the "moral law," the end of which is "love."[20] Holiness as the outworking of faith through love not only refrains from doing evil, but purposely does good. Wesley describes this as the negative and positive law of faith working through love or, in other words, external holiness. He also calls attention to inward holiness which he describes as "the purifying of the heart, the cleansing it from all vile affections."[21]

Although he refuses to drive a wedge between inward and outward holiness, Wesley nevertheless draws a contrast. Inward holiness for Wesley is an "immutable, invariable state."[22] Wesley uses the terms "non-degreed," "non-graduated," "unshaded," "non-quantified," and "unqualified" to explain that there is no more or less holiness; no superior nor inferior holiness; no best nor better holiness. On the other hand, there are many degrees of outward holiness, corresponding to many branches of Christian holiness, all with love as its foundation.[23]

Wesley's unique contribution to Christian theology and praxis is his interpretation of holiness as having an inward and outward foci, a remark-

---

17. Outler, *John Wesley*, pp. 22, 116.
18. Outler, *John Wesley*, pp. 159, 160, 243.
19. Outler, *John Wesley*, pp. 228, 229.
20. Outler, *John Wesley*, pp. 222-23.
21. Outler, *John Wesley*, p. 230. Here Wesley refers to 1 John 3:3.
22. Outler, *John Wesley*, pp. 371, 372.
23. Outler, *John Wesley*, p. 160.

able understanding promoted through arguments that are thoroughly grounded in Scripture.

Conclusion

A New Testament perspective on holiness is characterized by complexity. As "purity of heart and mind" holiness is not only the absence of negative traits, but it is also the presence of positive traits in the soul. Moreover, holiness is inward and outward, holistic and singular, corporate and individual. Holiness is finally perceived as present process, future goal, and present attainment.

Holiness in the Old Testament is, by contrast, a thoroughgoing trait that belongs solely to God. All other beings and objects are holy only in some derivative, extrinsic, and imperfect sense, and only in regard to external status and function.

Although the New Testament carries forward the Old Testament themes, it is nevertheless in the New Testament where holiness becomes emphasized as an intrinsic trait of the human soul as it is of the being of God. John Wesley captures this essential character of New Testament holiness, and achieves distinction with his emphasis upon its outward manifestation as works of love, mercy, and justice.

CHAPTER 3

Jesus and a Gospel of Holiness

David W. Kendall

As one who grew up in the Holiness tradition, it strikes me as odd that most Holiness teaching and preaching seldom visit the Gospels.[1] This is odd for several reasons. First, members of the Holiness movement would claim to be earnest Christians, intense and deep in our discipleship.[2] And yet we have seldom elaborated the deeper life in terms of the story of Jesus our Master. Second, we claim to be Bible-Christians, an expression Wesley used. That is, we hold a high view of Scripture and its inspiration and authority. And yet nearly half the New Testament, the half that tells the story of Jesus, has not often directly and intentionally informed our understanding of living a holy life. Third, our preferred mode of discourse on holiness has been oriented around Pentecost and Spirit-baptism/filling. To be sure, all the Gospels describe Jesus as the one who baptizes with the Holy Spirit.

1. I am affirming the four Gospels as primary source material for the story of Jesus. Though different in significant ways, they cohere in their presentations of Jesus and offer a solid basis for understanding the meaning of his life, death, and resurrection. The North American Holiness movement, as it developed from the nineteenth century on, has focused *primarily* on certain Old Testament themes and images drawn from the Torah and the prophetic literature, and in the New Testament primarily on the Pauline Epistles, the Pentecostal language and imagery from Acts, Hebrews, and 1 John. My intuition is that Gospel material became associated mostly with conversion and justification and less with the everyday life of the believer, and even less still with the call to holy living.

2. B. T. Roberts, founder of my own denomination, used the term "earnest" to denote the intense and passionate discipleship that characterized our movement at its inception.

In John's Gospel especially Jesus celebrated the Spirit's ministry within his followers as a gracious expression of divine self-giving that would make *Jesus* — his life, teachings, and way — gloriously clear to them. Yet, ironically, *our* focus on the Spirit's fullness has not consistently brought us to a place of holy preoccupation with the person of Jesus.

When you read the Gospels, however, it appears that Jesus has very little to say on the subject of holiness. The standard terms are seldom found. To begin, then, why does Jesus seldom address a theme so central for much of Judaism in the first century? Moreover, what does this fact imply for a tradition that seeks "to spread scriptural holiness across these lands"? In general terms, these pages aim at offering an answer.

Jesus had little to say about holiness for the same reason he had little to say about the Messiah. That is, the concept of "holiness" that prevailed in the first century could not be embraced or engaged without major critique and redefinition. Especially the redefinition, but also the critique, was closely tied to his own identity and mission in the world.

More particularly, then, I want to highlight some features of the notion of holiness that shaped the context for Jesus' ministry and outline Jesus' critique of those features. Next, I will explore briefly how Jesus redefined the concept of holiness around his own kingdom and mission in order to offer his followers the gift of a new and holy life. Finally, I will begin to draw out some of the ways the story of Jesus in the Gospels suggests a gospel of holiness that is truly "gospel," good news.

Holiness in the First-Century Jewish Context

How did Jews distinguish themselves from their unbelieving world? By what means did they live that clearly marked them as different — holy — precisely because they claimed to be people of the one true God? What markers or boundaries separated "holy" from "unholy"?[3]

---

3. In the section that follows I acknowledge my grateful indebtedness to N. T. Wright. See his *Jesus and the Victory of God* (Minneapolis: Fortress, 1996), especially pp. 383-428.

Land

The people of God lived in a land that was God's gift to them and to their descendants.[4] That land was "promised" to them and therefore special, unlike any other. The people of that special, holy land were themselves the holy people of God, and exile from the land called into question that identity. The long years of struggle to enter, subdue, and inhabit the land,[5] the yearning to return and reconstitute the nation as independent and free,[6] and the need to expel foreign, godless occupiers would necessarily set the stage for the final establishing of God's Kingdom in God's land and for God's people.[7] Such life as subjects of God the King in the holy land, with all attendant blessing, would be holy indeed.

Temple

The land became holy because it had been promised, set apart as a unique place. In particular, this land was the place of God's glorious dwelling on earth, with the Tabernacle/Temple as the locus of that dwelling.[8] As such, the Temple became the symbolic center of holiness. The Holy One of Israel had chosen the Tabernacle/Temple as the premiere place for disclosing his magnificent presence. Within the innermost sanctuary — the holy of holies — Israel's God was enthroned. From that throne the Holy One governed the universe. From that same throne, the Holy One provided a way for the unholy to draw near and to stay near. The priesthood and its administration of the sacrificial system of Israel offered atonement for sin and cleansing for defiling impurities. Atonement and cleansing became foundational for the people's life before God, for living in fellowship with God, and for enjoying the covenant blessings of God. Thus, the Temple and those who carried out its ministries on the people's behalf established, maintained, and guaranteed that God's people would be a holy people.

4. Among other passages see Genesis 12:1-3 and Psalm 105 as representative of numerous references to the centrality of the land for the people of God.

5. The period of Patriarchs, the Exodus, and entry into the land of Canaan.

6. The exilic and post-exilic periods.

7. The so-called inter-testamental period and first century before Christ.

8. See, for example, Psalm 48.

For this reason, the Temple carried profound social and political meaning, as the unique dwelling place of the Holy One and as the means for making God's people holy. Whoever built, maintained, and controlled the Temple achieved enormous status and power among the people. Likewise, whoever or whatever threatened the well-being or operation of the Temple was by that fact an enemy of God, God's people, and all that was holy.

Fidelity to Torah, or the Law

God's people in God's land under God's rule would live in ways unlike the peoples around them. The provisions of the covenant, with the interpretive body of tradition they generated, would certify the faithful as truly holy. Although first-century Judaism (even in Palestine) seldom spoke with one voice on matters of tradition, there was agreement that circumcision, adherence to dietary regulations of the law, and observance of Sabbath constituted the most prominent markers of a holy people. At the birth of a male child the community acknowledged and affirmed they were a covenant people — the difference cut in their very flesh. Every day their diet reminded them they were nourishing a life unlike that of other groups. And on the seventh day, while others carried on as always, they rested from their labor as their God had done in the beginning. Hallowing that day marked them as holy people. In the centuries preceding Jesus' life, these markers became critical to the people's self-understanding as people of Yahweh, the Holy One of Israel, and especially so once the nation experienced exile.

We could summarize these three markers of holiness in Jesus' day in the following three principles of holy living: (1) holiness requires a Kingdom life, (2) in the presence of the Holy One, (3) that is radically distinct from others outside God's Kingdom. When we express holiness in this summary way, however, we must not forget the very precise ways in which these expressions were understood by Jesus' contemporaries. In Jesus' day, "God's Kingdom" meant re-establishment of Israel as a geopolitical nation in the world. Moreover, to welcome and celebrate the presence of God dwelling among his people required the Temple and all that went with it. Finally, the uniqueness of God's people was conceptually joined with circumcision, clean foods, and Sabbath observance. Therefore, to speak of holiness in Jesus' day *necessarily* implied these features of common Jewish life.[9]

While there was room for some variation in understanding them, to call any of them into question would constitute a rejection of holiness itself and incur violent hostility. That, of course, is what Jesus did. He embodied and offered the world a different understanding of holiness. That different understanding led to his loving sacrifice, his mighty triumph over death, and a radically new life for his followers.

Jesus' Critique and Reorientation of Holiness

Israel's God, the Holy One, was king of the universe. Jesus' message announced that reality and invited people to enter a Kingdom life. Yet, the Kingdom was not Israel re-established; it was larger. It was not only the "Holy Land," but all land, indeed the whole earth.[10] And the way of the Kingdom was not that of Israel or any other nation of the world. Not by armed resistance or military struggle would the Kingdom come. Rather, the Kingdom comes by entrusting self and all to the care of the king, by seeking and surrendering to his way. It comes by repenting, by becoming like a child, and by rebirth.[11]

The Kingdom came not by violent striving but by grace and gift to all

9. Note that in the earliest mission of the church, these markers became contentious issues for the church — circumcision, foods offered to idols, and the observance of special days. It has been common to interpret these controversies as regarding conditions for salvation (particularly in Galatians), but the issue was more likely whether these markers would continue to be the markers of holiness for the people of God and whether embracing them offered a path to perfection. In this connection, consider Paul's question in Galatians 3:3, "having begun by the Spirit will you now be perfected by the flesh?" (ἐναρξάμενοι πνεύματι νῦν σαρκὶ ἐπιτελεῖσθε;). Here the issue seems more likely the path to "perfection" than to "salvation." Ironically, most of the North American Holiness movement rightly rejected such markers as conditions for "salvation," but then embraced them as markers of holiness, which was the very error that Paul sought to expose! Closer attention to the Gospels may have helped the movement avoid much of its legalism and its lingering impact.

10. Note that the third beatitude in Matthew 5, that announces blessing on the meek because they will inherit the earth, is drawn from Psalm 37:11, which referred to the land as that which God promised to his people. In Jesus' beatitude, however, "land" has been universalized — no longer limited to the land of promise but extending to the earth.

11. See among other references Matthew 18:1-4; 19:14; Luke 13:1-1-5; John 3:3.

who would receive it. According to Jesus, the Kingdom belonged especially to the poor — materially or otherwise — who relied not on worldly, human resources but on the riches of another world to which they became heirs. Not that the Kingdom was otherworldly. For Jesus Kingdom reality embraced the here and now, the very concrete life of people in relationship with God, others, and self.

Indeed, this Kingdom was among them, already a given, providing foundation and empowerment for another way of life. That other way was holy. To be sure, at some point God's Kingdom would prevail over all of reality, but until then the world of Jesus' first followers had been visited and occupied by a very different kind of realm and as its subjects they began to live a very different kind of life.[12]

Jesus called people to enter and to live such a Kingdom life. He invited people to come into the presence and dwell, to taste the fellowship of the Kingdom table, to leave behind former ways and begin anew in the company of his own.[13] Precisely in the context of this radical invitation to all, Jesus could pronounce forgiveness of sins, the arrival of salvation, and the presence of *shalom*. Similarly, he dared to utter words of woe on those who refused to see what he was doing and to hear his words of life.

The opponents of Jesus rightly interpreted his invitation into the presence as at best a rebuke of Temple, the priesthood, and their efficacy to atone for, and cleanse the people from, sin. At its worst, Jesus' welcome was simply a rejection of Temple, the priesthood, and sacrifice. All the Gospels tell of Jesus' rampage in the Temple and cite prophetic judgment to explain it.[14] The house of prayer for all nations had become a hideout for bandits, who robbed worshipers as they came to the Temple, but even more they robbed God by denying him the fruit of the nations streaming to the holy place to offer him worship. As the alternative, Jesus would be lifted up and

12. Although it is most common to regard the Kingdom of God in exclusively temporal and linear terms, the biblical conception of Kingdom is that of a present reality already present, overlapping and interacting with the space-time world of common, fallen human experience. Thus, the Kingdom is both present and "coming," yet its coming is not so much a function of time running out or reaching its goal, as it is the final manifestation of God's rule or order.

13. In Luke's Gospel especially the theme of table-fellowship and its connection with the full manifestation of the Kingdom is most clear — see such passages as Luke 14:1-14 with the parable it occasioned in 14:15-24; see also 13:22-30; 15:1-2.

14. See Matthew 22:12-13; Mark 11:15-19; Luke 19:45-46; John 2:12-16.

draw all people to himself. Referring to his crucifixion and resurrection Jesus had said, "Destroy this temple and in three days I will raise it up."[15] Although his opponents could never have made this connection, they correctly saw that Jesus' ministry posed a grave threat to the status quo.

Finally, Jesus' welcome into divine presence and call to a Kingdom life founded a community that lives in ways profoundly different from other communities. But it was not the case that Jesus simply rejected circumcision, food laws, and Sabbath observance, or other features of common Jewish life. Jesus rejected the connection assumed between these external forms and a heart set on God. His quarrel with the Pharisees was not that they marked holiness by observable behaviors or customs. In fact, a holy life by definition will always be distinguishable from other ways.[16] Jesus quarreled with the Pharisees' lack of integrity. Their outer forms of life, which might otherwise be well and good, did not flow from hearts soft toward God, surrendered and submissive to God's ways. To the contrary, often the outer forms provided cover for inner defiance of God or rejection of God's word.[17] Jesus had no patience for such pretense.

Jesus claimed that Israel's story came to its full God-intended meaning in his own identity and mission.[18] He came as the anointed of God, uniquely called to bring God's redemption to Israel and through Israel to the world.

15. John 2:18-22.

16. Among God's people as reflected in the Old Covenant it was simply a given that the people would live in ways that distinguished them from the peoples around them. This given was surely carried over into the life of the earliest churches, but in tune with the preaching and teaching of Jesus and the apostles. The North American Holiness movement has historically identified a number of distinguishing features of their life. It is common to dismiss these as simple legalism, but it seems wise to assess them in the way Jesus did, as I am suggesting. It is the assumed or presumed connection between the "markers" and a heart, not to mention life, which is in tune with God. In the New Testament literature the tables of virtues and vices become prominent markers of the new way of living among God's people. See, e.g., Romans 12; Galatians 5; Ephesians 4 and 5; Philippians 2:1-16; Colossians 3:1-17; 1 Thessalonians 5:12-24.

17. Jesus' stern rebuke of the Pharisees and teachers of the law in Matthew 23 is a case in point.

18. See the parable in Mark 12:1-12 and the risen Christ's references to the Scriptures as the subject of prophetic foretelling in Luke 24:25-27.

Jesus on Holiness

The retelling of Israel's story in the life and ministry of Jesus identifies the problem with the people of God as a heart-problem. Isaiah had said, "This people honors me with their lips but their hearts are far from me" (Isa. 29:13). Matthew's Jesus cites that very diagnosis in describing his opponents, the leaders of God's people (Matt. 15:8). Similarly, Jesus argued that people contract the worst forms of defilement not from contaminated externals but from inner corruption. Not from food that goes in, but from the wellspring of the heart "come evil thoughts, murder, adultery, sexual immorality, theft, false testimony, slander. These are what make a man 'unclean'; but eating with unwashed hands does not make him 'unclean'" (Matt. 15:19-20). He pronounced woe upon those who cared most about purity; they had become whitewashed tombstones outwardly, but rotting corpses inwardly.[19] They were, in fact, intensely concerned with image and profoundly lacking in substance. Their righteousness, Jesus insisted, was cosmetic. The beauty of their holiness was indeed only skin deep. Such inner corruption produced a hardness of heart. They could not fulfill God's original intent for their lives because of such hardness. Even the Torah made concessions to this heart-condition, so that the covenant of marriage could be easily broken, which in turn signaled the shattering of the more basic covenant God had made with his people. Through rebellion and defiance, Israel, God's choice vineyard, failed to produce at all, or suffered the plundering of its fruit under the judgment of God.

The mission of Jesus to Israel as Messiah exposed this heart-problem and offered God's answer. In Jesus, God fulfilled his promise of a new covenant inscribed on human hearts. If the law could be summed up in two great love commands, Jesus exposes the problem: 'You do not have the love of God in your hearts," and then offers the solution in his own loving sacrifice.[20] In response to that love, he calls his own to love as he himself loves.[21] Such love, filling up and then flowing from the human heart, expresses new covenant holiness.

19. See Matthew 23:27-30 for the full text.
20. See John 5:42; see also Luke 11:42.
21. See, for example, John 15:9.

The Good News of Holiness

Here is the gospel of holiness, according to Jesus. To address the human predicament of sinful bondage to the ways of death and the hardness of heart those ways develop, even among God's people, Jesus came as king of love and inaugurated a Kingdom of love that counters, and *will* conquer, every other kingdom.

Because Jesus brings a Kingdom of love, he extends loving welcome not just to some, but to all. Decent God-fearing fishermen, despised tax collectors, disgraced women of the village, and the disturbed, bedeviled lunatics lurking among the tombs — *all* no less than the distinguished guardians of the sacred traditions may come. All who waited for God's Kingdom had braced themselves for its shattering invasion into their midst. But no one expected the shocking assault of a loving invitation to whomever.

Response to his loving invitation drew people into gracious forgiveness. But this forgiveness was more than removal of guilt; it came as assurance that they were now somehow keeping divine company, somehow included in divine hospitality — at table, no less — somehow belonging to others and to God. With such belonging came a very different life. Strangely, they belonged to these others who had also been surprised by Jesus' invitation. They seemed to be a community held together by growing commitment to the One who spoke as from God. In time, he would call them family — brothers, sisters, aunts, and uncles — who hear and obey the word of God, a form of family that could include, but was not limited to or by, the other families that claimed them.[22]

Their new life was learned "on the go." They walked, literally and otherwise, with Jesus. He said, "Follow me!" and they did. In time, he sharpened the summons by demanding, "Deny yourself, take up your cross, and follow me." To the degree they understood, they did. Moreover, they listened as he pronounced blessing on those they and most everyone else had considered cursed before — the poor, the powerless, and the persecuted. They learned that the same love they had received *could* actually rule their

---

22. See the pericope in Matthew 12:46-50, Mark 3:31-35, and Luke 8:19-21, where Jesus calls into question the commitment to family on which his social world depended by stressing that his followers constituted a new family that has priority in the disciple's life. Against this background we should understand Jesus' statement about "hating" family as a qualification for discipleship in Luke 14:26.

lives. In fact, such love *must* rule, even when responding to enemies, even as they participated in the unfolding of God's plan for the ages and the nations. They began to understand that piety is for God and others, but never for self. As soon as piety serves self it degenerates into one more pathetic attempt to take glory that belongs only to God. They learned to trust the love that drew them into their new family. They learned that the One who loves them *truly* loves them — that is, he knows what they need and will respond to their needs. Because they are so cared for, they can live carefree. And they heard and learned many other facets of life in God's Kingdom of love.[23]

Somewhere along the way, it must have dawned on them that "This is not what we expected, but it is good." In fact, it wasn't what anyone had expected. This life was completely different, in a word, holy.

It was an active, engaged holiness. Following a king like no other meant doing things they had never done before in ways they would never have thought to do them. Indeed, they did the very things Jesus did — preached, healed, cast out demons, and invited other people to a kingdom life. If they were becoming like Jesus, that likeness could be seen most clearly as they interacted with one another. As they saw people in the way Jesus did, and as their hearts went out to them as Jesus' did, they did what they could in Jesus' name. They were becoming like Jesus in the most comprehensive sense.

That they were also *unlike* Jesus became clear as well. It did not become clear as the result of inner reflection, but as they sometimes found themselves jealous of one another's relative standing with Jesus, as they took offense at the rejection of people who had no interest in the good news, and as their heroic professions of allegiance to Jesus collapsed under the weight of trial and temptation.

Yet love conquered on their behalf. Love did not let them go. Love found them and reclaimed them, just as he had told them it would. And, in community, in the new family he had founded, they received the Spirit he promised them — the Spirit as Jesus' own indwelling and empowering presence to go as he went, to love as he loved, to replicate and reproduce the family here, there, and everywhere.

The good news of holiness from the story of Jesus is that Jesus contin-

23. In this paragraph I am suggesting that the so-called Sermon on the Mount was the first Holiness Manifesto.

ues this same journey and extends this same call with and to us. The story engages us. We are now called to follow, to find ourselves in the company of others who wish to follow, to find ourselves listening and learning and living in ways we never imagined for ourselves. We are called to discover in the following how it is that we are like and unlike this One, how it is that he meets us on the other side of a cross to breathe new life into us and our branch of the family so that we actually go, love, and act as he himself did.

This seems to me so important and truly good news. It has become common within the Holiness movement in North America to lament the decline of teaching and preaching about holiness. Then, to address our perceived need, we clamor and work to make up for what is lacking. Surely this present volume exploring the theme of holiness in the twenty-first century is itself a case in point. Those of us in a position to address this perceived need feel it as privilege, I think, but also as responsibility. We may even feel it as burden, a heavy burden. And yet the burden can be lightened and heaviness eased by the Jesus of the story who calls us to come, to see for ourselves, to walk trustingly with him and others to a new — holy — way of life. This call sounds like good news indeed.

Spreading Scriptural Holiness

Finally, how might this account of the story of Jesus with particular reference to a holy life challenge and inform us as we seek to "spread scriptural holiness across these lands"? Here are just a few possibilities.

First, Jesus' hesitancy to use the language and terminology that most commonly conceptualized holiness in his day, but had been corrupted by its religious handlers, should perhaps give us pause. To what have we wed the categories of a holy life that may, in fact, compromise that very life? One part of the answer: when our formulations of a doctrine become so important to us that we can no longer think about the doctrine or recognize its reality without using those formulations. I believe that many of the more traditional ways we have articulated a doctrine of entire sanctification have become dangerously formula-like for some among us.[24]

---

24. To illustrate: compare the paucity of references in the New Testament to "*entire sanctification*" with the tenacity with which some insist that the truth of this doctrine requires the use of this terminology!

Second, in Jesus' way the primacy of love is clear; this has been a hall-mark of classic Wesleyan teaching. In the Gospel story, however, that love extends to others in radically inclusive ways that profoundly threaten the neat moral/spiritual arrangements of the status quo. In what ways might we understand, embody, and share Jesus' love that would distinguish us with similarly radical and threatening consequence? Is Christ-like love our bottom line, and the most important aspect of holiness? It was for John Wesley, B. T. Roberts, and the earliest Holiness people. As we articulate the message of holiness in the twenty-first century, we will find that a return to love's primacy will connect well with many unbelievers.

Third, Jesus offers us little detail on the process and the steps that would lead a people to be truly holy. It would seem odd indeed if there were no steps and helps toward holiness. Likewise, how strange if there were no common patterns of life-experience observable among followers of Jesus to a holy life. As legitimate and helpful as identifying these may be, however, still Jesus offers little explicit help for doing so. Contrast that with a common tendency in our tradition to pin down the steps, as though getting it right (in this sense) and proclaiming it passionately somehow guarantees results. Jesus' way with people may suggest that this tendency is misguided.

Rather, Jesus' preferred model would include these basic components. He begins with a call to follow (or keep following); then, he summons to bear the cross, which means carrying it all the way to Jerusalem, a full identification with his death (as Paul would later express it, dying with Christ); and finally, he gives his Spirit to each within the community, empowering new life and impact on the world.[25]

Fourth, Jesus' way with people is tailor-made to each disciple's need. It also seems patient, even in the press of an urgent mission. He seemed satisfied to have his followers on the way, moving in the same direction with him, participating in the common life and ministry of their community. Does this suggest a shift of perspective from a primary focus on the progress already made in one's walk with God (marking the milestones passed) to a primary focus on the continuing walk in the same direction in close

---

25. This clearly observed pattern from the story of Jesus suggests to me the wisdom of holding our models of how we "perfect holiness in the fear of the Lord," to use Paul's phrase, more loosely while boldly calling, or joining Jesus in calling, people in some of the very same terms so common in the ministry of Jesus.

proximity to Jesus (keeping the eye on where he is going)? I wonder if most of the teaching and preaching of the Holiness movement hasn't led us to reflect on our condition more than to embrace the vision of a holy life. The Gospel story of Jesus would counsel us to focus more on the way and the goal, while affirming what we expect God will do. Such refocusing would keep us more open to the tailor-made approach of Jesus, and less likely to assume that God's way with one is God's way with all.

Fifth, Jesus' way of love is grasped and lived only in community. When the Lord deals with individuals — their lack of love, their misguided or sinful responses, and his call to love — his interaction with them typically plays out in the company of others. That is, actually becoming a loving person and actually expressing love occurs in the course of relating to others in the community. Especially in North America, but increasingly elsewhere, how do we embrace Jesus' love, and invite others to his way of love, in the cultures of our society and our churches when they are so enthralled with the private and the individual?

Sixth, the new way of life Jesus offers engaged the world and the powers, and those held in their grip. In reading the Gospel stories it is not possible to distinguish the inner God-awareness and God-likeness of individuals from their service and ministry toward others. Especially in John's story, Jesus stressed that his word came from the Father and his deeds were what the Father was doing. He entered into and completed a word and ministry already in progress on behalf of people caught in the historical, social, cultural, and religious realities that conditioned their lives. Now, as Jesus was sent, so he sends his own. How is it, then, that a holy people, Christ-like in character, could ever disengage their piety from the ongoing mission of Jesus? In my judgment we must make this connection between a holy life and the church's ministry much stronger than we have in the past.

Seventh, indeed, to use terminology now in vogue, Jesus' way was missional to the core — to confront, call, challenge, and change people as well as social, religious, and political structures by the power of love. More specifically, it was by the power of self-sacrificing love. Jesus really believed, and then lived, died, and rose again, in this way of love. That is how he brought victory to the world. Is it not at the core of the Jesus story and the ongoing Jesus movement that the followers of Jesus take this same unique — holy — way? That they distinguish themselves most clearly and powerfully by living and dying, at least to egocentric and ethnocentric living if not otherwise? And, that they trust this way of Jesus' costly love, as opposed to other political, social, military ways, and thus continue to conquer? Twenty-first-century holiness proclamation must place much stronger emphasis on specifically dying to a self-centered life and filling with divine love as the primary meaning of purifying from sin.

HOLINESS IN HISTORICAL AND
THEOLOGICAL PERSPECTIVE

Integrated Streams of Holiness: Christian Holiness and Unity, Ancient and Future

DON THORSEN

Ancient Holiness

"Holy" is an ancient term, used in Scripture to describe God. "Holy, holy, holy is the LORD of hosts; the whole earth is full of his glory," says Isaiah (6:3).[1] *Holiness* describes the holy condition or quality of God that sets God utterly apart from everyone and everything else. Moses and the Israelites sang these words to God: "Who is like you, O LORD, among the gods? Who is like you, majestic in holiness, awesome in splendor, doing wonders?" (Exod. 15:11). Scripture is full of descriptions of the holiness, perfection, and uniqueness of God, wholly different — wholly transcendent, wholly other — from God's creation and creatures.[2] Believers were awed by God's holiness and celebrated God's holiness in worship.[3] Throughout biblical times, holiness was prominent in their understanding of themselves as well as God.

"Holy" and "holiness" are also terms that repeatedly appear in descriptions of both believers and churches in history. From the formation of

1. Scriptural references in this essay will be from the New Revised Standard Version of the Bible.

2. Deuteronomy 32:4; 1 Samuel 2:2; Isaiah 6:3; Revelation 4:8. Note: This list of verses and following biblical references do not intend to prove the statements made. Instead they serve as representative verses of statements made, which need to be investigated in the context of the whole of Scripture.

3. 1 Chronicles 16:29; Psalms 29:2; 99:5; 103:1; 145:21; Isaiah 6:3.

the ancient church through the development of Roman Catholic and Orthodox Churches, holiness appeared central to Christian self-understanding. Protestant Reformers differed in their understanding of the holy and holiness, focusing on the sovereignty of God in providing for them. However, the terms remained no less central to the preaching and teaching of the Protestant Reformers.

The revivals of the seventeenth and eighteenth centuries revealed an emphasis in Protestantism upon becoming more Christ-like through the immediate presence and power of the Holy Spirit in the lives of believers. Puritans, Quakers, Pietists, Methodists, and the leaders and participants in the Great Awakening all focused on the dynamic, transformative aspects of salvation, including sanctification as well as justification. This focus upon the Holy Spirit continued in the nineteenth century through the Holiness movement and, in the twentieth century, through the Pentecostal and Charismatic movements. Perhaps, more than other Christian traditions, these have focused on the importance of holiness.

Despite this ongoing stream of holiness in church history, its understanding and prominence in contemporary churches has waned. In self-described Holiness churches, no less, the movement has been pronounced "dead" by Keith Drury.[4] Likewise, in Pentecostal churches, Terry Cross laments that the early holiness emphasis in Pentecostal churches has virtually disappeared.[5]

Unfortunately, Christians who claimed to be oriented toward holiness have been subject to beliefs, values, and practices that have hurt rather than helped biblical holiness. Too often, holiness was conceived and promoted in ways inimical to its historical roots as well as to Scripture. Rightly or wrongly, the promotion of holiness and holy living became identified with legalistic perfectionism and the eradication of sin, a preoccupation with instantaneous rather than gradual growth in holiness, and a privatized rather than a holistic and socially constructive understanding of holiness. Some of these caricatures occurred due to excesses within the various Holiness traditions. The more unflattering caricatures, however, occurred

4. Keith Drury, "The Holiness Movement Is Dead," presidential address presented to the Christian Holiness Association, 1994. Available online at http://www.drurywriting.com/keith/dead.footnoted.htm.

5. Terry Cross, "Justification, Sanctification, and Justice in the Wesleyan-Pentecostal Movement," paper presented at the meeting of the Commission on Faith and Order, Portland, Maine, October 14, 2005, p. 11.

by those from other Christian traditions. Due to theological and cultural differences, ignorance, and sometimes laziness, Holiness traditions were misunderstood and mislabeled. Consequently, talk about holiness waned inside as well as outside churches, including those in the greater Holiness tradition. Less and less did Christians identify themselves and their churches as representative of holiness.

Is There a Future for Holiness?

Is there a future for holiness? What will it look like? These are important questions for Christians and for churches that are a part — directly or indirectly — of a self-described Holiness tradition, and for all Christians who worship a holy God and believe that God has called them to be holy, however it may be conceived and accomplished.

Although holiness has too often been misunderstood and neglected, it remains a well-known descriptor of Christians worldwide and can unite them because of their common goals of worshiping God, who is holy, and of becoming more like God in who they are and in how they demonstrate love to others. In order for holiness to function in a way that unites Christians and churches, we need to remember its biblical roots. We need to remember its pervasive roots throughout church history in describing Christian spirituality. We also need to imagine its future potential in uniting Christians and churches that already share common goals.

We do not need to create a new movement under the banner of holiness. Nor do we need to try to prop up a particular Holiness movement or tradition. Instead we need to work toward uniting a broad and diverse group of Christians and churches, who have forgotten or neglected some of their core values, yet recognize the family resemblance of people called to be holy.

In reflecting upon church history as well as Scripture, it is not possible to discuss with sufficient breadth and depth all the dynamics of holiness, including holiness preaching, teaching, and practice throughout the centuries. The following discussion should not be considered exhaustive or descriptive of all the important streams of Christendom, not all of which directly reflect holiness themes. However, we may paint broad strokes in describing Scripture and church history that accurately highlight the prominence of holiness. We may also identify points of contact between various Christians and church traditions that highlight holiness and the ways in which it has been inextricably bound up with the whole of Christendom.

If God represents the source of holiness, then Christians need to explore, understand, and appreciate various streams of holiness they represent and promote. In so doing, they may end up finding ways to better unite and cooperate in their common goals of uplifting God, who is holy, and of becoming more like God in all dimensions of life.

You Shall Be Holy

Jesus is described as holy, and his works were holy.[6] Moreover, Jesus makes God's people holy. The apostle Peter said the following about Jesus and the people of God:

> Come to him [Jesus], a living stone, though rejected by mortals yet chosen and precious in God's sight, and like living stones, let yourselves be built into a spiritual house to be a holy priesthood . . . you are a chosen race, a royal priesthood, a holy nation, God's own people. (1 Peter 2:4-5, 9)

Once saved, believers are enabled to grow in holiness. It is God who chooses who and what is to be holy; likewise, it is God who chooses and calls his people to holiness.[7] In the Old Testament, holiness is conferred by the sovereign action of God in people's covenantal relationship with God.[8] In the New Testament, holiness is conferred by the sacrifice of Jesus and, subsequently, through reconciliation and relationship with him.[9] The Holy Spirit continues to work in and through the lives of believers, sanctifying them to love God with their whole heart, soul, mind, and strength, and to love their neighbors as themselves.[10] The human response to Jesus' atonement, of course, involves faith and repentance. It further involves

---

6. Luke 1:35; 4:34; Mark 1:24; John 6:69; cf. Acts 2:27; 3:14; 13:35.
7. Deuteronomy 7:6; 2 Chronicles 7:16; 1 Kings 9:3; Ephesians 1:4.
8. Exodus 19:5-6; cf. 1 Thessalonians 5:23.
9. 1 Corinthians 1:2, 30; Hebrews 10:10.
10. 2 Thessalonians 2:13.

obedience to the Holy Spirit in the many ways God wants believers to be, think, say, and act.

The idea of the holy and holiness appears throughout church history. From the patristic writers in the ancient church through the formation of the Roman Catholic and Orthodox Churches, Christians championed the holiness of God and the holiness to which God calls believers: "The LORD spoke to Moses, saying: Speak to all the congregations of the people of Israel and say to them: You shall be holy, for I the LORD your God am holy" (Lev. 19:1-2). However, the various streams of church development obeyed the call to holiness in different ways. In the ancient church, holy living occurred through prayer, fasting, and almsgiving.[11] In time, it was expressed in more specific and, at times, dramatic ways. The early martyrs such as Ignatius of Antioch and Justin Martyr were considered paradigms of holiness. Later, holiness was also thought to be expressed through apologetic writings, mystical pursuits, and more and more through monastic living. Those whose ministry it was to give order and leadership to churches as well as monasteries fulfilled "holy orders" because they were thought to be spiritually closer to God.

In Roman Catholicism, a variety of expressions of holiness and spirituality arose. Mendicant ministers promoted apostolic living through the Franciscan and Dominican Orders. Scholastics emphasized spirituality expressed through theological research and education, and mystics emphasized spirituality expressed through personal encounters with God by means of contemplation, visions, and other ecstatic experiences. More than ever the spiritual disciplines were promoted among the laity as well as the clergy in encouraging devotion to God, for example, through such writings as *The Imitation of Christ* by Thomas à Kempis. All the time holiness remained a central goal of Roman Catholicism.

Orthodox Churches also followed the call to holiness, though in somewhat different ways. Some pursued mystical spirituality, while others promoted the concept of *theosis* (deification), which emphasized the opportunity for all believers to participate in God. Such participation helped them grow more intimate in relationship with God. It also helped them become godlier in loving service to God and others. The use of icons was helpful in aiding believers in prayer and in nurturing their participation in

---

11. John McGuckin, "The Early Church Fathers," in *The Story of Christian Spirituality: Two Thousand Years,* ed. Gordon Mursell (Minneapolis: Fortress, 2001), pp. 31-72.

God. Icons helped to focus upon God in worship, in the spiritual disciplines, and subsequently in living holier lives. Like Roman Catholics, Orthodox Christians thought that believers could become more saintly.

Protestantism introduced new understandings of holiness, yet it remained a pursuit of theirs. Reformers such as Martin Luther and John Calvin talked about holiness more in terms of how God *imputes* it to believers than in terms of how God *imparts* holiness to them. To be sure, the Reformers recognized that God calls believers to be holy, but it is a holiness that is imputed or positional. That is, it is through God's "alien righteousness," according to Luther, that believers become holy, without which anyone will receive eternal life.[12] The Reformers' emphasis on the sovereignty of God elevated the role of God in all aspects of salvation, discharging believers from responsibility. Every aspect of salvation and the Christian life were thought to be due to divine predestination and election rather than to any word or deed on the part of people. Certainly, believers are expected to act righteously out of a sense of respect, praise, and thanksgiving to God. However, if they became more holy, then they were to give all the credit and glory to God. It is the responsibility of God, rather than people, to fulfill the biblical call to holiness.

Protestant developments subsequent to the Reformation went in more than a few directions, and it lies beyond the scope of this essay to investigate them, despite our interest and appreciation for their contributions. Although Protestants deeply appreciated the theological and ecclesiastical improvements they inherited from the Reformers, they took seriously the Reformation emphasis upon the need to be "always reforming." For the sake of this discussion, I want to focus on only two of the developments that occurred among Protestants after the Reformation. The first focus has to do with reassertions of the synergistic responsibility of people in cooperating with God's gracious initiation for salvation. Salvation, conceived this way, includes a sense of task as well as gift. The Reformers were thought to have gone too far in emphasizing the sovereignty of God at the expense of human freedom. The second focus has to do with Protestants reasserting the singular importance of sanctification as well as justification. Salvation, conceived this way, includes more emphasis on the ongo-

---

12. Martin Luther, "Two Kinds of Righteousness," in *Luther's Works*, vol. 31, *Career of the Reformer: I*, ed. Harold J. Grimm, trans. Lowell J. Satre (Philadelphia: Muhlenberg, 1957) pp. 297ff.

ing work of God through the Holy Spirit in the lives of believers in addition to the completed work of God through Jesus Christ and the atonement.

Ironically, these foci reflect a reintegration of the streams of Roman Catholic and Orthodox beliefs, values, and practices devalued by the Protestant Reformers. Like so many renewal movements, later adherents modify the reactive positions thought to be held by their forebears. In their place, more balanced positions are developed (or attempted) from all the contributing streams. In the abiding pursuit of God and God-likeness, Protestants after the Reformation sought a more balanced, presumably biblical, view of such issues as the responsible participation of believers for salvation, holistically conceived, as well as to the actual holiness to which God calls them.

Gift and Task

Theologically, one of the persistent debates about salvation has to do with the relationship between God's role in making people holy (gift) and people's role in its accomplishment (task). Throughout most of church history, there has been surprising agreement about how holiness — pertaining to sanctification as well as justification — involves both divine gift and human task. However, debate over this issue began in earnest with Augustine's opposition to Pelagius and the prospect of salvation by the merit of good works. Although we have none of his writings, Augustine portrayed Pelagius as advancing the primary responsibility of people for their salvation and for Christian living. Augustine strongly objected to Pelagian emphases upon human effort or merit for salvation. Due to the sin and depravity of people, Augustine thought that God alone was responsible for salvation. People are dead in sin and must rely entirely upon God's grace and election for gaining eternal life. God alone provides the holiness without which no one will be saved.

The ancient and medieval churches followed Augustine's theological lead in so many ways. However, in terms of the relationship between divine providence and human freedom, Christians held to more of a semi-Augustinian view. They emphasized the need for God to initiate, sustain, and complete people's salvation. Still, people needed to respond freely to God's offer of salvation, working synergistically with God. God gives grace to all, providing the wherewithal for people to choose or do what is necessary for salvation. This affirms both the primacy of God for salvation and the need for people to respond.

Both the Roman Catholic and Orthodox Churches affirmed semi-Augustinian views of divine predestination and human freedom, reflective of the majority of ancient church writers. Thomas Aquinas, for example, articulated how people have responsibilities both for their salvation and for living the Christian life. In addition to accepting God's gracious offer of salvation, mediated through the sacraments, believers are called to live virtuous, holy lives. The Christian life involves both gift and task, both divine grace and human faith, hope, and love. Accordingly, believers are called to plant seeds of holiness, though it is God — of course — who gives the increase (1 Cor. 3:6, 9).

Protestant Reformers such as Luther and Calvin reintroduced Augustinianism in their views of divine predestination and human freedom. As in Augustine's view, people were thought to be dead in sin, totally depraved, and bound to damnation. Salvation could come only by *sola gratia* (grace alone) and *sola fide* (faith alone) — hallmarks of the Protestant Reformation. To think otherwise was considered Pelagian and heretical, relative to biblical teachings. Grace was irresistible, and believers should not expect to do anything in order to attain their justification (or conversion) or growth in holiness apart from God's election.

Later Protestants acted to counterbalance perceived excesses in the Reformers. Among those excesses were their views of divine predestination and human freedom. James Arminius, for example, represents a key interpreter of Calvinism, who advocated a more semi-Augustinian view of people and their relationship with God. At the Synod of Dort (1611), followers of Arminius challenged the so-called five points of Calvinism, which championed the sovereignty of God in all matters of belief and practice.[13] Although Arminian ideas were condemned, their influence spread throughout the Protestant world.

Arminianism was largely accepted by the Church of England (the Anglican Church) and its offshoots, including Wesley and the Methodists. Wesley challenged Calvinistic views of divine predestination and human

13. The so-called five points of Calvinism include: (1) total depravity; (2) unconditional election; (3) limited atonement; (4) irresistible grace; and (5) perseverance of the saints. Together the first letters of the five points are summarized by the acronym TULIP.

freedom, considering the latter critical for his holistically conceived *ordo salutis* (order of salvation). Later developments in the Methodist and Holiness traditions continued to emphasize synergism and its significance for evangelism and missions as well as discipleship and the pursuit of holiness.

Other Protestant traditions affirmed synergism — in practice, if not in theory. Pentecostalism, for example, followed in the theological tradition of the Wesleyan and Holiness movements in several ways. One of those ways includes an emphasis upon how God wants to empower believers for holy living and for ministry as well as for conversion to Christianity. Certainly there are Pentecostal churches that follow other theological emphases, reflective of magisterial Reformers. Pentecostal beliefs, values, and practices are not uniform; they are diverse, despite their common emphasis upon the person and work of the Holy Spirit. Nevertheless, Pentecostals tend to emphasize both the sovereignty of God and human freedom, seeing the two as wonderfully complementary in fulfilling God's will for people. Indeed, they champion the empowerment that comes through the Holy Spirit, baptizing them in ways that result in a dynamic ministry of spiritual gifts.

Wesleyan, Holiness, Pentecostal Connection

Wesley considered holiness important for understanding both justification and sanctification. The Holy Spirit makes it possible through the various ways God graciously works in and through the lives of believers. Wesley thought that God's grace works preveniently in calling people to conversion. He further thought that God continued to work graciously for their justification and, subsequently, for their sanctification. Wesley was optimistic about the empowerment available through the Holy Spirit for entirely sanctifying those who earnestly consecrated their lives to God. He advocated holiness of heart and life that resembled the spiritual heritage of Roman Catholicism and Orthodoxy as well as what he believed Scripture taught about God's call to holiness. Wesley valued and encouraged people to read Roman Catholic and Orthodox authors as well as Protestants.

Wesley emphasized the person and work of the Holy Spirit in his ministry and writings because he thought that Christians needed to focus upon the dynamic ways the Holy Spirit acts in our day-to-day lives.[14] In reclaiming the importance of the Holy Spirit, Wesley thought that the Christian life was intended by God to be a dynamic time of personal growth in holiness as well as a dynamic time of ministry. Personally, believers had the privilege of a "second blessing" of the Holy Spirit, usually occurring subsequent to conversion.

Wesley discusses his views on sanctification at length in his treatise *A Plain Account of Christian Perfection.*[15] After conversion, God continues to work graciously in the lives of believers, calling them to live holy, Christ-like lives. Total consecration on the part of believers would be aided by God's grace through the Holy Spirit in sanctifying them through and through. This entire sanctification, which Wesley also described as Christian perfection, empowered believers to live lives of love for God with all their heart, soul, mind, and strength. It also empowered them to love their neighbors as themselves, ministering to their physical as well as spiritual needs. Indeed, Wesley conceived of entire sanctification in terms of perfecting a believer's intention to love as Christ had loved. The second blessing (or second crisis, subsequent to the crisis of conversion) did not result in sinless or absolute perfection; such a view was neither biblical nor realistic, based upon experience. As long as people live in this world, they are subject to the finitude, sin, and other forces — good and evil — that bind them. Despite these, Wesley was optimistic with regard to the degree God's Holy Spirit may purify believers in their intention to love God and others. Purity of intention, in turn, led to optimism with regard to the holiness they may achieve in who they are and what they think, say, and do. Such purity was expected to impact the world socially as well as individually, serving to overcome societal ills in addition to what people suffered individually.

The Holiness Movement

The Holiness movement in the United States promoted Wesley's emphasis upon holiness of heart and life. Phoebe Palmer and others such as Charles

14. For example, see Wesley's sermons on "The First-fruits of the Spirit," "The Witness of the Spirit, I," "The Witness of the Spirit, II," in *The Works of John Wesley*, vol. 1, Sermons I, 1-33, ed. Albert C. Outler (Nashville: Abingdon, 1984), pp. 233-47, 267-98.

15. John Wesley, *A Plain Account of Christian Perfection, as believed and taught by the Reverend Mr. John Wesley from the year 1725 to the year 1777* (Kansas City: Beacon Hill Press, 1966).

Finney, John Noyes, and Timothy Merritt made holiness the focus of their lives and ministries. Camp meetings, churches, and denominations arose that made holiness the focus of their Christianity. Some of the denominations that identified with the Holiness movement include the Wesleyan Methodist Connection (1843), Free Methodist Church (1860), Church of the Nazarene (1895), Pillar of Fire (1901), and Brethren in Christ (1910). Of course, the Holiness movement influenced more than these new churches. They also influenced existing denominations, and their influence increased through the turn of the century, outside as well as inside the United States.[16]

More than Wesley, the Holiness movement promoted the crisis experience of purification available to believers subsequent to conversion. In an instant, they thought, believers might experience quantum growth in their spirituality.[17] In describing entire sanctification (or Christian perfection), Holiness preachers and teachers referred to this second blessing as "baptism with the Holy Spirit."[18] Using phraseology derived principally from John Fletcher, Wesley's chosen successor, the Holiness movement promoted purification and piety in the lives of believers as well as in their ministries.[19] They did not intend that their holiness should be individualistic, privatized, or legalistic. On the contrary, like Wesley, they were active in spreading holiness that impacted people and society as a whole in addition to the more predictable areas of conversion and morality.[20] The Salvation Army, founded by William and Catherine Booth, more than other churches, promoted holiness that broadly ministered to the social, political, and economic well-being of people as well as to their spiritual well-being.

16. In England, for example, the first Keswick Convention met in 1875, promoting holiness, and the organization of the Salvation Army in 1878 represents one of the most prominent branches of the Holiness movement.

17. See Phoebe Palmer's *The Way of Holiness* (Wheaton, Ill.: Institute of Evangelism, Billy Graham Center, 1996).

18. For example, see Acts 2:2-4; 8:15-17; 10:44-47; 11:15-17; 15:8; 19:6.

19. See Laurence Wood's discussion of the influence of John Fletcher upon the Holiness movement in *Pentecostal Grace* (Grand Rapids: Zondervan, 1980), pp. 177-239.

20. Timothy L. Smith, *Revivalism and Social Reform: American Protestantism on the Eve of the Civil War* (Eugene, Ore.: Wipf & Stock, 2004).

Pentecostalism

Pentecostalism has done more than any Christian movement in church history to focus on the dynamic aspects of the person and work of the Holy Spirit. Most of the early Pentecostals came out of the Holiness movement and used its phraseology to articulate their full gospel experience of the gifts of the Holy Spirit.[21] Marked by speaking in tongues, prophecy, and other signs and wonders, Pentecostals quickly grew in size and influence in the Christian world, despite the general refusal of existing churches to accept their emphasis upon the gifts of the Holy Spirit. Like the Holy Spirit, they too were a holy movement of God, and holiness played a prominent role in their self-understanding and ministry. Sometimes called "holy rollers," Pentecostals emphasized holiness along with the fire (or power) of the Holy Spirit. Some claimed that baptism with the Holy Spirit represented a third crisis (or third work) in the lives of believers, subsequent to conversion. These were sometimes called Holiness Pentecostals. Others claimed that baptism with the Holy Spirit represented the second crisis, which included power for holy living along with the power of spiritual gifts. These tended to view baptism with the Holy Spirit as part of one, finished work of Christ in the lives of believers.

There were a variety of differences found among Pentecostals, since they largely consisted of independent churches that developed because existing churches did not welcome them. Nevertheless, holiness remained an important theme among Pentecostals. Pentecostalism is unique; there is nothing quite like it in church history. Yet it shares a family resemblance with the Wesleyan and Holiness traditions from which it emerged. To this day, Pentecostals often refer to themselves as "Holiness churches," if for no other reason than that they focus so intently upon the dynamic aspects of the person and work of the Holy Spirit — the Spirit who is Holy.

The Charismatic movement arose during the 1960s, and it represented a Pentecostal renewal within existing denominations. The denominations included more than Protestant churches; they included Roman Catholic, Orthodox, and Anglican Churches as well. Altogether, Pentecostal and

21. It is now commonplace to trace the theological and ecclesiastical connection between Wesley, the Holiness movement, and Pentecostalism. See Donald W. Dayton, *Theological Roots of Pentecostalism* (Grand Rapids: Zondervan, 1987), and Vinson Synan, *The Holiness-Pentecostal Tradition: Charismatic Movements in the Twentieth Century*, 2d ed. (Grand Rapids: Eerdmans, 1997).

Charismatic emphases upon baptism with the Holy Spirit, spiritual gifts, and lively worship services with contemporary choruses, music, and instruments transformed much of Christendom. Few churches today have escaped the valuable influence of Pentecostalism and the Charismatic movement in their broad-ranging emphases, theologically and ministerially. Throughout their existence, the Spirit, who is Holy, is uplifted and promoted in empowering believers in life, in church, in ministry, and in all aspects of the world. The Holy Spirit acts to make people holy individually, ministerially, socially, and in all other ways God wants to empower believers.

Integrated streams of holiness flow throughout church history, and not just through the Wesleyan, Holiness, and Pentecostal connection. It flows from Scripture, and its offshoots branch out like a delta with tributaries that meet, mingle, and then spread further. God, of course, is ultimately the one who unites Christians. Yet, terms, phrases, and other images can also serve to unify those with differences and also similarities. Holiness already serves as a word that many Christians use to describe a family resemblance among themselves, their churches, and their ministries. Despite its particular and sometimes peculiar, downright doleful connotations, holiness may still serve as a point of unity among Christians. It is a term both ancient in usage and future in potential for uniting Christians; it unites them in worship of a holy God and in living holy, Christ-like lives that impact people socially as well as individually, and physically as well as spiritually.

Varieties of Christian Spirituality

In contemporary literature on Christian spirituality, there is widespread recognition and appreciation for Wesley and for his emphasis upon holiness.[22] Especially within the Protestant tradition, Wesley represents a model of what is most often called holiness spirituality. Even if authors do

22. Information in this section and the next first appeared in a paper I presented entitled "Ecumenism, Spirituality, and Holiness: John Wesley and the Variety of Christian Spiritualities," Annual Meeting of the Wesleyan Theological Society, Seattle Pacific University, Seattle, Washington, March 5, 2005.

not agree with everything Wesley said, he is credited with representing an important spiritual impulse among Christians throughout church history.

A survey of contemporary literature on the subject of Christian spirituality reveals Wesley's prominence. In summary of such literature, let me list some of the typologies used by scholars to discuss Christian spirituality. For example, Richard Foster, who is Quaker, represents a prominent, contemporary authority in Christian spirituality. In his book *Streams of Living Water,* he outlines what he considers six "great Traditions — streams of spiritual life if you will — and . . . significant figures in each."[23] They are:

> The Contemplative Tradition, or the prayer-filled life; The Holiness Tradition, or the virtuous life; The Charismatic Tradition, or the Spirit-empowered life; The Social Justice Tradition, or the compassionate life; The Evangelical Tradition, or the Word-centered life; the Incarnational Tradition, or the sacramental life.[24]

In Foster's book as well as in other writings on the Christian life, Wesley figures prominently as a representative of holiness spirituality.[25]

Other typologies list a larger number of Christian spiritualities. Ben Campbell Johnson, a Presbyterian, lists seven types of spirituality. He lists Wesley, for example, as having an ascetic spirituality rather than a holiness spirituality per se, but the essence of the type remains the same. Gary Thomas, a Baptist, draws upon Carl Jung and Myers-Briggs "types" in identifying nine "spiritual temperaments," what he calls "sacred pathways": (1) Naturalist, (2) Sensate, (3) Traditionalist, (4) Ascetic, (5) Activist, (6) Caregiver, (7) Enthusiast, (8) Contemplative, and (9) Intellectual.[26] In this typology, Wesley and the Holiness tradition appear several places, as both ascetics and activists. While these typologies may not appeal to every-

23. See the foreword to Richard J. Foster, *Streams of Living Water: Celebrating the Great Traditions of Christian Faith* (New York: HarperSanFrancisco, 1998), p. xvi.

24. Foster, *Streams of Living Water,* p. xvi.

25. In the book *Authentic Spirituality: Moving Beyond Mere Religion* (Grand Rapids: Baker Academic, 2001), Barry L. Callen elaborates on each of the spiritual traditions identified by Richard Foster *(Streams of Living Water)* and highlights the holiness and Wesleyan dimensions in particular.

26. Ben Campbell Johnson, *Pastoral Spirituality: A Focus for Ministry* (Philadelphia: Westminster, 1988); Gary L. Thomas, *Sacred Pathways: Discovering Your Soul's Path to God* (Grand Rapids: Zondervan, 2000), p. 21; cf. pp. 26, 100-101.

one in the Holiness tradition, they reflect recognition of Wesley and the larger holiness embodiment of Christian spirituality.

The following list of Christian spiritualities is not intended to be exhaustive but representative of the different ways Christians find spirituality depicted in Scripture as well as how they live out spirituality in their lives:

Christian Spirituality
Academic
Activist
Charismatic
Contemplative
Ecumenical
Evangelical
Holiness
Sacramental

Most comprehensive studies of spirituality resist typologies and list a wide variety of Christian spiritualities, spanning the entirety of church history. Robin Maas and Gabriel O'Donnell, a Methodist and Roman Catholic respectively, offer more of a historical than typological list. They include patristic spirituality, monastic spirituality, mendicant spirituality, *devotio moderna* spirituality, Lutheran spirituality, Ignatian spirituality, Reformed spirituality, Carmelite spirituality, Anglican spirituality, Wesleyan spirituality, black spirituality, Marian spirituality, and feminist spirituality.[27] Of course, it would not take long perusing *The Westminster Dictionary of Christian Spirituality* to find literally dozens of distinctive Christian spiritualities.[28] In all these studies, Wesley remains a prominent and well respected leader — a crucial piece of the mosaic we call Christian spirituality.

---

27. Robin Maas and Gabriel O'Donnell, O.P., eds., *Spiritual Traditions for the Contemporary Church* (Nashville: Abingdon, 1990).

28. *The Westminster Dictionary of Christian Spirituality,* ed. Gordon S. Wakefield (Philadelphia: Westminster, 1983), passim.

Don Thorsen

Holiness and Unity

Holiness is a holistic, inclusive descriptor of Christian spirituality.[29] Why? Holiness implies wholeness and completeness as well as godlikeness. In the Bible, of course, God is referred to as being holy. Some consider the holiness of God as being representative of all God's perfections, of all God's transcendent characteristics.[30] In Scripture, Christians are repeatedly called to live lives of holiness. In the Old Testament, Leviticus 11:44a says, "For I am the LORD your God; sanctify yourselves therefore, and be holy, for I am holy." In the New Testament, 1 Peter 1:15 says, "Instead, as he who called you is holy, be holy yourselves in all your conduct." In the Sermon on the Mount, Jesus makes the most profound call to holiness when he says, "Be perfect as your heavenly Father is perfect" (Matt. 5:48). This call is to wholeness and completeness in every respect as well as to a moral conception of godliness, usually thought to be representative of holiness spirituality.

When holiness is viewed in relationship to the varieties of Christian spirituality, there is no reason to consider them in competition. On the contrary, it is not a matter of *either* holiness *or* some other form of spirituality, whether it is evangelical, sacramental, contemplative, or activist. Holiness may be understood in essence as embracing all the traditions of spirituality. It is a both/and relationship rather than one that is either/or. In fact, one could say that holiness, in the essential sense of the term, could be understood as a catchword that integrates all types of spirituality. Laurence Wood, for example, exemplifies this inclusive attitude in his writings on Christian spirituality. In his chapter on "Sanctification from a Wesleyan Perspective" in *Christian Spirituality: Five Views of Sanctification,* he speaks positively of the other four views, cultivating points of contact and cooperation rather than focusing on non-essential differences of opinion.[31]

Despite the inherent inclusivity of Wesley and his ideas of spirituality,

29. Randy Maddox shares this holistic concept of salvation and spirituality; see *Responsible Grace: John Wesley's Practical Theology* (Nashville: Abingdon, 1994), pp. 145-46.

30. For example, see Gustaf Aulén, *The Faith of the Christian Church,* 5th ed., trans. Eric H. Wahlstrom (Philadelphia: Fortress, 1960), pp. 102-6.

31. Laurence W. Wood, "The Wesleyan View," in *Christian Spirituality: Five Views on Sanctification,* ed. Donald L. Alexander (Downers Grove, Ill.: InterVarsity, 1988), pp. 95-132; cf. pp. 36-41, 83-87, 162-67, 197-99.

the Holiness tradition has often been sectarian in its theological as well as ecclesiastical manifestations. As mentioned, Wesley sometimes had difficulty accepting and cooperating with everyone who called themselves Christian, even with his "catholic spirit."[32] Likewise, proponents of the Holiness tradition — individually and collectively — have sometimes promoted fragmentation and schism more than ecumenism.

Nevertheless, holiness continues to embody an inclusivity that makes it an appealing point of contact with various traditions of Christian spirituality, outside as well as inside the Holiness tradition. In addition, it becomes an appealing point of contact for ecumenical dialogue, theologically and ecclesiastically. Proponents of holiness must remain humble; other traditions have equal rights in expressing their views of spirituality, especially in claims to holism reflected in their spirituality. Proponents of holiness must also remain open — genuinely open — to learning from other Christian traditions of spirituality. Wesley arguably remained open to learning from others when his views were demonstrated to be deficient or wrong.[33] Likewise, those of us in the Holiness tradition need to be humble, yet bold in uplifting the ecumenical value of holiness as a descriptor of Christian spirituality as well as Christian unity.

The Wesleyan Holiness Study Project represents one attempt to recover the ancient importance of holiness in Scripture and church history as well as its determination of the greater Holiness tradition.[34] The Wesleyan Holiness Study Project also represents an attempt to investigate the future potential of holiness for uniting Christians in their shared goals of worshiping a holy God and of living holy lives. Holiness, in fact, has surprising ecumenical potential that reaches far beyond the Holiness tradition to Christians worldwide.

32. See Wesley's sermon entitled "Catholic Spirit," in *The Works of John Wesley*, vol. 2, Sermons II, 34-70, ed. Albert C. Outler (Nashville: Abingdon, 1984), pp. 79-96.

33. Wesley said, "But some may say I have mistaken the way myself, although I take upon me to teach it to others. It is probable many will think this; and it is very possible that I have. But I trust, whereinsoever I have mistaken, my mind is open to conviction. I sincerely desire to be better informed. I say to God and man, 'What I know not, teach thou me.'" See "Sermons on Several Occasions," preface, in *The Works of John Wesley*, vol. 1, ed. Albert C. Outler (Nashville: Abingdon, 1984), p. 107.

34. The Wesleyan Holiness Study Project was a four-year (2004-2007) series of conferences held at Azusa Pacific University, Azusa, California, which discussed and promoted holiness. Led by Kevin Mannoia, numerous denominations historically, theologically, and ministerially related to one another sponsored the Wesleyan Holiness Study Project.

How Shall We Then Live?

The Wesleyan, Holiness, and Pentecostal traditions provide a Christian legacy that extends far beyond their respective theologies, ministries, and numerous adherents worldwide. How can we summarize that legacy? There may be no definitive answer. However, two things they do share in common are their goal to worship God, who is holy, and to promote holiness through the dynamic ways in which God's Holy Spirit works in and through the lives of believers. These goals are as essential to ancient Christianity as they are for the future of Christianity. Can holiness serve as term that unites Christians? Can it serve further as a term that unites other Christian traditions, Roman Catholic, Orthodox, and Protestant? Perhaps.

What holiness has going for it, ecumenically speaking, is the fact that so many Christians already refer to themselves and their churches as holy. Indeed, it is an ancient term, going back to Scripture and the earliest Christians, and there is no reason to suspect that its relevance will cease in the future. Christians today may not refer to themselves as being part of the Holiness movement, narrowly conceived. However, they describe themselves as holy — by the grace of God. So, what is needed is greater attention to understanding, appreciating, and promoting holiness. That attentiveness needs to occur in believers individually, collectively, and institutionally in churches and academic institutions as well as other Christian organizations.

How shall we then live? We should live as people who worship God, who is holy. We should live holy lives as God calls us to live. We should seek to understand God, God's holiness, and its relevance for integrating into our lives a vital, healthy, and comprehensive vision of Christianity. Its holistic nature challenges us to understand holiness in its potential for uniting those things so often disjoined. Charles Wesley, John's brother and co-worker in the Methodist movement, stated that he wanted to "unite the pair so long disjoined, Knowledge and vital Piety: Learning and holiness combined."[35] These words reflect John Wesley's holistic approach to Christianity, integrating aspects too often disjoined. William Abraham comments that Wesley had an unusual ability to hold in creative tension

---

35. Charles Wesley, "A Collection of Hymns for the use of the People called Methodists, 1780," Hymn 461, 1.5, in *The Works of John Wesley*, Oxford Edition (Oxford: Clarendon Press, 1983), vol. 7, p. 644.

aspects of Christianity that need integration: "faith, works; personal devotions, sacramental practice; personal piety, social concern; justification, sanctification; evangelism, Christian nurture; Bible, tradition; revelation, reason; commitment, civility; creation, redemption; cell group, institutional church; local scene, world parish."[36]

Integration does not occur at once; it is an ongoing process that continues among believers and churches from one generation to the next. As we come to understand and appreciate holiness more for what it can accomplish theologically as well as ministerially, then perhaps we can become more effective in promoting its relevance for unifying Christians. May it support and unite them in their common goals of worshiping God the Father, who is holy, and correspondingly of living holy lives as modeled for us by Jesus Christ and empowered by the Holy Spirit.

36. William Abraham advocates Wesleyanism in advocating the revival of Christianity worldwide. He argues that Wesley's significance rests largely on his ability to hold together elements in Christianity that generally are pulled apart and listed in isolation. Abraham presents this list of contrasting emphases that Wesley and his message of holiness integrate for a vital, healthy, and comprehensive vision of Christianity. See *The Coming Great Revival: Recovering the Full Evangelical Tradition* (San Francisco: Harper & Row, 1984), p. 67.

CHAPTER 5

The Social Vision of the Holiness Movement

WILLIAM KOSTLEVY

It is a fitting testimony to the work of scholars such as Timothy L. Smith and Donald W. Dayton that the significant role played by the Wesleyan Holiness movement in the history of antebellum reform has become common knowledge among students of American culture and religious history. In his landmark *Discovering an Evangelical Heritage,* a work which in part helped to define and deepen the missiological understanding of a generation of evangelicals, Dayton convincingly demonstrated that for nineteenth-century evangelicals, rooted in the Methodistic perfectionist currents, "Christian" mission included such important cultural mandates as the abolition of slavery and the empowerment of women and the poor. Dayton, understandably, defined the cultural mission of nineteenth-century evangelicals in terms that had immediate relevance to evangelicals shaped by the social crisis of the 1960s. Left unexplained in Dayton's work (which, it should be noted, made no claims to be exhaustive) were a constellation of related social issues which, taken as a whole, defined the moral universe for a significant segment within the Wesleyan Holiness tradition.[1] Primarily comprising Free Methodists, Wesleyan Methodists, United Brethren, and other Wesleyan Holiness folk who interpreted Wesley

---

1. Donald W. Dayton, *Discovering an Evangelical Heritage* (New York: Harper & Row, 1976). See also Dayton's postscript in the reissued edition, *Discovering an Evangelical Heritage* (Peabody, Mass.: Hendrickson, 1988). Also Timothy L. Smith, *Revivalism and Social Reform in Mid-Nineteenth Century America* (New York: Abingdon, 1957).

through the moral lens of Oberlin, Ohio, especially through the eyes of its most famous resident, evangelist Charles G. Finney, this body of so-called radical evangelicals insisted that in the mission of the church, revivals of religion and societal transformation were two indivisible parts of the same gospel.[2]

Highly critical of the sentimentality of Phoebe Palmer's shorter way to heart holiness, radical evangelicalism vigorously sought to purify church and state from such egregious sins as slaveholding, and in the years following the Civil War, racial prejudice, Sabbath desecration, complicity with the liquor traffic, and tolerating secret societies. Of these issues, the radical evangelical crusade against secret societies presents the modern reader with particular difficulties. Dismissed by a generation of scholars as either a typical expression of rural evangelical paranoia or a manifestation of "new" right extremism, the crusade nevertheless played a determinative role in the formation of the Free Methodist Church, the fragmentation of the Wesleyan Methodist Church following the Civil War, and the subsequent division of the United Brethren in Christ Church. Initiated by the venerable father of modern revivalism, Charles G. Finney, and led for a quarter century by ardent reformer and Wheaton College president Jonathan Blanchard, as late as the 1940s, the campaign was a crucial element in the mission of a diverse assortment of evangelicals who came together to form the National Association of Evangelicals.[3] In spite of its obvious cen-

2. The term "radical evangelical" is a creation of the author, but is partially dependent on Victor B. Howard, *Religion and the Radical Republican Movement, 1860-1870* (Lexington: University Press of Kentucky, 1990), and draws on discussions with David Bundy. As a loose coalition, the composition of the radical coalition varied over time. Among the useful lists of denominations, see that in "Coercion or Conscience," *Christian Cynosure* April 9, 1874; and in E. Ronayne, *Ronayne's Reminiscences: A History of His Life and Renunciation of Romanism and Freemasonry* (Chicago: Free Methodist Publishing House, 1900), p. 424.

3. A classic expression of what might be termed the "paranoid" interpretation of American evangelicalism is Seymour Martin Lipset and Earl Raab, *The Politics of Unreason: Right-Wing Extremism in America, 1790-1977* (Chicago: University of Chicago Press, 1978). Drawing on the writings of Richard Hofstadter, this work treats the participants of this campaign as part of a continuous stream of political extremism threatening the foundations of American society. In a discussion of the "moralistic Protestant creed" of the National Christian Association, Lipset and Raab conveniently ignore the organization's support for the civil rights of African Americans, Asians, and women while quoting features of the platform of the American Party that confirm the authors' prejudices. Although paranoia is certainly present in the National Christian Association, it is unfair to reduce the broad reform commitment of the NCA to such an ambiguous phenomenon.

trality to the Wesleyan Holiness experience, antisecrecy has received little attention from students of the movement. This is certainly not surprising. Lacking either the popular appeal of abolitionism and the women's movement or the biblical basis of Sabbatarianism, and presenting no clear health or social relevance such as temperance did, antimasonry does not seem to provide us with a usable past. Yet, following a suggestion by Robert Darnton that it is precisely where the past is most opaque that we most often find the key to the meaning of an alien cultural system, I will explore the cultural mission of radical evangelicalism as it interacts with one of the most explosive dimensions of nineteenth-century North American culture, women's changing roles.[4]

Although the origins of modern secret societies remain shrouded in mystery, Freemasonry, the forerunner and model for the secret societies, is generally believed to have been started in London during the early eighteenth century. With indirect roots in a medieval English guild of stonemasons, Masons included celebrated clergymen, professional men, and scientists ideologically tied to such Enlightenment concepts as deism, and to such related ideas as a natural morality and divine revelation apart from Scripture. Transported to New England late in the eighteenth century, Freemasonry frequently functioned as a vehicle of religious and political dissent, particularly for men who found in its elaborate rituals, code of ethics, convivial brotherhood, claims of universality, and oath-bound secrecy an attractive alternative to established Congregationalism's austere Calvinist orthodoxy.

During the early nineteenth century, alongside the spread of Masonry, evangelical Christianity also experienced rapid growth, especially among women. The evangelical emphasis upon heartfelt piety, moral responsibility, and corporate discipline led almost inevitably to a conflict with Masonry because the two movements had foundationally contradictory value systems.[5] Such a conflict erupted following the apparent abduction and murder, presumably by Masons, of William Morgan, a Batavia, New York, Mason who threatened to make public elements of the Masonic secret ritual. Even though no body was ever found and evidence was circumstantial,

4. Robert Darnton, *The Great Cat Massacre and Other Episodes in French Cultural History* (New York: Basic Books, 1984), p. 5.
5. The most useful work dealing with evangelical success among women is Curtis D. Johnson, *Islands of Holiness: Rural Religion in Upstate New York, 1790-1860* (Ithaca: Cornell University Press, 1988), pp. 53-66.

the controversy was exacerbated by the acquittal of four Masons by a jury which included Masons before court officials who were also Masons. Concerns raised by the publicity surrounding the Morgan incident caused lodge membership to plummet.

Primarily limited to the North, especially New England, and to areas with significant numbers of migrants from New England such as western New York, parts of Pennsylvania, northern Ohio, and Michigan, antimasonry was "a church-oriented protest against the Masons, a fraternal body believed to be undemocratic, anti-American, elitist, anti-female, a substitute religion," and subversive to the American legal system.[6] Forming themselves into a political party, antimasons gained immediate political success in New York, Vermont, and Pennsylvania. They passed a series of proscriptive laws limiting the order's rights in Vermont, Massachusetts, and Rhode Island. Most significantly, a generation of young political leaders, such as Thurlow Weed and William H. Seward in New York, Thaddeus Stevens in Pennsylvania, and William Slade in Vermont, emerged from antimasonic forays to play key roles in subsequent American political history.[7]

Many, including ex-Mason Charles G. Finney, believed the order had been dealt a mortal blow by the antebellum antimasonry movement. However, such hopes proved to be premature, as by the 1850s a Masonic revival was underway. In 1865, membership eclipsed its pre-Morgan figures, and continued to grow rapidly for the reminder of the century. In 1897, a writer in the *North American Review* estimated that every fifth, or perhaps eighth, man belonged to one of the country's seventy thousand fraternal lodges. This figure did not included the millions more who belonged to other organizations that included features of fraternal orders, such as the Grand Army of the Republic, the Knights of Labor, the Good Templars, the Grange, and mutual insurance companies. Comprised primarily of white, middle-class Protestant men or skilled workers — the high cost of initiation fees, annual dues, travel, uniforms, and ritualistic paraphernalia excluded most ordinary farmers and workers — secret societies, historian

---

6. A useful general outline of the history of freemasonry is found in Lynn Dumenil, *Freemasonry and American Culture, 1880-1930* (Princeton: Princeton University Press, 1984). The quotation is from William Preston Vaughn, "An Overview of Pre– and Post–Civil War Antimasonry," *Historian* 49 (August 1987): 495.

7. On the social significance of the antebellum antimasonic crusade, see Paul Goodman, *Towards a Christian Republic: Antimasonry and the Great Transition in New England, 1826-1836* (New York: Oxford University Press, 1988), p. 53.

Mark C. Carnes has argued, provided Victorian-era men with solace and meaning independent of the female-dominated evangelical religiosity of the late nineteenth century. As a consequence, the radical evangelical crusade against secret societies can be viewed as part of a gender-driven struggle to shape the spiritual direction of American society in the late nineteenth century. To understand that struggle, one needs to explore briefly both the masculine ideology of the lodge and the female dominance, or at least the perceived dominance, of evangelical Christianity. It is only within this context that radical evangelicalism's crusade for an egalitarian, interracial social order that enshrined the values of the temperance movement, the evangelical Sabbath as a day of rest, and the acknowledgment of Christ's authority over civil law can be properly understood.[8]

Rooted in the profound social changes introduced by the expansion of the market economy, such as urbanization and the increased sexual segregation of work, women assumed increased control of the domestic sphere.[9] Freed from the need to engage in economic production, middle-class women increasingly saw childrearing as a uniquely feminine vocation. Although legally inferior to men, women gained status as the moral guardians of the young. And increasingly, as the century progressed, courts recognized the preeminence of women in the childrearing process. As Carnes notes, even the popular pseudoscience of phrenology attributed to women special gifts of "love of home."[10] Unfortunately, at least in the eyes of many men, women failed to limit their nurturing role to the home. As the primary work force of the great benevolent empire that shaped American social life before and after the Civil War, at least in the North, women sought to extend the morality of the domestic sphere throughout society. Believing in the universality of the middle-class evangelical social values, evangelical women, and their male allies, established a series of social institutions, the most notable being the Sunday school, while actively supporting the feminization of the teaching profession, which was viewed as a natural extension of women's nurturing roles. Firmly committed to the

8. Mark C. Carnes, *Secret Ritual and Manhood in Victorian America* (New Haven: Yale University Press, 1989), pp. 1, 4.

9. See Nancy Cott, *The Bonds of Womanhood: Women's Sphere in New England, 1780-1835* (New Haven: Yale University Press, 1977), and especially Mary Ryan, *The Cradle of the Middle Class: The Family in Oneida County, New York, 1790-1865* (Cambridge, Mass.: Cambridge University Press, 1981).

10. Carnes, *Secret Ritual*, p. 111.

doctrine of female moral superiority, many evangelicals, both male and female, sought to expand women's roles, and rights, as a means toward the establishment of an evangelical cultural hegemony which enshrined such values as temperance, a single standard of sexual purity for men and women, and respect for the Lord's Day.[11]

Historians have only recently come to appreciate the extent to which middle-class men, the foot soldiers in the great capitalist market revolution of the nineteenth century, resisted the feminization of Protestantism. They did so in three ways: exiting female-dominated churches; co-opting evangelical denominations, most notably the Methodist Episcopal Church; and creating an exclusively male fraternal religion in the form of Freemasonry and other similar organizations. Frequently noted in the nineteenth century, men's declining participation in Protestantism was understood almost exclusively in terms of gender. In the words of British minister Dwight Pentecost, "Women naturally gravitate to the prayer-meeting and men . . . to the penitentiary." One writer insisted that men who viewed religion as "weak and womanish" had been deceived, by women presumably, into believing that restrictions against drinking, smoking, or the theater were essential ingredients of the Christian faith. This same writer also observed that the men who were not in the penitentiary were at "the Odd Fellows Hall, or at the grange, or club house . . . interested in every conceivable organization except the church of the Lord Jesus Christ."[12]

It was evident to all that growth of fraternal orders coincided with the male exodus from Protestant churches. Contemporaries were not reticent in noting the relationship. "The secret club-rooms of Boston which outnumber the churches three to one," Alice Stone Blackwell observed, "need to have the light turned on, that all may see the real character of these counterfeit religions that are keeping men from Christ." One of the most frequently observed sins of "lodge religion" was its deleterious effect on men's religious activities.[13] Equally troubling was the omission of Christ

11. The significance of the expansion of women's moral sphere is discussed in Barbara Leslie Epstein, *The Politics of Domesticity: Women, Evangelism, and Temperance in Nineteenth-Century America* (Middletown, Conn.: Wesleyan University Press, 1981), pp. 115-51. See also Carnes, *Secret Ritual*, pp. 107-16.

12. Quoted in Henry Allen Bridgman, "Have We a Religion for Men?" *Andover Review* 12 (April 1890): 388-96.

13. The quote from Alice Stone Blackwell appears in E. E. Flagg, "The New England," *Christian Cynosure*, December 3, 1891. Charles Blanchard, son of antisecrecy leader Jonathan

from virtually all lodge rituals. This omission, which occurred at a time when Protestant worship was increasingly Christ-centered, was rooted in the rationalism of the Enlightenment and justified on the grounds that lodge religion had a universal character that exceeded the bounds of Christianity, a claim made ironic by the fact that virtually all lodge members were white, male Protestants. At the same time, the rituals of the new women's auxiliaries such as the Eastern Star and the Rebekahs, male creations to allay women's opposition to fraternal orders, included references to Christ and urged women to follow his example. Apparently while the self-sacrificial model of Christ was an unworthy, and certainly unmanly, model for men it was appropriate, even normative, for women.

Not surprisingly, fraternal orders vigorously endorsed gender-specific roles for men and women. As Carnes has noted, the literature of fraternal orders extolled the "old-fashioned mother" who discharged her innately female tasks exclusively within the domestic sphere while eschewing any desires to enter the male world of politics, business, or of course the lodge.[14]

Recognizing the immense popularity and power of evangelical faith, fraternal orders were usually content to affirm the compatibility of the faith of the lodge with that of the churches, albeit claiming that the religious teachings of the lodge were universal as opposed to evangelicalism's particularity. Although usually circumspect in their criticisms of evangelicalism, one Masonic editor did suggest in 1872 that since churches were attended mostly by women, women should possess a greater voice in their affairs. After all, the author noted, men had their own Masonic religion.[15]

Among the key players in fraternal orders' co-opting of evangelicalism were the large numbers of Protestant ministers and leading laymen active

---

Blanchard, made the observation that the few denominations which opposed secret societies, such as Reformed Presbyterians, Christian Reformed, German Baptists, and Swedish Methodists seemed to have more involvement of men in the life of the church. See his *Modern Secret Societies* (Chicago: National Christian Association, 1915), p. 276. Two of the many articles in the *Christian Cynosure* which link the lodge to male religious indifference are Alexander Thompson, "Where Are the Men?" *Christian Cynosure*, March 3, 1892, and E. E. Flagg, "New England Letter," *Christian Cynosure*, June 30, 1892. An interesting article that ties Masonic lodges to the decline of religious among Jews is Tony Fels, "Religious Assimilation in a Fraternal Organization: Jews and Freemasonry in Gilded-Age San Francisco," *American Jewish History* 74 (June 1985): 369-403.

14. Carnes, *Secret Ritual*, pp. 79-90.
15. Carnes, *Secret Ritual*, p. 61.

in lodges. Lodges' recognition of the importance of ministers was reflected in the practice of not charging them initiation fees or annual dues. Ministers, in turn, frequently served as lodge chaplains, wrote fraternal rituals, and, when necessary, took leading roles in the suppression of congregational and denominational outbreaks of antimasonry. By the end of the century significant numbers of Episcopal, Methodist, and Baptist clergy belonged to fraternal orders.[16]

Interestingly, the least antimasonic evangelical denomination in the North was also the largest, the Methodist Episcopal Church. In America, Methodism's reticence in confronting Masonry dated from the Morgan era, when the church was notably absent from the antimasonic movement. Even before the Civil War, Methodists such as B. T. Roberts, the founder of the antimasonic Free Methodist Church, insisted that the growing doctrinal latitude in the Methodist Episcopal Church was rooted in the explicit universalism of Masonic religion. By the 1870s Methodism had suppressed antimasonic outbreaks in western New York, Michigan, and Indiana. Critics of Methodism suggested that the denomination's reticence in opposing slavery, moral compromises with wealth, and the desire for respectability were in part the result of the co-opting of the church by worldly Freemasons.[17]

These critics were also not unaware that the popularity of the Methodist Church paralleled the popularity of the lodge. Antisecrecy publications detailed Methodism's silence and its all-too-frequent cooperation with fraternal rites. Noting Methodism's toleration of a Masonic cornerstone-laying ceremony at Methodist-related Evanston Female College, the *Christian Cynosure*, the major antisecrecy publication of the post-Civil War era, noted that it was certainly ironic that an order that excluded women would be allowed such privileges. "But Masonry is popular," the writer observed, "and is not the M. E. Church par excellence the popular church of the day?" Not all radical evangelical women were willing to tol-

16. Carnes, *Secret Ritual,* p. 74. See also Dumenil, *Freemasonry in American Culture,* p. 54.

17. On Roberts's views, see B. T. Roberts, *Why Another Sect: Containing a Review of Articles by Bishop Simpson and Others on the Free Methodist Church* (Rochester: Earnest Christian Publishing House, 1879; repr. New York: Garland Publishing Co., 1984), pp. 44-63. In 1892 the *Christian Cynosure* estimated that 20 percent of the pastors in the Methodist Episcopal Church were Masons. Theses statistics are verified by a Masonic survey of clergy who were Masons in New York. See Dumenil, *Freemasonry in American Culture,* p. 54.

erate such compromises. In 1880 a Methodist woman from Iowa wrote the *Christian Cynosure* that all faithful women should follow her lead by severing all ties with Methodism, since the church included such a large proportion of male members who were Freemasons. As Carnes implies, radical evangelicals did not worship the same commercial spirit as the petty bourgeoisie populating Methodism and the rapidly increasingly fraternal orders.[18]

An understanding of the social vision of radical evangelicalism begins with the iconic father of the so-called Second Great Awakening, Charles Grandison Finney, a figure of mythic proportions. It is understandable that one's view of Finney frequently determines one's attitude toward evangelicalism. Deeply committed to the conversion of sinners and the spiritual renewal of Christians, Finney had a social vision which continues to elicit vigorous debate. Astonishingly, it is still assumed, albeit frequently by scholars whose only introduction to the extensive corpus of primary materials documenting Finney's ministry is *Lectures on Revivals of Religion,* that shortly after his arrival at Oberlin in 1835 he retreated from whatever narrow social vision he had. This view rests largely on the assumption that the conversion of individual sinners, although useful as a mechanism of social control, is fundamentally incompatible with systemic social reform, and, more substantially, that Finney's attempt to discourage Theodore Weld from the recruitment of Oberlin students as antislavery lecturers was rooted in a rejection of reform. In fact, as Timothy Smith and Donald W. Dayton have demonstrated, Finney's commitment to reform continued unabated. The actuality that some at Oberlin exceeded Finney in their commitment to an egalitarian social vision says little about the extent or character of Finney's own commitment to reform.

From the beginning of his ministry, Finney emerged as a powerful spokesman for the expansion of women's roles. Employed as a missionary

18. *Christian Cynosure,* July 11, 1871. Sarah Smith, "A Woman's Plea," *Christian Cynosure,* May 30, 1880. See also *Christian Cynosure,* October 4, 1870; January 14, 1892; March 21, 1871. See Carnes, *Secret Ritual,* pp. 31-32. On fraternal ties to the introduction of the market economy, see Goodman, *Towards a Christian Republic,* pp. 34-53. On the early Methodist responses to secret societies, see William Henry Brackney, "Religious Antimasonry: The Genesis of a Political Party" (Ph.D. diss., Temple University, 1976), pp. 133-37. One example of Methodism's handling of antimasonic agitation is found in Lucia Cook, *Sunbeams Among the Mysteries: Ten Unanswered Arguments. Free Masonry Speechless* (Elkhart, Ind.: self-published, 1871).

by the Oneida Female Missionary Society, his early evangelistic success was made possible by the existing network of women's missionary societies, aid groups, and prayer groups. His insistence that women be allowed to pray and speak before so-called promiscuous audiences (i.e., audiences of men and women), the most controversial of the new revivalistic measures that have long been associated with his name, represented a significant expansion of women's roles. Closely allied with evangelical women, Finney's ministry was frequently resisted by men who resented the time-consuming church meetings, visitations, and the confrontational style of Finneyite revivalism, such as the anxious bench and praying for sinners by name. In one notable but hardly unique instance, a man reported that Finney had destroyed the tranquility of his home by stuffing his wife with tracts, alarming her fears, filling her days with meetings, and convincing her that she was "unevenly yoked."[19]

It is within the context of Finney's lifelong commitment to the evangelical women's culture and the expansion of women's roles that his highly publicized, but little understood, crusade against Masonry needs to be interpreted. Often left unsaid, especially by scholars who have little interest in Finney after 1835, is the assumption that his antimasonic foray in the late 1860s is the reactionary rambling of an aged and disillusioned revivalist.

Initially serialized in the widely circulated evangelical periodical, the *Independent,* Finney's writings on Masonry are remarkably consistent with his mature theological reflections from the 1840s.[20] Rooted in the doctrine of "disinterested benevolence," i.e., God's requirement of supreme and impartial love of God and neighbor, i.e., humankind, Finney argued that Masonry required partial benevolence, or benevolence toward a clique of young, able-bodied white men. Insisting that issues of race and gender were crucial in understanding the inadequacy of Masonic benevolence, Finney reminded his readers that lodge benevolence excluded women, old men, deformed men, and African Americans. Quoting at length from an article in the *American Freemason* which indicated that African Americans were unfit members of lodges as a result of "their depressed social condi-

19. Quoted in Paul Johnson, *A Shopkeeper's Millennium: Society and Revivals in Rochester, New York, 1815-1837* (New York: Hill and Wang, 1978), p. 108.

20. Evidence from Finney's correspondence suggests that the letters of concerned women were responsible for Finney's entrance in the antimasonic movement. See Leonard I. Sweet, *The Minister's Wife: Her Role in Nineteenth-Century American Evangelicalism* (Philadelphia: Temple University Press, 1983), pp. 213-14.

tion, and general want of intelligence," Finney suggested that the partial benevolence of the lodge betrayed the oppressed and violated Christian morality. As he wrote, "God accepts nothing that does not proceed from supreme love of Him and equal love for fellow-men . . . that is all mankind." "Whatever does not proceed from love and faith is sin," Finney argued, "but Masonry teaches no such morality. . . . The motive urged by Masons is, . . . to honor each other. . . . They are pledged not to violate the chastity of a brother Mason's wife, sister, daughter, or mother; but they are not pledged by Masonry . . . to abstain from such conduct with any female. . . . Nothing short of universal benevolence is acceptable to God."[21]

Finney was in the twilight of his career as a reformer and revivalist when he published his exposé of Freemasonry. But his views were shared by a large segment of the northern evangelical community. In October 1867, eighty-seven delegates, representing ten denominations, met in Aurora, Illinois, to organize the National Christian Association (NCA). The primary national body opposed to secret societies, the NCA selected Jonathan Blanchard, president of Wheaton College, as its president. Deeply committed to the antisecrecy movement, Blanchard was a dedicated reformer, and a confirmed champion of evangelical women's culture and the expansion of women's roles.

From its inception, the NCA was dominated by such radical evangelical denominations as the United Presbyterian Church, the Reformed Presbyterian Church, Wesleyan Methodist Church, Free Methodist Church, United Brethren Church, and assorted radical Congregationalists and Baptists. Perfectionist in temperament and doctrine, radical evangelicals advocated strict discipline and the expulsion of sinners who used intoxicants (including in many cases tobacco), owned slaves, or belonged to oath-bound secret societies. Committed to societal perfection, as they understood it, they believed that a perfect society existed where human laws were in harmony with divine laws, and where God's law was the law of the land. Not given to vague generalities, the platform of the American Party, the political arm of the NCA, called for full equality for African Americans, through the vigor-

---

21. Charles G. Finney, *The Character, Claims, and Practical Workings of Freemasonry* (Chicago: Ezra A. Cook, 1893), pp. 187, 211-12. The immediate cause of Finney's writings was the organization of a Masonic lodge in Oberlin in 1867 and subsequent applications of several Masons to join First Church in Oberlin where Finney was pastor. See William E. Bigglestone, *Oberlin: From War to Jubilee, 1866-1883* (Oberlin, Ohio: Grady Publishing Co., 1983), pp. 47-52.

ous enforcement of the Thirteenth, Fourteenth, and Fifteenth Amendments; justice for Native Americans; the banning of economic monopolies; prohibition of the sale of intoxicants; the use of the Bible in the public schools; the enactment of the so-called Christian Amendment, a popular evangelical proposal that would have added an amendment to the U.S. Constitution recognizing the U.S. as a Christian nation; and revocation of lodge charters. Given such a platform, it is hardly surprising that the American Party was a dismal failure at the polls. By 1892 one embittered NCA constituent, after noting that the so-called Christian nations were the most dangerous nations in the world, and that the United States government oppressed its native population, supported the liquor traffic, assisted economic monopolies, and was as warlike as Turks and Zulus, suggested that to place the name of God on the constitution of such a people was like taking the name of the Lord in vain. Interestingly, this author, having abandoned his faith in political action and the Christian Amendment movement, looked forward in expectation to a kingdom of righteousness inaugurated by the premillennial advent of the Savior himself.[22]

Proud of the label "radicals," the old abolitionists, who were the primary constituency of the NCA, were firmly committed to the creation of a bi-racial and egalitarian social order. As the Committee on Secret Societies and Temperance of the Wisconsin Conference of the Wesleyan Methodist Church observed in an 1870 report that linked the Ku Klux Klan and Masons with the denial of civil rights to African Americans, "Our committee believes that the only normal relation of man to man is fraternal equality. Hence all central governments, or organisms, whether social, civil or ecclesiastical, which put few in the place of power, and many in dependence and subjection, are violent transgressors of the spirit and precepts of holy religion." In fact, the intensity of their rhetorical attacks on Masonry becomes more intelligible when one understands that radical evangelicals believed that a Masonic conspiracy lay behind the Southern rebellion. Fearful of the consequences, radical evangelicals believed that the positive results of the war which followed, the liberation

---

22. On the NCA, see Richard S. Taylor, "Seeking the Kingdom: A Study in the Career of Jonathan Blanchard, 1811-1892" (Ph.D. diss., Northern Illinois University, 1977), pp. 504-73; and Robert Wayne Smith, "A Study of the Speaking in the Anti-Secrecy Movement, 1868-1882, with Special Reference to the National Christian Association" (Ph.D. diss., State University of Iowa, 1956), pp. 27-30. On the NCA platform, see *Christian Cynosure,* July 9, 1874, and July 8, 1880. The last quote is from J. W. Wood, "What Constitutes a Christian Nation?" *Christian Cynosure,* July 14, 1892.

of African Americans, was in the process of being betrayed by a second Masonic-inspired conspiracy under the direction of the Klan.[23]

The radical evangelicals' opposition to fraternal orders was deeply rooted in gender-related issues. Firmly convinced of the moral superiority of women, radical evangelicals saw a direct link among the lodge, liquor shop, gambling den, and brothel. Replete with horror stories of male moral failure resulting from lodge involvement, radical evangelicals rejected the concept of a separate women's sphere while urging men to follow the pure examples of their wives, mothers, and sisters. Using ridicule and mock initiation ceremonies, NCA lecturers, who frequently endured assaults and the disruptions of vigilantes, particularly relished such passages as the provision from the ritual of Blue Lodge Masonry, in which the one being initiated promised not to be at the initiation of a "woman, an old man in dotage, a young man in nonage, an atheist, a madman, or fool." As Charles Blanchard noted, the classification of women with atheists and idiots would be repulsive, if it were not so ridiculous. In a similar manner, one antimasonic writer, responding to a Masonic argument that admitting women to all male lodges would destroy the purity of the lodge, wryly noted that if such were the case, fraternal orders had an obligation to aid in the moral elevation of womankind. As such humor makes explicit, radical evangelicals believed the economic, social, political, and religious separation of men and women had an especially deleterious effect upon men. For men this was not a popular position in the late nineteenth century.[24]

Although differences did exist among the NCA's constituency concerning women's roles in church and society, an observation that should not de-

23. See especially George Candee, "The Relation of Masonry to the KKK," *Christian Cynosure*, November 29, 1877, and also Taylor, "Seeking the Kingdom," pp. 530-31. For the remainder of the century, radical evangelicals supported efforts to educate African Americans, urged boycotts of businesses which continued to discriminate against freedmen, and embarked on a program of southern evangelization. For example, see "Southern Mission Fund," *Christian Cynosure*, July 30, 1887. Radical evangelicals were serious about their opposition to racism. In an antisecrcy novel, Elizabeth E. Flagg noted that fraternal orders such as the Odd Fellows barred Chinese, Polynesians, Indians, any mixed bloods, anyone of African descent, and all women. See E. E. Flagg, *Between Two Opinions; or, The Question of the Hour* (Chicago: National Christian Association, 1885), p. 13.

24. See Charles A. Blanchard, *Modern Secret Societies* (Chicago: National Christian Association, 1915), pp. 107-13; F.E.T., "Woman's Influence on Secret Lodges," *Christian Cynosure*, September 28, 1871; "Tenth Anniversary of the NCA," *Christian Cynosure*, November 1, 1877; and "Why Can't a Woman Be a Mason?" *Christian Cynosure*, December 13, 1870.

tract from the fact that radical evangelicals among Free Methodists, United Brethren, Friends, and Wesleyan Methodists were some of the earliest and most persistent supporters of women's rights, the group fervently believed that the expansion of women's social influence would "drive drunkenness out of politics" and usher in an age of economic prosperity and social righteousness. Noting that "the rum party" provided the chief opposition to women's suffrage, New England antisecrecy leader Elizabeth E. Flagg suggested that besides closing saloons, women's votes would result in literary renaissance and the destruction of the Democratic Party. Her evidence included the reigns of the Queens Elizabeth and Victoria and, especially significant, the overwhelming Republican composition of Wellesley, while, sadly, considerable support for the Democratic Party existed at Harvard.[25] "What fruit do we find the sheepskins-aproned fraternity bring forth," one woman wrote in 1877, "let every neighborhood of the lodge testify. Let every criminal court testify. Let the poor, the blind, the lame, and women testify. It seems to be that Freemasonry assumes to build up caste contrary to the Bible."[26] Among the many male leaders of the NCA who supported women's suffrage were B. T. Roberts, United Brethren Bishop Milton Wright, and Jonathan Blanchard, while in 1874 the NCA endorsed women's suffrage in principle. Specifically rejecting the notion of women's sphere, women served as delegates to NCA conventions, as members of committees, and as convention speakers.[27] Strong, although not completely conclusive, evidence suggests that the majority of the NCA's constituency were women.[28]

From the inception of the crusade against secret societies, radical evangelical women urged their sisters to educate themselves concerning the dangers of fraternal orders and actively to oppose such orders. Women were urged to refuse to marry lodge members and to warn sons and husbands about the perils of lodge membership. The reasons women members gave for opposing secret orders appear similar to those given by men. Primary among them were the deleterious effects of lodges upon men's piety, the

---

25. E. E. Flagg, "New England Letter," *Christian Cynosure*, May 12, 1892. One of the most persistent NCA tactics was to attempt to tie secret orders to the economic interests of the liquor industry. For an example, see E. E. Flagg, *Masonry vs. Prohibition* (Chicago: Christian Cynosure, n.d.).

26. S.M. "A Woman's View of Masonry," *Christian Cynosure*, November 15, 1877.

27. See "Dr. Storrs on Woman's Sphere," *Christian Cynosure*, November 13, 1879.

28. Carnes, *Secret Ritual*, p. 80. See also Smith, "A Study of the Speaking in the Anti-Secrecy Movement," pp. 91-97.

sufferings caused to families of lodge members by husbands' and sons' absences, and the financial hardships resulting from money spent on lodge regalia, travel, and dues. Some suggested that the rapid increase in the divorce rate was directly tied the growth of fraternal orders. One writer, not given to subtlety, noted that the foolish woman who supported her Masonic husband "must not be surprised to find that her bosom companion sometimes turned aside from the lodges of male secret societies to visit those female secret societies." Other women saw fraternal orders as detrimental to democracy and its ceremonies as breeding grounds for militarism.[29]

In Chicago, the center of the NCA, the Woman's Christian Association of Chicago operated a dispensary, staffed by six female physicians, an employment bureau for women, and a boarding house. The organization reported that in three years nearly two thousand visits to homes of the poor had been made in the greater Chicago area. The visitors surveyed needs while distributing medicine, food, and clothing.[30] Although no NCA women served as lectures or field agents, women were very active as writers and played an especially important role in building coalitions with other reform groups, most notably the WCTU. The NCA endorsed WCTU president Francis A. Willard and her so-called do everything policy, a plan by which the WCTU refused to concentrate exclusively on temperance and pushed a wide ranging social agenda including sexual purity, total abstinence from liquor and tobacco, opposition to Sabbath desecration, support for the arbitration of all international disputes, and the enfranchisement of women of all nations.[31] Willard, who was a long-time family friend of the Blanchards, initially encouraged the NCA to be a participant in the annual WCTU-sponsored reform conference which met at a Methodist camp near Chicago. A monument to the social vision of evangelical women, the motto of the Lake Bluff Convocation was "a free platform —

29. The quote is from "Unhappy Marriages," *Christian Cynosure*, September 16, 1880. On lodges and militarism, see "What One Women Sees," *Christian Cynosure*, July 7, 1892, which quotes an article by Hannah Bailey, superintendent of the Department of Peace and Arbitration of the WCTU. The significance of Bailey is discussed in Ian Tyrrell, *Woman's World, Woman's Empire: The Woman's Christian Temperance Union in International Perspective, 1889-1930* (Chapel Hill: University of North Carolina Press, 1991), pp. 170-90. See also P.M.K., "A Woman's Protest," *Christian Cynosure*, October 9, 1879, and Mrs. E. S. Sutphen, "A Sister's Prayer," *Christian Cynosure*, October 23, 1879.

30. "Woman's Christian Association of Chicago," *Christian Cynosure*, June 20, 1880.

31. See "WCTU Woman's Pledge," *Christian Cynosure*, December 3, 1891.

only bigotry, intolerance, and discourtesy excluded." One NCA participant praised Lake Buff as a place where "the most radical reforms and advanced sentiments on all reform questions are uttered from its platform."[32]

As in any reform movement, conflict was inevitable. Willard's vision, the creation of a great reform coalition including labor, agriculture, and all temperance organizations, even encompassing groups committed to secrecy such as the Knights of Labor and the Good Templars, was strongly resisted by the NCA and their radical evangelical colleagues. The conflict which existed beneath the surface for some time finally exploded at Lake Bluff in 1887 when Francis Willard, after several months of open NCA criticism of the WCTU, unceremoniously dropped from the program a public NCA forum on secret societies while adding a presentation by the Knights of Labor. Coming only months after Willard had addressed a conference of the Good Templars which celebrated the reuniting of the American and international branches of this order which had divided in 1876 because Americans barred African Americans from membership, the action represented a serious blow to the many members of the WCTU who believed secrecy was an important tool in an ongoing campaign to silence women's voices. Later in the year, E. E. Flagg wrote Mary Blanchard that the women's suffrage club in Wellesley, Massachusetts, was controlled by Masons, who even were responsible for nominating candidates for the local school board. Other concerns were more immediate. Warning women that involvement with secret labor orders could lead to wine suppers and late-night treks to saloons, Anna E. Stoddard wrote, "Did it ever occur to you, my dear sisters of the W.C.T.U., that young men and middle-aged have been, and are being drawn into associations whose practices are of such a character as to tend to draw them from paths of sobriety and rectitude?"[33]

By the mid-1880s few women were taking such warnings seriously, and the rapid growth of all secret orders, including women's orders, suggests that Willard's course was certainly pragmatic. But in fairness to radical evangelicals, the acceptance of secrecy by the WCTU, during a period when secrecy was not infrequently used for racial and economic advantage, did represent a retreat from the vision of an open, interracial egalitarian social order.

32. M. A. Gault, "Lake Bluff Convocation," *Christian Cynosure*, July 14, 1887.

33. See "Good Templars Reunion," *Christian Cynosure*, June 9, 1887, and the discussion in the *Christian Cynosure* in July 1887: E. E. Flagg to Mary Bent Blanchard, December 23, 1887 (Jonathan Blanchard Papers, Wheaton College Archives), and Anna E. Stoddard, *The Foe in Hiding* (Chicago: Christian Cynosure, n.d.), p. 2.

One of the most notable contributions of women to the postbellum antisecrecy crusade was the antisecrecy novel. Written exclusively by women, this literary genre expressed the anxieties and fears of radical evangelical women confronting the secret foe. In such novels, the prayers of faithful evangelical women overcome the indifference of Masonic grandfathers, husbands, sons, and boyfriends. In *A Woman's Victory, or the Query of the Lodgeville Church,* the fasting and prayer of a faithful wife drives her indifferent Masonic husband to read antimasonic literature. Realizing that the lodge, which happened to meet above a saloon, is the reason the community fails to experience revival, the husband invites an antimasonic lecturer. A struggle ensues, and an antimasonic church is organized. Revival immediately occurs, the family's two worldly daughters are converted. The lodge is closed, which in turn results in the saloon being forced out of business, followed by the local billiard hall. In the course of the novel, evangelicalism, antisecrecy, and evangelical women's culture are vindicated against the moral and spiritual indifference of the lodge.[34]

The most important antisecrecy novelist was Elizabeth E. Flagg. Associated with Wellesley College, and active in the WCTU in New England, Flagg was a tireless reformer committed to temperance, women's suffrage, the rights of Indians and Chinese, the rights of labor, and the defense of the Sabbath. In her most important antisecrecy novel, *Between Two Opinions; or, The Question of the Hour* (1885), Flagg tells the story of a young American worker, Nelson Newell, a victim of a Catholic father, and his beautiful fiancée, Martha Benson. The novel is dominated by the themes of ethno-cultural conflict. The protagonists include Martin Treworthy, an associate of John Brown and veteran of the Civil War who is described as "a dash of Yankee, the Puritan, and backwoodsman"; Stephen Howland, a lawyer, prohibitionist leader, and faithful son of New England; Martha, a radical Presbyterian who is active in the WCTU; Mrs. McGowan, a radical Scotch-Irish Presbyterian covenanteer; and Peter Snyder, a converted Irish rum dealer who emerges at the end of the novel leading a Salvation Army contingent. The antagonists include Felix Bassett, a dishonest Odd Fellow; Gerrish, an Irish dynamiter and conspirator; and Schumacher, a German socialist.[35]

34. Jennie L. Hardie, *A Woman's Victory, or The Query of the Lodgeville Church* (Chicago: National Christian Association, 1884).

35. Flagg, *Between Two Opinions,* pp. v, 91-99, 120, 144.

Throughout the novel, it is impossible to separate the themes of gender and cultural conflict. Consistent with radical evangelicalism's vision of an egalitarian social order in which men and women share the same reform agenda, the notion of a separate woman's sphere is dismissed. "I don't care what people say about 'woman's sphere,'" Stephen Howland's mother exclaims, "it is always right where God puts her." "Women followed Jesus to the cross," one heroine notes, "I think I could follow him to the polls."[36] Such sentiments were shared by many radical evangelical women. For them, women's suffrage was laden with salvic and even eschatological power. It was assumed that morally superior and empowered women, with their male allies, would create a social order which enshrined the values of temperance and social purity. Rooted in the notion that women everywhere shared the same interests and moral perspective, Flagg's novel bitterly assailed secretive and exclusive lodges as places bereft of women's influence. As a result, women such as Flagg, saw secrecy, especially male secrecy, as an attempt to deny God's desire for American society which was a society in which culture flourished, and women and children were free from abusive men.

It is easy to dismiss the moralistic and paternalistic, or perhaps more correctly maternalistic, social vision of radical evangelicalism. A product of Victorian sentimentalism, its prudish, especially pre-Freudian, character makes the social vision of radical evangelicalism easy to excuse as excessively legalistic and rooted in religious intolerance. However, such caricatures fail to appreciate the legitimacy of radical evangelicalism's gender-based critique of nineteenth-century fraternal orders. Interestingly, the demise of radical evangelicalism in the twentieth century seems to have coincided with the decline of a gender-based critique of secret orders. As other theological traditions increasingly shaped the NCA and related bodies, women's issues ceased to define the antisecrecy crusade and even such stalwart radical evangelical denominations as the Wesleyan Methodist and Free Methodist Churches became shaped by theological traditions which had little understanding of the egalitarian roots of an earlier Finneyite social vision.[37]

---

36. Flagg, *Between Two Opinions*, p. 109.

37. In the twentieth century the NCA was increasingly dominated by the Christian Reformed Church, while continuing to have ties to Wheaton College and the Wesleyan Methodist Church. During this period gender seems to have played little role in evangelical critiques of secret fraternal orders.

CHAPTER 6

Holiness: Sin's Anticipated Cure

DIANE LECLERC

It is my purpose in this chapter to be a catalyst for conversation about the subjects of sin and salvation, broadly defined. On sin specifically, it has been stated, "That Wesley regarded human nature as corrupt is too well known to need proof."[1] Wesley himself writes, "If therefore, we take away this foundation, that [human beings are] by nature foolish and sinful . . . the Christian system falls apart at once."[2] According to Wesley, the doctrine of original sin must never be rejected nor neglected as the condition of humanity or as a reality of human experience. This much, at least, is clear. Yet as Robert Chiles has argued, the scholarly assessments of John Wesley's doctrine of original sin differ.[3] At first glance, this may appear surprising; Wesley did in fact write a lengthy and detailed treatise on the theme, *The Doctrine of Original Sin*. Because it covers historical, sociological, existential, and scriptural evidence for the doctrine, it gives the appearance of being a clear and comprehensive treatment of the subject. However, its rhetorical style — which counters the treatise of his "heretical" opponent almost point by point — distracts from its systematic value and raises the possibility of varied restatements of its less prominent themes.

1. Umphrey Lee, *John Wesley and Modern Religion* (Nashville: Abingdon-Cokesbury, 1936), p. 120.

2. John Wesley, *The Doctrine of Original Sin*, in *The Works of John Wesley*, ed. Thomas Jackson (London: Wesleyan Methodist Book Room, 1831), vol. 9, p. 194.

3. See Robert Chiles, *Theological Transitions in American Methodism: 1700-1935* (New York: Abingdon, 1965), pp. 121-22.

There are multiple and diverse interpretations of the significance of Wesley's doctrine of sin, specifically his view of original sin's consequences — i.e., the extent of human depravity. My own work intentionally disrupts an Augustinian interpretation of Wesley's understanding of sin[4] by examining his understanding of sin as found in his letters to women. And yet, in the catholic spirit, if you will, I agree that what is most vital is Wesley's dependence on a strong hamartiology for his soteriology, even if I disagree with other interpretations of its expression. The point is that we affirm and attempt to express the reality of sin.

As we have come to understand rather recently, there has been a shift from a "modernist" to a "postmodernist" theoretical framework that, although it is conceptual, has all sorts of connections to real life. This presents the theologian with the task of correlation — communicating religious truth to a new context. It is a means by which we can speak the "truth" without losing its dynamic character. And this is how I interpret the task of the Wesleyan Holiness Study Project — to correlate the truth of "holiness theology" with the emerging postmodern situation. And yet even here, with a boldness about the absolute necessity of the attempt, a humility remains. I wonder, even at my relatively young age, whether I have an accurate or even adequate grasp of the situation to which I attempt to speak. It may well be that in the time it takes to complete our project, the language that we choose to communicate holiness may *miscommunicate* holiness. All language is metaphorical, certainly all language about sin. And yet, again, to discard any attempt to communicate will necessarily keep the gap unbridged. This is why I write here. I sense, very strongly, that this next generation could in fact be the generation that abandons belief in sanctification. In my inquiries, I have discovered that it has not been miscommunication that fuels their apathy. Rather, it has been silence. "Holiness" and "sanctification" are foreign concepts to my students. While I grew up struggling with my peers to reconcile the abuses of the doctrine of "perfectionism" with our own existential lives, this generation is not struggling at all, for they have been given little with which to struggle. Yes, it may well be that in our efforts here we may not communicate perfectly; we may well miss the mark. But at least we are aiming and shooting at the mark of meaningful communication. We must speak, lest

---

4. See especially Diane Leclerc, *Singleness of Heart: Gender, Sin, and Holiness in Historical Perspective* (Lanham, Md.: Scarecrow Press, 2001).

our doctrine of holiness become a nice, quaint, but antiquated part of our story.

In 1958 (long before *A Theology of Love*), Mildred Bangs Wynkoop penned an unpublished work entitled *An Existential Interpretation of the Doctrine of Holiness.* Interestingly, her words there seem prophetic here:

> Paradox and tension exist in all living situations. These are not things to be deplored. Creativity can only thrive in tension. The abortive demand for premature intellectual peace is death to thinking. We are not attempting to solve difficulties but to restore them so that in the wholesome contest between doctrine and life, dynamic and productive and sanctified Christian activity may thrive and expand. Perhaps, we had better explain this. Committed as deeply as the author is to that which the doctrine of holiness means to life, there is the most painful concern growing daily in respect of the limited hearing which the doctrine receives. . . . More serious yet is the fact of a growing spiritual indifference among holiness people. Perhaps others also struggle with the weight of disinterest but, to us, who, filled with the Holy Spirit presumably, ought to be the example of the world's solution to indifference, the lack is of particular seriousness. In a word, the problem seems to resolve itself into a statement such as this: the doctrine of holiness has not made adequate provision for the human element in life. (pp. 2-3)

"Existentialism" is a means by which Wynkoop addresses the very problem she sets forth. In a serious attempt to make "adequate provision for the human element in life" and to avoid speaking of the most experiential of all doctrines only in the abstract, I turn to existentialism myself, where I have found language that, intriguingly, also communicates and resonates with my students. I would suggest that the "needs" of the postmodern for relationality, his or her search for meaning, and the quest for an experientially based spirituality (that has given rise to new liturgical theories) have already found expression in Wesley's emphasis on experiential life and faith, and in Søren Kierkegaard's exististential expression of the nature of sin. I am hopeful that placing them in correlational dialogue will bring edible fruit which in turn correlates to our situation now and in our future.

A Wesleyan-Soteriological Dialogue with Søren Kierkegaard's *Sickness unto Death:* Some Introductory Remarks

I wholeheartedly affirm Randy Maddox's assessment of Wesley's understanding of sin and his belief that one of the strongest metaphors found in Wesley for salvation is that of healing of a disease. Salvation is "therapeutic." I, with Maddox, find deep resonances between Wesley and the Eastern Fathers on this point[5] (which carries over today in resonances with nuances with Orthodoxy's theological scheme). This way of conceptualizing sin as disease correlates with Wesley's optimism about (sanctifying) grace, envisioned as a deeply (progressive) cure. The metaphor offers great benefit. And yet this more Eastern perspective can be criticized for being "light" on sin, so to speak, even to the point of interpreting the Fall as a rather understandable consequence of Adam and Eve's immaturity. Similarly, it is possible to so emphasize the potentiality of the restoration of the *imago Dei,* as to under-stress the degree of the distortion. In light of

---

5. See Randy Maddox, *Responsible Grace: John Wesley's Practical Theology* (Nashville: Kingswood, 1994). For support of the theory of seeing Wesley as more Eastern, see, e.g., Arthur MacDonald Allchin, "Our Life in Christ, in John Wesley and the Eastern Fathers," in *We Belong to One Another: Methodist, Anglican, and Orthodox,* ed. Arthur MacDonald Allchin (London: Epworth, 1965), pp. 62-78; Paul M. Bassett and William Greathouse, *Exploring Christian Holiness,* vol. II, *The Historical Development* (Kansas City, Mo.: Beacon Hill Press, 1985); Ted A. Campbell, *John Wesley and Christian Antiquity: Religious Vision and Cultural Changes* (Nashville: Kingswood Books, 1991); Ted A. Campbell, "John Wesley and the Asian Roots of Christianity," *Asian Journal of Theology* 8 (1994): 281-94; Seung-An Im, "John Wesley's Theological Anthropology: A Dialectic Tension Between the Latin Western Patristic Tradition (Augustine) and the Greek Eastern Patristic Tradition (Gregory of Nyssa)" (Ph.D. diss., Drew University, 1994); David C. Ford, "Saint Makarios of Egypt and John Wesley: Variations on the Theme of Sanctification," *Greek Orthodox Theological Review* 33 (1988): 285-312; Luke L. Keefer, "John Wesley: Disciple of Early Christianity," *Wesleyan Theological Journal* 19 (1984): 23-32; Randy Maddox, "John Wesley and Eastern Orthodoxy: Influences, Convergences and Differences," *Asbury Theological Journal* 45 (1990): 29-53; K. Steve McCormick, "John Wesley's Use of John Chrysostom on the Christian Life: Faith Filled with the Energy of Love" (Ph.D. diss., Drew University, 1983); John G. Merritt, "'Dialogue' Within a Tradition: John Wesley and Gregory of Nyssa Discuss Christian Perfection," *Wesleyan Theological Journal* 22 (1987): 92-116; Albert C. Outler, "John Wesley's Interests in the Early Fathers of the Church," in *The Wesleyan Theological Heritage: Essays of Albert C. Outler,* ed. Thomas C. Oden and Leicester R. Longden (Grand Rapids: Zondervan, 1991), pp. 55-74; Mark Anthony Smith, "John Wesley: A Pattern of Monastic Reform" (Ph.D. diss., University of Kentucky, 1992); and Howard Synder, "John Wesley and Macarius the Egyptian," *Asbury Theological Journal* 45 (1990): 55-59.

this, the hamartiological insights of persons such as Augustine, Luther, Calvin, Søren Kierkegaard, Karl Barth, and Reinhold Niebuhr should not be overlooked. Although the West has too closely connected "forensic" salvation with such views of sin, making them almost inextricable (thus making salvation fractional), it would serve us well to grapple with the depth of human sinfulness offered by such views. In doing this, Wesleyanism's optimism regarding an actual transformation of "nature" can only gain in strength. It is an anxious, fractured self that finds wholeness. As a means of connecting a Western view of sin with a more robust soteriology found in the East, I will place Søren Kierkegaard and Wesleyan theology in dialogue.

One more note before I begin. In recent poststructuralist theology, the "self" has often been seen as a theological "evil" with *community* being its redemptor. "Self" is an illusion, some go so far as to say. If, by self we mean the Enlightenment self, then I stand against it as a concept. The problem is that it is only those who possess themselves in this modernist sense who can "crucify" it. For those who have never known the power of selfhood because of any number of oppressions, selfhood is the very sign and symbol of liberation, in even a spiritual sense. I contend that the self and the community should stand in "equilibrium" — as a balanced polarity enabled by the Spirit. We could get stuck here in debate. If only for the sake of going on, allow me to use the concept of the "self" as a viable and even necessary metaphor when talking about sin.

Kierkegaard on Sin

According to Søren Kierkegaard, humanity is born into an existentially anxious reality, one that is dependent upon its creation even before the need to reference sin. This reality is prototypically found in Eden, but it is in every individual. While Adam is unlike us in that he was the first (the first always being different from his progeny), this difference has a quantitative character rather than qualitative. "[A person] belongs to nature, but not to nature alone, for he [sic] is poised between nature and some other realm, and he is subject to imperatives which neither realm can explain of itself. He is material, yet spiritual; he is determined, yet free; he is derived like the rest of nature from what came before him, and yet, unlike anything else in nature, he alone is responsible for creating himself."[6] This causes anxiety. But the human is really "anxious about nothing." Kierkegaard defines anxiety as a disposition that results from the relationship of the synthesis of body and psyche, mediated by the spirit. In this synthesis, the self is aware of the freedom of potentiality; he or she is "able." But the self is also aware of his or her destiny and fixedness. And awareness of ability *and* limitation causes anxiety. It is the place where the finite touches the infinite, where the temporal touches eternity, where necessity touches freedom. This state of ambiguity gives rise to the temptation to "fall" to one side of the polarities or the other. This created situation is the human predicament, to which we will return.

But first, simply to remind us, when we try to define a human being, it is not enough to state what is universally human about her or him. Kierkegaard, as it is well known, is equally concerned for the individual as individual. And the individual possesses all that is personal and unrepeatable about him or her. "And this is where our difficulties begin, for although we can define what is human about him [sic] . . . we know next to nothing of how individual selves come about in their infinitely varied and unpredictable idiosyncrasy."[7] Our "true" selves are only potentialities in the structure of our being — potentialities that may or may not become actual in the living out of our lives. We still may be authentic, though not perfected selves; we are always becoming. But it is hard to understand how even this comes about. How does a self, a particular individual, "emerge from a chaos of living material" and reflect its own unique qualities, let alone reflect on itself? It is here that Kierkegaard turns to the synthesizing agent, the spirit. He conceptualizes the self as a highly individualized pattern which has emerged from the synthesis of the "soulish" and the bodily by the spirit. The spirit is what enables the self's consciousness of itself. The emergence of self-consciousness is derived from and maintained by the will. It is with the will that the predicament of existential anxiety (and its necessary fall) moves forward to actualize sin. And anxiety becomes despair.

Kierkegaard states, "The self cannot of itself attain and remain in equilibrium and rest by itself, but only by relating itself to that Power

---

6. George Prince, *The Narrow Pass: A Study of Kierkegaard's Concept of Man* (New York: McGraw-Hill, 1963), p. 35.

7. Prince, *The Narrow Pass*, p. 35.

which constituted the whole relation."[8] Without this Power, sin is an inevitable (but not necessary) movement. In *Sickness unto Death*, he extensively elaborates on "despair" as sin. Obviously, despair is not to be equated with sadness or melancholy, or even immobilized hopelessness. There is activity even in the inactivity of "willing not." Despair is an activity of the will that emerges from the spirit, when the self fractures toward the bodily or toward the psychic, disrupting the synthesis between the two. It is a lack of equilibrium which expresses itself in one side of the polarity to the neglect of the other.

Kierkegaard elaborates on the forms of the sickness. Specifically, despair can be viewed through polarities, such as those of infinitude/finitude, possibility/necessity, and eternal/earthly. Those who sin to the side of infinity idealize themselves as limitless in their potential and are fantastical. But rather than reaching infinity, these persons are carried out away from themselves, thus preventing them from being able to return to their true selves. Their hubris, then, comes before their actualized fall. "Now if possibility outruns necessity, the self runs away from itself, so that it has no necessity whereto it is bound to return. . . . Possibility then appears to be the self ever greater and greater, more and more things become possible, because nothing becomes actual."[9] This form of despair Kierkegaard calls defiance. And this represents the generalized understanding of sin found in Augustine and his theological successors. But Kierkegaard offers more. On the other hand, persons can despair toward finitude, or the earthly. "This form of despair is: despair at not willing to be *oneself*; or still lower, despair at not willing to be *a* self; or lowest of all, despair at willing to be *another* than himself. . . . He swings away entirely from the inward direction which is the path he ought to have followed in order to become a true self."[10] Kierkegaard calls this form of sin weakness. The point of his

---

8. See Søren Kierkegaard, *The Sickness unto Death*, trans. and ed. Walter Lowrie (Princeton: Princeton University Press, 1954), p. 147.

9. Kierkegaard, *Sickness unto Death*, p. 169.

10. Kierkegaard, *Sickness unto Death*, pp. 186, 189. Italics mine. Some work has been done on Kierkegaard's famous footnote that genders the forms of despair. Trying to be a self by oneself, Kierkegaard names the "manly" form of despair. The opposite despair, the despair of not willing to be a self at all, he names the "womanly" form of despair. Man attempts to overcome the anxiety of selfhood by forcing the poles of infinitude and possibility. Woman, on the other hand, relinquishes herself to the poles of finitude and necessity. Woman, according to Kierkegaard, gives herself away, thus losing her true self. The man, in

lengthy discussion is to claim that while the expressions of despair might differ, the self is fractured, incapable of being its self by itself. The self is itself only by relating to the Power that constituted the self to begin with. In other words, every self stands in need of God.

For those, then, who despair over willing to be a self by defiantly exerting their supposed limitlessness, they must will to be a self *related* to the Power. For those who despair over willing to be a self by weakly not willing to be a self at all, they must will to be a *self* related to the Power. The whole point for Kierkegaard is that sin, whether defiance or cowardice, is disabling. It manifests itself in countless ways.[11] It is impossible to break free of the predicament alone.

The value of this paradigm for an understanding of sin today is that it addresses the situation. Specifically, most of my students come from dysfunctional backgrounds that truly disable their ability to relate to others well or, in some cases, keep them from being empowered even to claim a self. The thirst for meaningful selfhood and a healthy relationality, as well as the need to fill their experiential void, is something I encounter almost daily in my students. Kierkegaard can aid in understanding their predicament. Wesley can aid in providing a hopefulness that their lives can change.

---

contrast, defiantly attempts to maintain himself independently and egotistically, despairingly determined to be himself. But again, woman attempts to be rid of herself by losing herself in another. "Defiance" and "weakness" are Kierkegaard's final labels for the masculine and feminine forms of despair, respectively. See Kierkegaard, *Sickness unto Death*, p. 144. Working closely with the Danish text, Sylvia Walsh interprets a key passage in Kierkegaard: "In abandoning or throwing herself altogether into that which she devotes herself, woman tends to have a sense of self only in and through the object of her devotion. When the object is taken away, her self is also lost. Her despair, consequently, lies in not willing to be herself, that is, in not having any separate or independent self-identity." Sylvia Walsh, "On 'Feminine' and 'Masculine' Forms of Despair," in *International Kierkegaard Commentary: The Sickness Unto Death*, ed. Robert L. Perkins (Macon, Ga.: Mercer University Press, 1987), p. 124.

11. But what of a person who feels no despair, who seems unconscious of the predicament? He writes, "Unawareness is so far from removing despair, or of transforming despair into non-despair, that on the contrary, it may be the most dangerous form of despair." Kierkegaard, *Sickness unto Death*, p. 177.

A Wesleyan Response

Prevenient Grace

The problem with any system, even Kierkegaard's (which he would, of course, resolutely deny is a system!) is that it is bound to its own presuppositions, presumptions, and theories, and to its own language. It is not my aim here to defend the whole, but to explicate the parts that are valuable for our purposes. What we gain from Kierkegaard is a sense of the depth of sin, and the intricacies of how it affects our entire being, particularly in our ability to relate. Despair, as an intentional act of the will, brings about existential estrangement. "The state of being in sin is worse sin than the particular sin, it is the sin emphatically, and thus understood it is true that the state of remaining in sin is continuation of sin, is a new sin."[12] This continuation then leads to the sin of despairing over one's sin. It can also lead to despairing over the forgiveness of sin. "God offers reconciliation in the forgiveness of sin. Yet the sinner despairs, and despair acquires a still deeper expression."[13] In other words, even in the offer of mercy, despair discounts the self to itself as too far gone. This deep estrangement fragments the self from itself, it severs our intended relationships with others, but most important, it keeps us from God, even if we glimpse God's reconciling call. It is our sin that keeps us believing that anything can conquer sin.

As we have said, Adam and Eve were created with an ontological structure that would lead to anxiety over being themselves. It was the presence of God that kept anxiety at bay.[14] But when they gained knowledge of good and evil, a new level of consciousness made them aware of their anxiety. In this anxiety over "nothing" they fell.[15] What became

---

12. Kierkegaard, *Sickness unto Death*, p. 237.

13. Kierkegaard, *Sickness unto Death*, pp. 244-45.

14. In Kierkegaard's words, in a "dreaming" state.

15. I would suggest that ironically, it was Eve who sinned defiantly, and Adam who "lost himself" in another, namely, Eve. Perhaps the consequences of the Fall were a reversal of this first tendency. Augustine himself contemplates this. "So we cannot believe that Adam was deceived, and supposed the devil's word to be truth, and therefore transgressed God's law, but that he by the drawings of kindred yielded to the woman, the husband to the wife . . . man could not bear to be severed from his only companion, even though this involved a partnership in sin." Augustine, *The City of God* (New York: Random House, 1950), p. 459. Adam

"shame" was their attempt to hide from God. They *sought* estrangement out of their shame. And God allowed it, and symbolically removed them from Eden.

According to Kierkegaard, we are born with an anxiety that is quantitatively different from our first parents, and thus born with such a sense of dread that sin becomes actual as we "inevitably" attempt to deal with its weight — by willing to be a self defiantly, or by resisting to be a self at all.[16] In this paradigm, the pressing need of explaining transmission fades. Also does the problem of justifying a God who holds us accountable for sin we cannot help but commit, because we are already corrupted at birth. While anxiety is our predisposition, and while this dread accumulates over time, it is possible to read Kierkegaard as saying we become responsible for sin only as we actualize it through the will.

Long seen as foundational to Wesley's entire theology, the concept of prevenient grace has largely been assumed rather than explicated. Its significance can be seen when overlaid on Kierkegaard's concept of despair. Kierkegaard's ideas help us envision the devastating estrangement experienced by human beings. Wesley's understanding of prevenient grace helps us envision the potentiality for something different. Fundamental to Kierkegaard's beliefs regarding humanity is its inability to rectify the situation in which it finds itself. God is the only means by which a fractured self is given any potentiality for change. "A self face to face with Christ is a self potentiated by the prodigious concession of God, potentiated by the prodigious emphasis which falls upon it for the fact that God also for the sake of this self let Himself be born, became man, suffered, and died."[17] Clearly, Kierkegaard does not believe that we will never actualize any of this God-

---

seems to be the one "loving the creature more than the creator." But his punishment reverses the tendency. This is reinforced by countless patriarchal anthropologies through the centuries. See, e.g., Hegel's scheme which places man as the symbol for that which is spiritual and woman for that which is bodily, or earthly.

16. One of the questions in scholarly debate over Kierkegaard's conception of sin is the question of whether anxiety, or dread, is itself sin, or only the precondition that elicits temptation. Or more plainly stated, is there an experiential reality of the "pull" of original sin before sin is personally actualized? Is dread this pull? The problem is that Kierkegaard seems to state that this preconditional dread breeds a type of dread that is sinful. Dread multiplies. Where does dread become despair? In my analysis, dread is the precondition and the pull of original sin. Despair only arises when the will breaks the synthesis of the spirit that relates the self to the self. This has relevance to the Wesleyan understanding of intentionality.

17. Kierkegaard, *Sickness unto Death*, pp. 244-45.

given potential. And yet, while Kierkegaard is certainly not Pelagian in his understanding of sin, it is possible to interpret him as quite Pelagian in the quest for salvation. By what means are we saved?

> How then can this act come about? It can be performed, [Kierkegaard] says, only by means of a relation to God. This relation is achieved when man's powers are organized and integrated together in one totalitarian resolve towards God in an act of "conscious" seriousness and deep intent to believe, to choose God as He presents Himself in His "unbelievable" paradoxicalness in the God-Man, together with the life-view and the teaching associated with Him. This calls for an absolute act of will; and the sheer strain of willing-to-believe tenses the will to the breaking-point, heightens self-consciousness, and draws the self into a new synthesis, making it a fully effective basis for all future activity and development. But if a man refuses this supreme task . . . the self remains a broken system, and is simply developing itself in terms of its own radical weakness. Kierkegaard sadly remarks that a man will only exert such an act of will under extreme pressure, and only when he is brought to that dark frontier where an unavoidable decision must be made.[18]

Here we find his understanding of the "leap" into the abyss and of "infinite resignation" which leads to the potential of being a "knight of faith." But we find no way of explaining in Kierkegaard's view how these steps of faith are possible except as an act of the human will. It is we who leap toward reconciliation in faith. While we can find in Kierkegaard a Christ who suffered for us, we really do not find the mechanism by which we have faith to begin with, nor to explain how faith overcomes estrangement.

If it is the presence of God that effectively vanquishes despair, is it we who must find our way into that presence, or is there a condescension toward us, even in our existential estrangement? It is here, I believe, that the power of the concept (and certainly the reality) of prevenient grace solves the problem of Kierkegaard's apparent salvation-seeking Pelagianism. It is also a concept that will aid our own holiness people.

We have not understood grace. As much as we talk about being saved by grace through faith, and not by works, our tradition has often fallen to-

18. Price, *The Narrow Pass*, p. 40.

ward the side of our own efforts as we misconceive both the nature of holiness and the nature of God. And yet, how do we avoid the dangerous conclusions we seem to reach? How do we avoid our tendency to reduce sin to behaviors we are to avoid (often quite avoidable in our own strength)? How do we avoid our tendency to reduce holiness to our own attempts to live "sinlessly"? And how do we avoid the legalisms that ensue? We must first understand the depth and pervasiveness of sin. But we must also understand the pervasiveness of grace in the world and in our hearts, even before we exercise faith. Prevenient grace can explode our superficiality regarding sin, and the nature of salvation.

It has been suggested that the best way to understand prevenient grace is pneumatologically. In other words, this grace is not a "substance" any more than sin is a substance. We are better served to envision prevenient grace as the activity, even presence, of the Holy Spirit. Unlike Kierkegaard, and other Western thinkers, Wesleyan theology believes that the sinful predicament into which we are born is not the only factor in our human situation. If we are pulled by an original sin (dread) that has accumulated throughout history, there is a counterbalancing pull toward life and away from self-destruction. I will be bold enough to say that the presence of God, through the gracious activity of the Holy Spirit, *enables* the will, not to save itself, but to move toward God. This is different than Kierkegaard's conceptualization of the activity of the will (which is simultaneously fallen, yet responsible for the leap). We have *free will* because we have been graced by the very presence of God.[19]

The concept of prevenient grace is also crucial in our understanding of the *imago Dei*, and in our understanding of "true humanity." Mildred Bangs Wynkoop and others have defined the image of God as our capacity for loving relationships. H. Ray Dunning elaborates by speaking of our relationships with God, others, ourselves, and the earth.[20] If we hold to

19. I am tempted to say here something about "God is in the presence of sin" through prevenient grace as a means of countering the unfortunate message conveyed, that is, that when we sin God leaves us for God cannot be present to sin. I will have to flesh this out elsewhere.

20. I agree with his relational "quadrilateral" here, but strongly disagree with his interpretation of the last two. For one, he has missed the potential of speaking of the environmental imperative others have found in Wesleyan thought. See H. Ray Dunning, *Grace, Faith, and Holiness* (Kansas City, Mo.: Beacon Hill, 1988).

Kierkegaard's scheme, a fractured self is incapable of relating to others without great distortion.[21] The Wesleyan concept of prevenient grace allows for the possibility of genuine love for others, even before the concept of *agape* is ever introduced to them. In this way, we can affirm loving acts in the world as coming from the grace of God, even if the loving individual is not a Christian. Important also is our understanding that the *imago Dei* is not obliterated in the Fall. It has simply yet to be progressively "actualized" through the (sanctifying) grace of God.

Jesus Christ is both the source and the example of the perfected "image of God." But in him, we not only see the image of God, we also see perfect humanity, in an even "better" sense than a pre-lapsarian Adam or Eve. I believe this has been neglected in our tradition — the goal of being truly human. In the scheme of Kierkegaard, in sin(ning) there comes a radical break between true humanity and the human situation.

> [Our] basic condition makes ultimate self-improvement impossible. This is the force of the Greek phrase from Aristotle meaning "in terms of possibility," e.g., as the oak-tree is in the acorn, the chicken in the egg. . . . The self we desire to become is not even potentially present, and all efforts to develop it from the existing basis are futile, until the self is in "equilibrium." Then, and only then, does the self exist "in terms of possibility," present in itself an ideal basis for satisfactory development. . . . "Becoming" can now take place.[22]

Thus Kierkegaard believes that it is only after being in a saving relation to the Power that constitutes the self that potentiality is even offered. There is no acorn at all before "salvation." It would serve us well to agree with Kierkegaard at this point, for it will help us avoid such problematic language of "human nature" and "depraved nature" and the need to distinguish them. True humanity is not even potentially present in those who actualize despair. But, rather than waiting for salvation for the potentiality to be restored, Wesleyan theology opens up the possibility of true human potential in those who have yet to find equilibrium. Prevenient grace, then, gives us our potential. Our very nature changes in terms of its potentiality

21. To the degree that Kierkegaard envisions the purest form of love as love for a dead person! Only if the person is dead are we free from all self-interest that seeks to use the other for personal gain. See Kierkegaard's *Works of Love*, available in several editions.

22. Price, *The Narrow Pass*, p. 40.

immediately from the moment of birth (life). Further, according to Wesley, our potentiality is not simply that of the first humans. Wesley clearly states in his sermon "What is Man?" that our potential is now even greater since Christ came to earth. We can become more than Adam or Eve ever could. While prevenient grace gives us the "acorn," our potential begins the process of actualization most acutely at the moment of our second birth. It is here that the process that we have called "healing" truly begins. And yet in this scheme, "healing" does not really encompass the scope of the internal change. At this point we will sacrifice one of Wesley's metaphors for another: that of New Creation.

Saving Grace: New Creations

Pure potentiality begins to be actualized when we are related to the Power that constitutes the self. In the more traditional sense than my use above, prevenient grace (the Holy Spirit) "woos" us toward this relationship with God; it also draws us toward our true selves. To despair at willing to be a self defiantly, and to despair at not willing to be a self, is to existentially know our "nature" as estranged. It is not that we have a human nature and a sinful nature somehow mingling within us, warring against each other until one is "eradicated" from our being. This metaphor simply does not work. But if we take Kierkegaard's understanding of existential estrangement seriously, we will see that what needs to happen in us is to be created anew. Perhaps the best explanation of Wesley on New Creation comes from Theodore Runyon in *The New Creation: John Wesley's Theology Today*. I have neither the time nor the space here to attempt a full examination of the breadth of value in this metaphor for salvation. But one passage will be helpful:

> Wesley was convinced that when the re-creative Spirit is at work real changes occur. Not only are we granted a new status in Christ through justification but God does not leave us where we were; God inaugurates a new creation, restoring the relation to which we are called, to mirror God in the world. . . . [There is real as well as relative change, says Wesley]. The relative change is that change in the way of being related brought about through our acceptance by God and is absolutely essential to everything that follows. But what fol-

lows, the real change, is the beginning of the new creaturehood, the *telos* toward which salvation is directed.[23]

It is for this reason (the belief in real change beginning at regeneration) that Wesley so highly values the experience of new birth. He complained against those who would minimize its power to change inward and outward sin. To use words applied to Wesley on this point, new birth not only justifies, it is our *initial sanctification* that enables us to progress toward our new *telos*. In Kierkegaard's words, because we are now in relationship with God, we find the evasive equilibrium that keeps the bodily and the psychic balanced by the spirit, or Spirit. And in the presence of God, we keep anxiety at bay, and find ourselves free from the bondage of accumulated dread. Our relations with God, others, ourselves, and the earth move toward not only authentic selfhood, but toward our true selves, as we "come about" in our unique unpredictable idiosyncrasy.[24] We *find* ourselves in God. New birth, then, begins a new life to be lived in sanctifying grace.

Sanctifying Grace: Infinite Resignation?

Central to another of Kierkegaard's primary works is the story of Abraham and Isaac. Kierkegaard refers to Abraham's infinite resignation of Isaac.[25] It is through this resignation that Abraham becomes a true knight of faith (or in some of his other words, where he moves to "Religion B" — a place beyond one's own ethical attempts at goodness). There are interesting parallels between this idea of resignation and many stories in our Holiness past that perhaps still have value. One example is offered.

A daughter, Eliza, was born to Phoebe Palmer on August 28, 1835. Palmer describes her as particularly beautiful and winsome. When the infant was eleven months old, her mother had a type of premonition. This premonition of "not being with her long" came true, but not through some childhood illness; the tragedy was even greater. A crib fire, started

23. Theodore Runyon, *The New Creation: John Wesley's Theology Today* (Nashville: Abingdon, 1998), p. 71.

24. See footnote 11 above.

25. It is fascinating in Kierkegaard to parallel Abraham's story to that of his own, in the relinquishing of Regina.

through apparent carelessness with a candle by a servant, took the "angel to heaven." Palmer records that she retired alone that night. "While pacing the room, crying to God, amid the tumult of grief, my mind arrested by a gentle whisper, saying, 'Your Heavenly Father loves you. He would not permit such a trial, without intending that some great good proportionate in magnitude and weight should result.'"[26]

"Palmer came to understand these losses as more than just random occurrences: they were acts of God which had a purpose."[27] The fullest spiritual utilization of their meaning, however, was still yet to come. It would be another year before Phoebe Palmer finally reached that "day of days" — her term for her own experience of entire sanctification. There was one last "idol" to be relinquished. Palmer's interpretation of Eliza's death obliged her to seek even more diligently the experience of entire sanctification. After several key events, including the sanctification experience of her sister, Sarah Lankford, Palmer reached a day where she determined to fast and pray unceasingly until her struggle was resolved.

Only when she was willing to place on the altar her husband and children did she finally sense that "all on the altar of sacrifice lay" and that entire sanctification was imminent. Thus, "her path to holiness had entailed a gradual weaning of affection, first for her children and then finally for her husband. . . . Sanctification came only when she was able to obey the Christian injunction to reserve her highest love for God."[28] In the theology of the Holiness movement, "original sin" is identified as that which prevents complete devotion to God. But in the story of Palmer and others, in a very real way, this Abraham-like infinite resignation (i.e., consecration) enabled true selfhood. In the end, it left women in particular with a radical freedom to become.

Unfortunately, this early idea of consecration was replaced by language of self-crucifixion, which still lingers in our midst! And yet, it is not only that it is antiquated; it is destructive to the whole message of salvation. The self is certainly not to be crucified if we understand "selfhood" as God's intention for our creation. But if the "self" in the metaphor of cruci-

---

26. Richard Wheatley, ed., *The Life and Letters of Mrs. Phoebe Palmer* (New York: Walter C. Palmer, 1876), p. 31.

27. Harold Raser, *Phoebe Palmer: Her Life and Thought* (Lewiston, N.Y.: Edwin Mellen, 1987), p. 38.

28. Anne C. Loveland, "Domesticity and Religion in the Antebellum Period: The Career of Phoebe Palmer," *The Historian* 39 (1977): 438.

fixion is intended to represent depravity within us, we once again stumble into the danger of two competing natures. There is no other crucifixion necessary other than the "ram" provided by God. To forget the *life-giving* work of Christ is to minimize the efficacy of grace, to empty the Christian life of love, and to disempower us again back into our estrangements. We lose sight of the *telos* available to those who "see" the presence of God. But for those who have responded to prevenient grace, have become new creations, and have increasingly actualized their created potential through God's sanctifying work, holiness expressed in love can have an existential reality in their hearts and lives as those who relate to the One who constitutes us all. I will end with Wynkoop's words:

> Salvation has to do with the whole disrupted relationship. Being a disruption in the sight of God and in the hearts of [people], the central concern is to correct that relationship. Nothing less can be dignified by the term salvation. The alienation must end. Only God can do this. This we know, in Christ the estrangement ended. We must meet God with a single-hearted love. Any duplicity, or mixed motives, make cleansing fellowship impossible. Christ's sacrifice of Himself on the cross not only made God's approval of us possible but makes a pure heart also possible. Sin is in this life possible of correction. Alienation is ended between God and [us]. The antithesis of loving God is not a state, nor is holiness a state, but an atmosphere daily, hourly, perhaps even momentarily, maintained in the presence and by the power of the Holy Spirit. This calls for the deepest measure of participation. But the participation is not a strained, unnatural, fear-inspired thing, but the whole person committed to God with abandon. This does not put an impossible burden on the human psyche, nor does it require any particular measure of maturity, ability, or knowledge. But it does ask for growth and nurture and a deepening spiritual sensitivity that never ends.[29]

29. Wynkoop, *An Existential Interpretation of the Doctrine of Holiness* (n.p., n.d.), pp. 254-56; edited.

HOLINESS IN MINISTRY

CHAPTER 7

Holiness and the Five Calls of God: Holiness in Postmodernity

HOWARD A. SNYDER

Times and cultures change. Is the holiness message still relevant in a so-called postmodern age? Or in a post-postmodern age? I believe it is. Paradoxically, however, the relevance of the holiness message for today becomes clearest when we first go back and look anew at what the Bible says about the holiness message, examining it in light of the questions and challenges of today.

The church has always been the most prophetic when it has rediscovered the relevance of the "eternal gospel" (Rev. 14:6) for a new age.[1] My thesis here is that the biblical message of holiness is pointedly and powerfully relevant to the world in which we live. But to understand God's call to and provision for holiness, we must see it within the context of the whole call of God. What does it really mean, biblically, to speak of the whole gospel for the whole world? Too often we pull apart things that should be held together. The need for biblical comprehensiveness is especially important when it comes to the subject of holiness. Holiness should mean wholeness, the integrity of heart and life. Therefore we should pay close attention to the full scope of God's call upon our lives, upon the church. We want to see, for instance, how the call to salvation, the call to ministry, and the call to holiness all fit together as one story, making one picture.

I am structuring my thoughts around what I am calling the five calls

---

1. Unless otherwise indicated, all biblical quotations are from the New Revised Standard Version (NRSV).

of God. We will examine what the Bible says about God's intent for humanity and for his creation. We are called to holiness. But that call is part of a larger intention of God to bring salvation in its fullness. We need to understand the call to holiness, and the grace of holiness, in the context of the full biblical witness of God's intention for people, cultures, and in fact the whole creation.

We will examine these five calls of God more or less in the order in which they appear in the Bible — that is, in a history-of-redemption sequence. There is a story here. We can trace it through Scripture, and even up to today and into the future, postmodern or not. God is up to something, and he graciously calls us to be part of this great work. We are a called people. The final goal is "a new heaven and a new earth," the kingdoms of this world becoming "the kingdom of our Lord and of his Messiah" (Rev. 11:15). Then "every knee [shall] bend, in heaven and on earth and under the earth, and every tongue . . . confess that Jesus Christ is Lord, to the glory of God the Father" (Phil. 2:10-11).

If we are to play the role God intends in this great drama, we must be a holy people. In fact, God calls and invites us to share his nature and his holiness, for his own good pleasure and purposes.

What then are these five calls of God? And what do they have to do with holiness? We begin with the first one we find in Scripture: the call to earth stewardship. This may at first seem a strange place to begin, but you will soon catch the drift of the story.

First: The Call to Earth Stewardship

We read in Genesis 2:15, "The LORD God took the man and put him in the garden of Eden to till it and keep it." The New International Version renders the commission as to "work . . . and take care of" the garden. This is a commission of course to all humankind, both men and women, not just to males. In the Genesis 2 account "the woman" has not yet been created, but the joint commission is clear in Genesis 1:26-28. "God blessed them, and God said to them, 'Be fruitful and multiply, and fill the earth and subdue it; and have dominion over the fish of the sea and over the birds of the air and over every living thing that moves upon the earth'" (v. 28).

"Dominion" here clearly means stewardship or nurturing management, not selfish exploitation.[2] John Wesley understood this very well. He wrote of this passage, "Man, as soon as he was made, had the whole visible creation before him, both to contemplate, and to take the comfort of." Made in God's image, man and woman have "the government of the inferior creatures" and are "as it were God's representative[s] on earth."[3] This is why Wesley says in his sermon "The Good Steward": "The relation which [humankind] bears to God . . . is exhibited under various representations," including that of sinner. "But no character more exactly agrees with the present state of man than that of a steward. . . . This appellation is exactly expressive of his situation in the present world, specifying the kind of servant he is to God, and what kind of service his divine master expects of him."[4]

Affirming man and woman as stewards of God's good gifts, including the created order, thus is basic biblical teaching. It has been fundamental in Christian history and theology, though more or less emphasized or neglected in various traditions.[5] The call to earth stewardship predates the Fall. It is an early commission given to all humankind — therefore, today, to all nations, peoples, and governments, and not just to Christians. But sound biblical exegesis, viewing the combined callings of God, bids Christians in particular to be committed to protecting and nurturing the physical environment. As Prof. Sandy Richter eloquently points out, the sense of Genesis 2:15 is that the Lord God put the human in the garden to serve and guard it. She writes that "the larger message" of the creation accounts is clear:

2. The dominion theme can be and often has been misinterpreted theologically, whether in so-called dominion theology or in an uncritical acceptance of a free-enterprise capitalism shaped by Enlightenment assumptions. The biblical meaning must "dominate" our hermeneutics here; biblically the meaning of dominion depends totally on the character of the Triune Creator and the nature of the image and reflection of God in humanity and the whole created order.

3. John Wesley, *Explanatory Notes on the Old Testament*, vol. 1 (Bristol: William Pine, 1765), p. 7.

4. John Wesley, Sermon 51, "The Good Steward," in *The Works of John Wesley*, vol. 2, Sermons II, 34-70, ed. Albert C. Outler (Nashville: Abingdon, 1985), pp. 282-83. Cf. Wesley on Luke 16:1, *Explanatory Notes on the New Testament* (London: Epworth, 1958). Wesley is here of course using "man" in the inclusive sense of "all humankind," men and women.

5. See Alister McGrath, *The Re-enchantment of Nature: Science, Religion and the Human Sense of Wonder* (London: Hodder & Stoughton, 2002).

The garden belongs to Yahweh, but [humankind] was given the privilege to rule and the responsibility to care for this garden under the sovereignty of their divine Lord. This was the ideal plan — a world in which [humankind] would succeed in constructing the human civilization by directing and harnessing the amazing resources of the planet under the wise direction of their Creator. Here there would always be enough, progress would not necessitate pollution, expansion would not demand extinction.[6]

Earth stewardship may also be called creation care.[7] It is the faithful human nurture and management of the God-created order. For Christians, creation care is an integral part of the faithful following of Jesus Christ and the worship of the Holy Trinity.

This then is the first of the five calls of God. We may view earth stewardship or creation care as the broadest circle of God's call. It is a call to all humanity. All men and women were and are called to care for God's good earth, thus fulfilling their mandate to be God's regents on earth. We are to serve and honor God by caring for his creatures; to worship and glorify God by our work and our enjoyment of the garden God planted.

To understand God's call to holiness, then, we need first to understand the context within which that call comes: the call to earth stewardship. But this in turn leads us to the second call of God.

Second: The Call to Covenant Peoplehood: Repentance, Faith, Obedience, Community

The second biblical call we must consider is the call to covenant peoplehood. This call appears in Scripture after the Fall, though it is implicit earlier, as God's abiding intent.[8] It is the beginning act in God's initiative to restore and heal a fallen creation. It is foreshadowed by the call of

6. Sandra Richter, "Stewardship of the Environment: A Christian Value" (unpublished paper, Asbury Theological Seminary, 2004).

7. *Creation Care* is the name of the quarterly magazine of the Evangelical Environmental Network, available online at http://www.creationcare.org.

8. Genesis 1–2 shows that humankind living responsibly, worshipfully, and joyfully in covenant communion with God in the world he created was always the divine intent.

Noah to build the ark,[9] but the call to peoplehood really begins with the call of Abraham and Sarah in Genesis. It continues through Isaac and Jacob and then expands as Israel becomes a nation. We know well the Genesis and Exodus stories. God liberates Israel from slavery in Egypt and forms a covenant people for himself. He gives his people not only his law — itself a revelation of God's character — but a whole way of life, an identity and a future as God's special people.

The Bible is explicit that this call was for God's glory and for the sake of all peoples and nations. The call is the expansion, partial fulfillment, and development of God's word to Abraham: "In you all the families of the earth shall be blessed" (Gen. 12:3; cf. 18:18; 28:14; Ps. 72:17). Since humankind went astray, rebelled, and wandered from God, Yahweh raised up his own people, a holy people called to serve him both in worship and in witness. In the Old Testament this witness was largely in the form of a contrast society among the nations — his "peculiar people" and "priestly kingdom."[10] But the Hebrew Scriptures also signal a broader, expanding, "centrifugal" mission to the nations.[11] This of course is the background of Jesus' great commission in the New Testament to "be my witnesses in Jerusalem, in all Judea and Samaria, and to the ends of the earth"; to make disciples of all nations and peoples.

Notice especially the two main elements of this call: covenant and peoplehood. *Peoplehood:* The call is not just to individuals. Rather it is a call to form, be, and act like a people — a human community in solidarity internally and with God. And *covenant:* The call is not simply to be just any kind of people; simply one more people group among the nations and ethnicities of the earth. The point is to be a people in covenant with God — so closely connected with Yahweh that their actual way of life is shaped more by God's character than by the nations and cultures all around. God's people are to be salt and light — so faithful in their love-relationship with God and in their revelation of his character that they season, heal, and illuminate the world rather than taking on the world's flavors or being dazzled by the Klieg lights of the world and its enticing show.

9. The call to Noah is a call to and promise of preservation of the earth, and thus reinforces the call to earth stewardship.

10. Deuteronomy 14:2; 26:18; Titus 2:14; 1 Peter 2:9, KJV; Exodus 19:6.

11. See Ralph D. Winter and Steven C. Hawthorne, eds., *Perspectives on the World Christian Movement*, 3d ed. (Pasadena: William Carey Library, 1999), especially "The Historical Perspective," pp. 195-370.

In Scripture, the call to covenant peoplehood is unmistakably a call to holiness. This call to holiness for God's covenant people is explicit and emphatic, and I'll say more about it a bit later.

Notice also that the call to covenant peoplehood is a call to repentance, faith, obedience, and community. Because of sin, we cannot simply of our own initiative become God's people. Here we face the biblical teaching about human rebellion and waywardness — the deep stain of sin that requires the healing medicine of salvation through Jesus Christ. The call is to be the redeemed people of God, the community of the Spirit, in the world. I do not need to elaborate these truths here, but we need to be clear about them. The call to covenant peoplehood is a call to transformation and healing — to turn from evil and alien ways to truly be the people of God on the basis of the provision God has made available through Jesus Christ.

The call to peoplehood is thus the call to salvation — to accept the healing offer of salvation that God graciously makes in Jesus Christ by the Spirit. This is a call God now makes to everyone, everywhere. God "now . . . commands all people everywhere to repent" (Acts 17:30); to "repent and believe" the Good News (Mark 1:15). It is the gospel call to all nations, tribes, languages, and peoples. In this gospel age of the Spirit, especially, this means that those who are called become also those who call. God commissions his called people to be his co-workers in the calling of the nations to Christ.

In terms of the five calls of God I am outlining here, we may view covenant peoplehood as a second circle inside the larger circle of the call to earth stewardship. The creation-care call is a call to all humanity, as previously noted. We see in Scripture, especially in the New Testament, that this "peculiar" call to covenant peoplehood ultimately also extends to all humanity. In the Bible the peoplehood call proceeds progressively from the call to Abraham and Sarah, to the whole people of Israel, to the ever-expanding Body of Christ, and thus to all peoples everywhere. So we represent this second call of God as the circle of covenant peoplehood within the initial circle of earth stewardship.

Third: The Call to God's Reign:
Allegiance and Loyalty

Jesus said, "I tell you the truth, no one can see the kingdom of God without being born again" (John 3:3, TNIV). But not everyone who is born again sees the Kingdom of God! For many born-again Christians, the call to covenant peoplehood exhausts the meaning of God's call to humanity. Many people who have been converted to Jesus and the church have not yet been converted to Christ's Kingdom. That requires a deeper, more comprehensive conversion. So much of the church thinks it is called only to be the church — that is, to be a community or organization that says, "Jesus Christ is our Savior," and that's it. A sort of religious club, or a lifelong waiting room for heaven.[12] This is sad, for it misses another essential divine call. Listen to Jesus' remarkable words: "Seek first the kingdom of God and his righteousness" (Matt. 6:33, ESV). Pray every day, "Your kingdom come, your will be done, on earth as it is in heaven" (Matt. 6:10, ESV). John Wesley comments that we should pray, "May Thy Kingdom of grace come quickly, and swallow up all the kingdoms of the earth! May all [humankind], receiving Thee, O Christ, for their King, truly believing in Thy name, be filled with righteousness and peace and joy, with holiness and happiness, till they are removed hence into Thy Kingdom of glory, to reign with Thee for ever and ever."[13]

This, then, is the call to the Kingdom of God — the call to God's reign. It is a fundamental biblical call. Scripture is all about God's reign, even where the precise term "Kingdom of God" is not used. The Bible is a book about God's sovereign providential oversight; his beneficent government; his loving care and sure purposes; and his concern with righteousness and justice. The Kingdom call therefore concerns *allegiance* and loyalty. God's call upon us Christians is a call not only to repentance and faith; it is also the call to an allegiance above all other allegiances and a loyalty that trumps all other loyalties. It is a call not only to be God's church but also to serve his Kingdom.[14]

---

12. This is of course a distortion of biblical ecclesiology, which in the person of Jesus Christ and the Holy Spirit is always linked with the Kingdom of God and thus with Kingdom mission.

13. Wesley, *Explanatory Notes Upon the New Testament*, on Matthew 6:10, p. 37.

14. The Kingdom call may be seen as part of the call to peoplehood, as suggested for instance by Exodus 19, 1 Peter 2, and many other passages. But because Christian theology (both popular and academic) in the West, especially, tends to drive a wedge between church

Christians today, says N. T. Wright, "need to think afresh through the issues of what allegiance to Jesus means in practice."[15]

At one level "Kingdom of God" is really a metaphor reflecting a cultural context of monarchy — and most nations today don't have kings. The United States rebelled against England to get rid of the king, so as a nation it has no king, at least officially. Thus for Americans the concept "Kingdom of God" may lack concreteness.

But the truth of God's reign is not confined to nations that have actual kings or queens. Faithful biblical exegesis shows that a broad web of key scriptural themes and metaphors weave together to teach us what the Kingdom of God really means. These themes all make essentially the same point: God is "high over all," the one to whom we owe total obedience and loyalty. Yet he is a God of love whose rule and care are life-giving and beneficent. This is essential teaching, relevant in every cultural context.

More than a God who demands obedience, however, the Holy Trinity is the Lord who *promises* the Kingdom of God in its fullness. He is the *shalom*-promising God, the one with healing medicine for our bodies and souls; our land and all earth's cultures. The Bible makes the same point through various metaphors and word pictures — for example, the eloquent statement in Colossians 1:20 that through Jesus Christ "God was pleased to reconcile to himself all things, whether on earth or in heaven, by making peace through the blood of his cross." If we are well grounded in the Old Testament, we will not read New Testament references to *peace* without thinking of the rich Old Testament meaning of *shalom*. The Kingdom of God is the reign of *shalom* because of the nature and character of the Triune God.

The Kingdom call is a call to Kingdom values and virtues, Kingdom ethics — to really live in the world so that we become *sunergoi*, "co-workers" toward the visible manifestation of God's reign on the earth.[16] It is a call for the church to live out the meaning of God's reign within our particular sociocultural contexts. It is a call to Kingdom loyalty and alle-

and Kingdom, we today in our contemporary context get a more faithful understanding of God's call by making the Kingdom call explicit.

15. N. T. Wright, *The Challenge of Jesus* (London: SPCK, 2000), p. x.

16. Glen H. Stassen and David P. Gushee, *Kingdom Ethics: Following Jesus in Contemporary Context* (Downers Grove: InterVarsity, 2003).

giance — pledging allegiance first and above all to Jesus Christ and his purposes, thus viewing all other identities and allegiances as secondary.

So our allegiance is to the Triune God and therefore to intentional solidarity with his people, our sisters and brothers in Christ throughout the earth. Loyalty to God's reign thus trumps national loyalty. As a Jesus-follower, my highest allegiance is not to my nation or party or president or state or social or ethnic group, but to Jesus Christ and the righteousness and justice of his reign. God's Kingdom redefines, for example, the meaning of "homeland security." It calls us to the primary task of discerning the difference between Kingdom allegiance and a proper national patriotism — a high-priority task for American evangelicals today, as well as for Christians in other lands.[17]

Jesus was explicit that the Kingdom call is a call to the justice and righteousness of God's reign. The Kingdom thus calls us to social and economic justice — to righteousness and justice in family and neighborhood, in and among the nations and families of the earth.[18] It is a call particularly to the poor and oppressed of the earth, for Jesus himself said, "The Spirit of the Lord is upon me, because he has anointed me to bring good news to the poor" (Luke 4:18-19).[19]

In terms of the five calls of God, we picture this Kingdom call as a third circle within the larger circles of earth stewardship and covenant peoplehood. It is not however a lesser or more restricted call; just the opposite. It is a call that is intended to — and in fact *will* — penetrate to the farthest circumference, accomplishing God's overall, underlying, penetrating, constant purpose: That in all things, all places, all spheres, God may be glorified, his creation gladly serving and praising him.

This also is a call ultimately to the whole human race. But it proceeds through covenant peoplehood. That is, while people and nations and cul-

---

17. This is true for Christians everywhere, but especially for those in contexts where ethnic pride or national identity threatens to compromise Kingdom allegiance. If the shoe fits . . . !

18. In my book *Kingdom, Church, and World* (Eugene, Ore.: Wipf & Stock, 2001), I show how the biblical Kingdom of God theme ties together many other biblical themes, including *shalom*, sabbath, jubilee, land, justice for the poor, and city of God.

19. It is clear from this as well as the larger biblical context that "poor," "captives," and "oppressed" here include all forms of poverty, bondage, and oppression. The terms should not be limited either to exclusively spiritual or to solely political or socioeconomic categories.

tures everywhere are under God's sovereign government, it is God's special people, the church, who are called to be the initial visible embodiment of the Kingdom of God — the community of the King.[20] The church is called to be God's subversive agency in the earth, constantly working — much of the time below the radar screen of the media — to witness to and actually speed the coming of the Kingdom of God in its fullness.

So we may picture this call of God, this Kingdom call, as a third circle within the calls to covenant peoplehood and earth stewardship.

Fourth: The Call to Specific Ministry: Gifts and Particular Vocations

The church has often discussed this call in terms of "vocation," or of "being called into the ministry." But how are we to properly understand this call biblically? How does it relate to the call to holiness? Are only "ministers" called to minister, or to live a high standard of holiness?

We know that Jesus Christ called the twelve apostles. Paul said numerous times that he also was "called to be an apostle" (Rom. 1:1; 1 Cor. 1:1). In the Old Testament we read of God calling Moses, David, Deborah, Esther, and Jonah, for example. These were all called to fairly specific ministries. They received calls unique to their lives and contexts.

Jesus called twelve apostles, but clearly these were not the only persons he called into ministry. He called many disciples, though relatively few apostles. Many men and women, many slaves and some masters, many poor and some rich responded. By the help of the Holy Spirit and the discipling process of the Christian community, these Jesus-followers were able to discern and live out God's special call on their lives.

Behind this reality of the New Testament church is an amazing, and socially unsettling, teaching of Scripture: *Everyone called to salvation is called also to minister.* Every man and woman, boy and girl whom Jesus calls to be a disciple he calls as well to be his ministering servant. No exceptions; no distinctions on the basis of wealth, class, gender, intelligence, physical characteristics, or ethnic or national identity. This is revolutionary! And the choice is up to the sovereign Spirit, not to us.

20. Howard A. Snyder, *The Community of the King*, rev. ed. (Downers Grove: InterVarsity, 2004).

If we are rightly to understand the gospel and the call to holiness, we must also understand the call to particular ministry. The Bible gives us a rich and fully practicable theology of the ministry of the whole people of God. We need to mine it, understand it, and apply it in all our churches. This is absolutely essential if the church is to be the agent of God's reign as Jesus intends, and to be his holy covenant people.

Unfortunately, most of the literature on ministry that has accumulated over the centuries assumes that the subject of ministry concerns only the ordained ministry. This is grossly misleading. It is not possible to understand biblically the meaning of the church's ordained ministry if we do not see such more specialized ministry within the context of the universal call to ministry — the call God graciously extends to every believer to be a minister and servant *(diakonos)* of the Good News.

Scripture reveals a clear and rich doctrine of the ministry of the whole people of God. The teaching rests on three pillars. All three have Old Testament roots and are elaborated in the New Testament as essential aspects of the New Covenant in Jesus and the new age of the Spirit. Here are the three pillars:

First, the *priesthood of believers* (1 Peter 2:4-10). Old Testament Israel was called to be "a kingdom of priests," God's priestly people among the nations. Within this general call was the more restricted Levitical priesthood.

This Old Testament history lies behind the New Testament teaching. We learn in the New Testament, particularly in Acts and Hebrews, that the New Covenant brings two key changes to the Old Testament priesthood. On the one hand, the priesthood is narrowed to just one person: Jesus Christ, our great High Priest, through whom we have salvation and receive the call to discipleship. But at the same time the priesthood is expanded to include all believers — fulfilling the original intention of a faithful, holy, priestly people in the earth. To be a Christian is to be a priest of God.

This is just what Israel's prophets foretold. Peter announced on the day of Pentecost,

> This is what was spoken through the prophet Joel: "In the last days it will be, God declares, that I will pour out my Spirit upon all flesh, and your sons and your daughters shall prophesy, and your young men shall see visions, and your old men shall dream dreams. Even upon my slaves, both men and women, in those days I will pour out my Spirit; and they shall prophesy." (Acts 2:16-18)

In other words, all Christians now live in the Pentecostal dispensation when the Holy Spirit has been poured out on all believers — precisely so that we can be God's witnesses, King Jesus' priestly people in the earth.

Second, Jesus' high priestly work and the pouring out of the Spirit open the door to another foundational pillar: *the gifts of the Spirit.* Just as every Christian is a disciple, so every believer receives special gifts for ministry. No one left behind; no one left out. As everyone is a priest, so everyone is spiritually gifted.

The doctrine of the gifts of the Spirit clarifies a key point. While we are all priests, we do not all have the same priestly ministry. "There are varieties of gifts, but the same Spirit; and there are varieties of services, but the same Lord; and there are varieties of activities, but it is the same God who activates all of them in everyone. To each is given the manifestation of the Spirit for the common good" (1 Cor. 12:4-7). One universal priesthood, but diverse gifts.

Here is the beauty of Christian community! Socially and politically speaking, this is the most radical teaching in Scripture because it says that *no one* — only the Holy Spirit — is authorized to determine who receives which gifts. As we look at Christian movements down through history, we see the amazing way God has raised up the most unlikely of leaders (from a worldly viewpoint). Repeatedly society has expressed the same puzzlement we find in Acts 4:13 — "When they saw the boldness of Peter and John and realized that they were uneducated and ordinary men, they were amazed and recognized them as companions of Jesus." This was the only explanation the Jewish leaders could find: these troublemakers had hung out with Jesus.

The Bible is explicit in both Testaments that this is precisely God's strategy. As Paul summarized it in 1 Corinthians:

> Consider your own call, brothers and sisters: not many of you were wise by human standards, not many were powerful, not many were of noble birth. But God chose what is foolish in the world to shame the wise; God chose what is weak in the world to shame the strong; God chose what is low and despised in the world, things that are not, to reduce to nothing things that are, so that no one might boast. (1 Cor. 1:25-29)

This is true generally, and it is true specifically with the gifts of the Spirit. So in the New Testament we see that God has ordained a whole variety of gifts and ministries. All Christians are gifted, but not all have the same ministry.

How then are we to understand the role of what the church usually calls "ordained ministry"? The key passage is Ephesians 4:11-13. The Lord Jesus ordained a diversity of gifts so that "some would be apostles, some prophets, some evangelists, some pastors and teachers, to equip the saints for the work of ministry, for building up the body of Christ, until all of us come to the unity of the faith and of the knowledge of the Son of God."

Finally, the third pillar supporting the biblical doctrine of ministry is the call to be *servants of Jesus Christ.* In the Old Testament we read of people like "Moses the servant of God" or "David the servant of the Lord." But now, in the New Covenant in Jesus Christ, we are all God's servants. We are all called to servanthood — to what the New Testament calls *diakonia.*

The call to be servants and ministers of Jesus Christ teaches another key truth. It reveals the spirit, the attitude and character, the incarnational manner in which ministry is to be carried out. Jesus' words, "As the Father has sent me, so I send you" (John 20:21), were not meant for the first apostles only. They set the model for all ministry in the name of Jesus Christ.[21]

Here then is our commission to ministry. We are all — each one of us — called as *priests* of God, *gifted* by the Spirit, and sent as *servants* of Jesus Christ.

We may view this comprehensive call of God — the call to specific ministry — as a fourth circle within the calls to earth stewardship, to covenant peoplehood, and to the Kingdom of God. These other calls then clarify and amplify our understanding of what ministry is. Ministry is not just "church work" but is all that Christians faithfully do to show the truth of God in all areas of life and culture — arts, science, economics, politics, creation care; the full range of Kingdom concerns. In and through all of these dimensions pulses the great apostolic concern to reach people with the transforming love of Jesus Christ and form faithful Jesus-like communities of the Kingdom of God.

---

21. As Peter, John, Paul, and other New Testament writers emphasized — e.g., Philippians 2:1-15; 1 John 2:6; 1 Peter 2:21-23.

Fifth: The Call to Holiness:
Trinitarian Love

We come now to the flaming heart of our concern, and the heart of the Good News: God's call to holiness. This is the call to know God in his fullness; to enter into the fellowship of Triune, self-giving love.[22]

This is the call — and the amazing, gracious invitation — to "participate in the divine nature" (2 Peter 1:4, NIV) — to know the Holy Trinity, Father, Son, and Holy Spirit, who allows us to enter into gracious fellowship with him such as otherwise we cannot even imagine. God "has given us . . . his precious and very great promises, so that through them [we] may escape from the corruption that is in the world because of lust, and may become participants of the divine nature" (2 Peter 1:4).

Mind-blowing as it sounds, holiness means sharing the very character of God — communion with the Trinity. This is precisely what Jesus prayed for in John 17:

> Holy Father, protect them in your name that you have given me, so that they may be one, as we are one. . . . Sanctify them in the truth; your word is truth. As you have sent me into the world, so I have sent them into the world. And for their sakes I sanctify myself, so that they also may be sanctified in truth.
>
> I ask not only on behalf of these, but also on behalf of those who will believe in me through their word, that they may all be one. As you, Father, are in me and I am in you, may they also be in us, so that the world may believe that you have sent me. The glory that you have given me I have given them, so that they may be one, as we are one, I in them and you in me, that they may become completely one, so that the world may know that you have sent me and have loved them even as you have loved me. (John 17:11, 17-23)

Here Jesus beautifully blends the call to holiness, participation in Trinitarian love, and mission in the world. This is what true biblical holiness, understood within the five calls of God, really means! The call to holiness is to be understood within the larger story of the other four calls — because God is one and his plan is one.

---

22. I am assuming here a comprehensive doctrine of the Trinity which I do not take the time to spell out.

A key reason, in fact, for the call to holiness is so that we may faithfully and graciously fulfill the other four calls. These earlier calls give us a fuller understanding of the larger context and the ethical and missional implications of holiness — what it really can mean to pursue what Wesley called "all inward and outward holiness."

Let us consider, then. What would it mean for us, for the church empowered by the Spirit and inspired by the example of Jesus and "all the saints," to live out the manifold call of God in postmodern society, and globally?

Holiness and Earth Stewardship

This is most fully understood in the context of the call to holiness. The creation-care mandate is an integral part of the heart-call of God. The more we share the character of God, the more we are concerned with God's concerns. So we want to fulfill the call first given to Adam and Eve to tend the garden. We want to preserve, nurture, and protect the physical environment, playing our part in helping it thrive to the glory of God and for his creative, esthetic, and redemptive purposes — as well as for our own survival!

What does earth stewardship lived to the glory of God mean today, in practical terms? It means everything from recycling paper and plastics and caring for church property according to good environmental principles here locally, to supporting larger efforts to protect endangered species and combat global warming and the disasters it is bringing to the world's poor. Consuming less energy and supporting public policies that help protect God's good earth: this is practical holiness. These are not mere secondary or peripheral ethical concerns, nor are they primarily political issues. They are good old-fashioned holiness issues.

Can we develop Jesus communities that practice creation care? Of course we can! It's simply a matter of the vision and the will. We can show once again in history that we can be God's people in God's land, practicing the principles of jubilee.

Creation care means, as well, the care of our bodies as part of holy and holistic living — a theme strongly emphasized by John Wesley, E. Stanley Jones, J. C. McPheeters, and Frank Bateman Stanger, among many others.

Our bodies were created by God, as were marriage and the family, so these are part of our earth-stewardship mandate.[23]

Holy people are those who feel deeply about all the creatures God has made. We notice a curious thing about the great saints of God, even some who were very otherworldly and saw little value in material things. Many of them saw God manifest in nature and were very sensitive to the well-being or the suffering of all living creatures. Francis of Assisi and John Wesley are, of course, prime examples.

So, holy people tread lightly and joyfully on the earth. Living in reciprocal harmony with God, they seek to live in harmonious reciprocity with God's good land. (Having just returned from a week or so in Cambridge, England, and noting the tide of bicycles there, I found myself wondering how we here in our own community could be more bicycle- and walker-friendly!)

In our age when we are learning the mysteries of earth and space as never before, we should be even better in our applied holiness in the sphere of earth stewardship than the church has been in the past.

Holiness and Covenant Peoplehood

Here the implications of holiness are fairly obvious but very profound. We are called to holy, loving, covenant community, and it is the sanctifying Spirit of God who makes this possible.

Covenant peoplehood reminds us that holiness, while personal, is not first of all individual. It is primarily social, as Wesley insisted. That is, it concerns the character of the Christian community, and of each of our lives within it. Thus sanctification is not in the first instance the sanctification of the individual person but the sanctification of the Body of Christ. As Jesus' physical body on earth was holy, so the Body of Christ on earth is

23. The issue here is *stewardship*, biblically understood. The biblical doctrine of stewardship is based on two correlative principles: responsible care for the entirety of the material world entrusted to humankind (including time, money, and the physical environment), and responsible stewardship of God's "manifold grace" (1 Peter 4:10). By the Spirit God grants us "supernatural" grace as the necessary resource for his people to be good stewards of the "natural" world. By the faithful Spirit-empowered stewardship of grace Christians in their stewardship of God's world are able to counteract the downward pull (entropy) of sin and its effects in the world.

to be holy — loving God with all its heart, mind, soul, and strength, and loving its earthly neighbors as itself. Holiness therefore means loving, mutually accountable community, the sanctification of the Body of Christ. This is the key to maintaining our own individual moral and ethical integrity. Holiness as personal experience is most healthily entered into in the context of Christian community.[24]

The New Testament says this in many places, but perhaps nowhere more plainly than in Ephesians 5:19-21 — "Be filled with the Spirit, addressing one another in psalms and hymns and spiritual songs, singing and making melody to the Lord with all your heart, giving thanks always and for everything to God the Father in the name of our Lord Jesus Christ, submitting to one another out of reverence for Christ." Jesus calls us to live in community with God and one another because God wants to share his very loving, holy, compassionate, merciful, gracious, out-reaching self with us — thus to make us like himself, like Jesus Christ.

Practical holiness as a matter of covenant peoplehood therefore means attention to the priorities and structures of biblical *koinonia* — building healthy, holy, and just community. It means affirming the gifts and fruit of the Spirit; practicing ministry and mission as taught in Scripture and modeled by Jesus Christ. Through the Holy Spirit we will find ourselves actually fulfilling Jesus' words that his followers would "also do the works that I do and, in fact, . . . greater works than these, because I am going to the Father" (John 14:12). We will find ourselves fulfilling Jesus' call to serve others, not just ourselves, and we will see that this is rooted in the very character of God. The more we grasp the meaning of the Trinity and Jesus' incarnation, the more we see that holy love (true Christianity) is all about relinquishing status for the sake of lifting others.

Christians are to be specialists in building covenant community to the glory of God. In regeneration we receive the very life of God so that we may do this. Building healthy missional community is in fact a major focus of New Testament teaching. Note how much of the New Testament is devoted, not to exhortations or strategies for evangelism or mission, but to building community that truly is the Body of Christ. Why is this? Because the biblical writers knew that covenant communities which truly incarnate the character of Jesus Christ would in fact do Jesus' work and fulfill God's

24. This was of course a key discovery of John Wesley and the early Methodists as they developed the community/discipling structures of society, class, and band.

mission in the world. It is that simple and that profound. The community-building that Paul and the other New Testament writers focus on is the Spirit's missionary strategy.

The call to covenant peoplehood means both learning about the nature of healthy community and how to build it, and practicing healthy, accountable community within our churches. We need to care for one another as genuine Christian community wherever we are. We are first of all sisters and brothers in the Body of Christ, hopeful but vulnerable, and that reality and identity transcends all other identities and distinctions. Jesus said much about this in instructing his disciples to walk as he walked.[25]

Holiness and the Reign of God

Holiness people are Kingdom of God people — if they are biblically grounded. Our Kingdom vocation means living for God's larger global and eternal purposes. As the old hymn puts it, "Only one life; 'twill soon be past — only what's done for Christ [and his kingdom] will last." Holiness in a postmodern age means holy, healthy living for the sake of the Kingdom of God.

Holiness means living the reality God's reign *now* in this present age. This was the great new insight that came to E. Stanley Jones in the 1930s. Jones was raised in the Holiness tradition; he was a Holiness missionary. But after visiting Russia in the heady days of communism's utopian vision, Jones came to realize that he had no adequate theology of the Kingdom of God now, in this age, this present time. He was troubled, and out of that questing came two of Jones's most prophetic books: *Christ's Alternative to Communism* (1935) and *Is the Kingdom of God Realism?* (1940). The Christian alternative to communist utopianism, Jones said, is the liberating biblical vision of the Kingdom of God. And yes, the Kingdom of God is *realism* — the way the world was made to be — not just *idealism* in the sense of some unattainable ideal.[26]

So E. Stanley Jones concluded that the gospel is not only about "the unchanging Christ" but also about "the unshakable kingdom." The gospel con-

---

25. See especially Matthew 20:25-28; 23:8-11; John 13:1-17; 1 John 2:6; 1 Peter 2:21-25.
26. E. Stanley Jones, *Christ's Alternative to Communism* (New York: Abingdon, 1935); E. Stanley Jones, *Is the Kingdom of God Realism?* (New York: Abingdon, 1940).

cerns a Person and a Plan — Jesus Christ and his Kingdom — and the two must be held together in our theology and in our lived discipleship. This is holiness lived within the sphere and the forward pull of the Kingdom of God.

So it must be for us. The work of the sanctifying Spirit is to make us Kingdom-of-God people — people who, like Jesus, incarnate the reality and priorities of God's reign in our personal lives, our families, our economics, and our politics.

Holiness and Particular Vocation

The call to holiness is the call to so open ourselves to God's Spirit that his gifts and graces flow and flourish in our lives. This also is a key part of holiness. Lived holiness is what Hebrews 10:24-25 is talking about: "Let us consider how to provoke one another to love and good deeds, not neglecting to meet together, as is the habit of some, but encouraging one another, and all the more as you see the Day approaching." Holiness means life empowered by the Holy Spirit so that what is said of Jesus in John 3:34 becomes true also of his disciples: "The one whom God has sent speaks the words of God, for God gives the Spirit without limit" (NIV).

Holiness means each of us finding our own vocation within, and guided by, the Body of Christ. In this way we each make precisely the contribution to God's Kingdom purposes that the Spirit intends. Understanding vocation in terms of the larger vision of God's reign, not narrowly in terms of church ministry, is part of the ecclesiological meaning of holiness. Our ministry for Jesus Christ is Kingdom ministry — our whole life and witness in the world — not just church ministry.

How do we come to experience this holiness, this deeper life in the Spirit? It comes through receiving the cleansing, empowering presence of the Holy Spirit by faith and obedience. Here pastors, disciplers, and other leaders have a keen responsibility to lead believers into the deeper life in the Spirit.

The Wesleyan emphasis on Christian perfection, or perfecting, holds together two vital emphases at this point. First, the goal (the *telos*) of Christian community, and of each of our lives within community, is always to grow up into the fullness of the character of Jesus Christ. This is the central point of Ephesians 4:7-16 and like passages which speak of the church as the Body of Christ, animated by and filled with the Spirit.

Second, this walking in the Spirit is to be our present experience, not just a future hope. We need to help one another enter into the fullness of the Spirit, to be filled with and walk daily in the Spirit of Jesus. Generally, as Wesley taught, this deeper dimension of Spirit-life comes as a distinct experience subsequent to conversion, though (as Wesley acknowledged) it may be experienced more gradually or less perceptibly — and thus possibly through multiple fresh fillings (or deeper workings) of the Spirit. For most people, it seems, this *process* of growing in the Spirit is enlivened or activated by *crisis* points, more or less perceptible, along the journey.

If our holiness teaching is to be practical and lived, we should not lose this key crisis and process link. Today's stress on gradual growth and on character and moral development is helpful and it is true, I think, that the nineteenth-century Holiness movement at times overemphasized crisis and underplayed process in the work of sanctification, particularly in some branches of the movement. But today we may face the opposite danger of overemphasizing process, either in reaction to Pentecostal/Charismatic emphases or in reaction to our own history. It would be un-Wesleyan as well as unbiblical to lose the crisis/process nexus.[27]

As a practical matter of preaching, discipleship, and growth, we need to help believers understand the deeper life of the Spirit that is available to them in Christ. We should give believers opportunities to enter into that deeper life — to confront the dividedness of their own hearts and enter into the fullness, wholeness, and integration *in Christian community* that is our inheritance in Jesus Christ and is a foretaste of that communion we will enjoy in the heavenly kingdom. This was Wesley's concern, and it should be ours.

So this is the call to holiness in relation to the other calls discussed earlier. I emphasize again: it is the Spirit's infilling that supplies the power, the energy, the effective movemental impulse that enables the church and each of us as Jesus' disciples to fulfill the other calls God extends to us.

We may view this fifth call of God — the call to holiness — as the central circle among all God's calls. This is the heart of our vocation, for it is the call to the heart of God. It is the call to love the Lord our God with all our heart, strength, soul, and mind, and thus to love our neighbors as ourselves. It is the central, the capacitating, the essential equipping call — the

---

27. The Wesleyan understanding of holiness, properly understood, also maintains the dynamic biblical link between faith and works (as for instance in Eph. 2:9-10, Phil. 2:12-13, and Gal. 5:6).

call that enables us to live out our gifts and callings; to see and serve his liberating reign; to be God's covenant people; to care for the good earth. Thus responding willingly to all God's calls, the church and each of us personally glorifies God and serves the world through the gifts Christ bestows (cf. 1 Peter 4:10-11; Romans 12).

Since holiness touches and penetrates every sphere of life, we could just as well conceive of holiness not as the inner circle, but as an outer circle that includes all the other calls of God. It is the dynamic work of the Spirit that penetrates all dimensions of life.

This vision thus is dynamic, not static. It is movement, like the wind of the Spirit. It is going somewhere — to the fulfillment of God's mission and the coming of God's reign in all its fullness. It is active and dynamic, for the Spirit draws us forward in mission in the spirit and character of Jesus. We can therefore reframe the picture as follows, showing how God by his Holy Spirit leads and draws the church into the fulfillment of mission in all its dimensions.[28]

Postmodern Holiness?

How does this biblically grounded conception of holiness respond to the challenges of postmodernity? In four ways.

First, *holiness is holistic.* It meets the human need for a way of life that reaches all dimensions of our existence. Even though postmodernity is famously hostile to holism and "metanarratives," yet people sense the need for an existence which at some deep level is whole.

Second, *holiness is particular.* It recognizes the uniqueness of each person created in God's image; that the Holy Spirit works uniquely in each individual, cleansing, empowering, and granting gifts that especially fit each person's needs, capacities, and cultural context — without becoming self-preoccupied or overly individualistic.

Third, *holiness is narrative.* It is not first of all an abstract idea, philosophy, or theology. It is a story about what God has done for us and how our own stories find meaning but also self-transcendence within the story

---

28. I have in mind here also the ecclesiological model depicted in Darrell L. Guder, ed., *Missional Church: A Theological Vision for the Sending Church in North America* (Grand Rapids: Eerdmans, 1998).

and personal reality of the Triune God who sent Jesus Christ into the world in the power of the Holy Spirit to fulfill God's plan.

Finally, *holiness is life*. It is experience. It is not first of all a doctrine but a love relationship with God in Jesus Christ and the Spirit. Thus holiness is community — *koinonia* with God and with one another in a new kind of fellowship, the church, which simultaneously lives in two worlds — the one we now see visibly around us, and the one which is to come and which in fact is constantly, invisibly, penetratingly around us right now. Holiness is *undividedness* — the life in which, lost in God, we find ourselves. And thus finding God's love in us, we reach out and find others.[29]

Conclusion

On a warm October afternoon, my wife Jan called me outside to see something strange. The sun was shining; golden leaves were falling from the hickory trees. I went out and looked, but all I saw was scattered leaves drifting down.

"I see only some leaves falling," I said, "obeying the law of gravity."

"Look higher!" she said. "Way up in the sky."

I looked higher — and saw something I'd never seen before. Thousands of leaves high above our tree, fluttering and floating and drifting upward and away in all directions. Heading up and outward, not down to earth.

"What happened?" I asked.

Just moments earlier, she said, a gust of wind had swept up through the tree, driving a cloud of leaves high in the sky where they floated and scattered, not returning to earth. The leaves had conquered the law of gravity by a superior force — a breath of wind that had lifted them from the branches and scattered them far and wide.

Aha, I thought. Now I get it. This is a lesson for the church! How can the church overcome the deadening gravity, the weight of sin, self-centeredness, bureaucracy and institutionalism, rigid and obsolete structures? There is a way — the breath of the Spirit of God. "The wind blows where it chooses, and you hear the sound of it, but you do not know where it comes from or where it goes. So it is with everyone who is born of the Spirit" (John 3:8).

29. Holiness is the opposite of what the Bible calls being "doubleminded" (e.g., James 1:7).

Brothers and sisters, we can look higher!

The five calls of God may seem like demands, but they are really the breath of the Spirit. They not only drive us; they lift us, call us higher, call us to such faithfulness, ministry, love, and joy as has hardly entered our minds and imaginations.

But we have to be open to the Spirit. We have to place ourselves in God's currents. Like those autumn leaves, the church can soar and scatter its witness to the world, in the name of Jesus and the power of the Spirit.

The five calls of God are the compound call of the Spirit. *By the Spirit of the living God,* Jesus-people today can:

- be filled with all the fullness of God in Christ, living holy, devout, pure, healing lives, being Jesus' counterculture and contrast society in witness to the world;
- exercise a beautiful and effective array of ministries and callings, according to the diversity of the gifts of the Spirit;
- be God's Kingdom people in the world, living in full allegiance to Jesus and his reign — Spirit-endowed co-workers for the Kingdom of God;
- live as a faithful covenant people, building accountable community, growing up into Jesus Christ, embodying the spirit of God's law in holy love;
- care for the garden, this good earth, God's gift in trust to us, working in faith, hope, and confidence for the healing of all creation, being the leading edge among the nations for the care and feeding and eventual reconciliation of all things — things visible and invisible; things in heaven and on earth.[30]

This is what holiness — life in the Spirit in response to the fivefold call of God — means in a postmodern world and within earth's diverse cultures. We must be a holy people. For God says, it is "not by might, nor by power, but by my Spirit" (Zech. 4:6) that he fulfills his designs.

In faithful response to the fivefold call of God we learn more fully what the words mean: "They that wait upon the LORD shall renew their strength; they shall mount up with wings as eagles; they shall run, and not be weary; and they shall walk, and not faint" (Isa. 40:31).

---

30. E.g., Ephesians 1:10, 22; 3:9; Colossians 1:16-20; Hebrews 1:2-3.

CHAPTER 8

Transformed by Grace:
The Beauty of Personal Holiness

CHERYL BRIDGES JOHNS

You may have seen the bumper sticker that reads, "Christians aren't perfect, just forgiven." This bumper sticker is a symbol of modern Christianity. It symbolizes our resignation to continual failure and sin, with a "debt paid in full" stamp affixed at the end.

Yes, God accepts us anyway, in spite of our failures, but because God loves us he is not content to leave us in a state of brokenness. God's desire is to restore us to the beauty and wholeness for which we are created.

Personal holiness is a testimony to God's transforming grace. It is a journey, with God and in God. This journey, going from grace to grace, reverses the destruction of sin and makes possible a new way of being in the world. In a real sense, we are transformed into an image of restored creation. As a living icon we show forth to others this new way.

Personal holiness is grounded in the depths of transformational grace. It is not a legal code of ethics nor is it a static state of perfection. As a journey it is fueled by love and sustained within the logic of a crisis-development dialectic.

Transforming Grace

For John Wesley the effects of sin went beyond guilt. Sin created inherent corruption, and like a virus spread throughout the created order. As a result of the corruption caused by sin, humankind and the whole creation is in need of restoration. Harold Lindstrom points out that inasmuch as sin is "regarded as an illness, it follows that salvation will be seen primarily from a subjective-medical rather than an objective-judicial angle. Salvation is called a healing."[1]

A therapeutic understanding of salvation is grounded in a robust theology of grace. What has the power to heal and to restore but the grace of God found in Jesus Christ? For John Wesley this grace is able "to repair that total loss of righteousness and true holiness sustained by the sin of our first parent."[2] Anything less than "the renewal of our soul in the image of God . . . is no other than a poor farce, and a mere mockery of God."[3]

Grace, then, is the agent of God's healing and restoration. But we must remember that this grace is not an impersonal force sent by God to humankind. Rather, as Mildred Bangs Wynkoop points out, it is "a personal expression of God's nature."[4] As such, grace is God's self reaching out in mercy and love toward humankind.

Contrary to the idea of grace as a state or as a judicatory degree, covering or substituting for human sinfulness, it is to be seen as deeply personal and relational. It allows us to see the face of God and to participate in the Triune life. Grace is the great repairer of the *imago Dei*.

Grace does not merely offer solace; it is power. It is the power to effect real, inherent change. Transformational grace takes many forms, depending on the nature of the corruption of sin. First, there is "preventing grace," that measure of light and goodness that "enlightens every man that cometh into the world."[5] Preventing grace or prevenient grace is a strong power. It is recognized as inherent goodness and the ability of all people to do good works and live in honor and integrity. It is the grace that sustains life.

The ever-flowing stream of grace calls for human response. As the beloved hymn reminds us, grace is that which teaches our hearts to fear, and that which relieves our fears. We are saved by grace, sanctified by grace, and empowered by grace. The response to grace is to give ourselves to God

---

1. Harold J. Lindstrom, *Wesley and Sanctification* (Nappanee, Ind.: Francis Asbury Press, 1996), p. 41.

2. "Original Sin," in *The Works of John Wesley*, ed. Thomas Jackson (Grand Rapids: Baker, 1984), 6:64.

3. "Original Sin," p. 64.

4. Mildred Bangs Wynkoop, *Theology of Love: The Dynamic of Wesleyanism* (Kansas City: Beacon Hill, 1972), p. 197.

5. "Working Out Our Own Salvation," *Works*, 6:512.

in faith and in "holy, active, patient love."[6] We are co-laborers with God in the work of redemption. Active faith — faith working in love — opens the door for us to become not only recipients of God's grace but channels as well. In this sense holiness is at the same time deeply personal and widely social.

Crisis-Development Dialectic

Successive development is a key element of Wesley's thinking. He counted by degrees: degrees of enmity to God, degrees of self-denial, degrees of growth in holiness, degrees of faith, and degrees of contemplation of God.[7] Yet, while growth in grace is by degrees, there is also the dynamic of God's interruptions or interventions. As power, God's grace intervenes between the degrees, disrupting our known world in such a way as to compel us forward. To be holy we need both crisis and development. Our spiritual journeys are characterized by this dialectic.

Means of Grace: Development

Wesley understood that grace had to be actualized in daily life. It had to be developed and cultivated. The "means of grace" were spiritual disciplines designed to enable people to respond in faith to God's grace. They function to "advance toward holiness" and to "conduce to the knowledge and love of God."[8] Wesley divided these means into two categories: instituted means of grace and the prudential means of grace. Instituted means of grace are those disciplines that are revealed in the life of Christ. Prudential means of grace allow for the fulfillment of the social and relational aspects of the gospel. Instituted means of grace include the disciplines of prayer, fasting, Scripture reading, the Lord's Supper, and Christian Conference. Prudent Christians (hence the term "prudential") also attend to works of mercy and charity.

First and foremost of the instituted disciplines is prayer. For Wesley,

6. "The Great Assize," *Works*, 5:185.
7. Lindstrom, *Wesley and Sanctification*, pp. 120-21.
8. "The Means of Grace," *Works*, 5:186, 188.

prayer is "the grand means of drawing near to God."[9] Prayer is the means of entering into the heart of God and participating in the Divine Life. Richard Foster describes prayer as "coming home to that for which we were created."[10]

This type of prayer is more than "something we do in order to produce the results we believe are needed, or, rather to get God to produce the results."[11] It is dynamic of a deep personal relationship with Christ. Wesley had a very organic and dynamic understanding of prayer:

> As it is continually received by faith, so it is continually rendered back by love, by prayer, and praise, and thanksgiving — love and praise and prayer being the breath of every soul which is truly born of God. And by this new kind of spiritual respiration, spiritual life is not only sustained but increased day by day.[12]

It is this "spiritual respiration" that makes possible a life of holiness. Prayer becomes a dynamic process of mirroring — much like the give and take between mother and infant. Just as the face of the mother mirrors back to the young child love and praise, so too in prayer we are folded into the arms of God whose face reveals our true selves. We know that we are beloved and we respond in love and delight.

Prayer is not a one-dimensional activity. There are many forms of prayer and each form deepens our life in God. As we grow in Christ we will be led into the wonderland of prayer. There we find prayers of adoration, prayers of tears, intercessory prayer, meditative prayer and many other forms. Oh, the height and depth and breadth of prayer! It is the Christian's highest vocation, but often we fail to enter into its mysterious depths. This grieves the heart of God. Speaking of this grief, Foster observes:

> Today the heart of God is an open wound of love. He aches over our distance and preoccupation. He mourns that we do not draw near to him. He grieves that we have forgotten him. He weeps over

9. John Telford, ed., *The Letters of the Rev. John Wesley* (London: Epworth, 1960), vol. 4, p. 90.

10. Richard Foster, *Prayer: Finding the Heart's True Home* (San Francisco: HarperSanFrancisco, 1992), p. 1.

11. Robert Mulholland, *Invitation to a Journey: A Road Map for Spiritual Formation* (Downers Grove: InterVarsity, 1993), p. 105.

12. "The Great Privilege of Those That Are Born of God," *Works*, 5:226.

our obsession with much-ness and manyness. He longs for our presence.[13]

Attending to Scripture

The daily reading of Scripture is another powerful means of grace. The Bible provides the objective horizon by which we measure our lives. But the Bible is not merely objective, propositional truths. It is Spirit-Word, meaning that the Scriptures convey both the Word of God and the presence of God. God's Word is eternally married to God's presence. Reading the Word of God, therefore, is the means of encounter with God. There is never Truth with the capital "T" apart from Personal with the capital "P."

For Wesley, reading the Bible was an act of worship: "Here then I am, far from the busy ways of men. I sit down alone: only God is here. In his presence I open, I read his book; for this end, to find the way to heaven."[14] In Scripture we encounter God, but we must also keep in mind that the Bible is a literary document and meant to be read as such. For that reason, reading the Bible inductively enables us to see the literary structure and beauty of Scripture. Inductive Bible study entails treating the books of the Bible as whole literary units. Instead of reading chapter by chapter we read it book by book, breaking down each book into smaller literary units. The paragraph unit becomes the basic unit of study. This is essentially several paragraphs that are tied together around an event or a theme. Most contemporary versions of the Bible break down the text into paragraph units, giving headings over each unit.

Seeing the Bible as literature reveals to us the beauty and organic unity of the text. It helps us see the main points, avoiding focusing on tangents. It keeps us from reading into the text our preconceived ideas. Our growth in holiness is given steady, consistent guidance from a reliable source. Do not substitute reading about the Bible for reading the Bible. Read it as you would a good book, looking for the main points, repetitive themes, and unique twists in plot. Read it as an act of worship, knowing that the text is a means of encountering Truth.

Whenever we approach Scripture we should be prepared for the sub-

13. Foster, *Prayer*, p. 1.

14. *Standard Sermons, Consisting of Fourty-Four Discourses Published in Four Volumes* (London: Epworth, 1967), p. vi.

ject/object eclipse. It is a sleight of the Spirit's hand whereby the text ceases to be primarily the object of our inquiry and becomes the subject. In this eclipse, or figure-ground reversal, we as the human subjects become the objects. Suddenly we are being read and interpreted by the Spirit-Word. Transforming grace flows into our lives during this eclipse. It is a wonderful, scary, and worshipful moment when we realize that the text has turned on us and the eyes of God are gazing into our very souls.

Another means of attending to Scripture is to participate in the life of a congregation where the Scripture is read and the Word is preached. Whenever the Scripture is read in a worshiping community there is an awareness that the members of the congregation stand together under the authority of the text. "Hear this Word!" cried the prophet Amos to Israel. So too we are to call congregations to hear and to respond to God's powerful, all-knowing Word.

Preaching was a major aspect of Wesley's ministry and it is still a powerful means of conveying the gospel. The act of preaching brings about another mysterious figure-ground reversal, similar to that which happens in Bible study. Anointed preaching joins the words of the preacher with the Word of God in such a manner as to convey the power and presence of God. Growing in holiness means attending to the preaching of the Word. We thus open ourselves to the disruptive and convicting grace of God.

Fasting: Hunger for Righteousness

Wesley included fasting as one of the five instituted means of grace. It is a practice that many people find strange and most all of us find difficult. Yet, its benefits are numerous. First and foremost fasting helps us realize our total dependence upon God. It is God, not food, who is the source of our life. It is God who sustains us and God who provides our daily bread.

One reason that we human beings have difficulty maintaining a life of personal holiness is our inability to give our desire over to God. Our desire is wounded by sin and as a consequence seeks its own good. Wounded desire manifests itself in greed and gluttony. It tells us that we deserve to have what we want. If we want something, if we desire something, we should act upon that desire.

Fasting is a discipline that helps in the healing of desire. Wesley saw it as a means of increasing purifying grace, "drawing our affections to things above; to add seriousness and earnestness to our prayers; to avert the wrath of God, and to obtain all the great and precious promises which he hath made to us in Jesus Christ."[15]

There are many forms of fasting. Some practice total abstinence from food, while others celebrate partial fasts. Today, we may need to fast from media in order to draw our affections to things above. The media is a source of wounded desire. It provides images of ourselves and tells us stories about ourselves that are often contrary to God's story.

When fasting is linked with prayer, it can open the space for a great feast in the presence of God. It offers opportunities for God's desire for us to be met with our desire for God. Deep will call to deep and in this sacred meeting the beauty of holiness will shine forth.

The Lord's Table: The Real Presence of Christ

All too often Protestants have neglected the power of the Eucharist in effecting holiness of heart and life. In our reaction to Roman Catholic theology of transubstantiation, which teaches that the elements of bread and wine actually become the body and blood of Christ, we may fail to properly acknowledge the real presence and power of Christ at the Lord's Table.

Wesley attempted to forge a third way between the Protestant emphasis upon the freedom of the Spirit and the Catholic emphasis on visible means of grace. In the space of worship grace is experienced through the presence of the living Christ by the power of the Holy Spirit, but grace is also experienced through the practices that serve as visible means of transformation.

Steve Harper points out that Wesley had a threefold understanding of Communion.[16] First, it is a *memorial meal.* It is "meant to recall an event so thoroughly that the event comes alive, anew and afresh in the present."[17] Second, the Lord's Supper actualized *the real presence of Christ:* "By his own choice the risen Christ is truly present whenever the Lord's Supper is observed. Christ does not come through the bread and cup: he comes

---

15. *Works,* 5:357-58.

16. Steve Harper, *Devotional Life in the Wesleyan Tradition* (Nashville: The Upper Room, 1983), p. 37.

17. Harper, *Devotional Life in the Wesleyan Tradition,* p. 37.

through the Spirit."[18] Third, Wesley understood Communion as a *pledge*. "The presence of the sacrament in the church now is an assurance to Christians that the heavenly banquet awaits us after death."[19] Also, as Harper notes, Wesley saw "our reception of the elements as one tangible contact with the great cloud of witnesses who have preceded us."[20]

Christians should come to the Lord's Table on a regular basis. While it may not be daily or weekly, it should be frequent and regular. It is our "strength for the journey," moving us forward as we go from grace to grace.

Footwashing: Cleansing on the Journey

The practice of footwashing, while not followed by all Christians, is a sacramentally powerful rite that signifies the need for ongoing post-baptismal cleansing. In many ways, this ritual is penitential. It often includes confession and tears as weary Christians realize how dirty and broken their lives have become. Mutual confession is practiced, and grace to heal and forgive comes through the cleansing water and the tender hands of believers.

Participants in footwashing serve as agents of cleansing and healing as well as recipients of that grace. In this sense, footwashing conveys the power of the priesthood of believers. Practiced in the context of a worshiping community it gives visible expression to the grace found in the body of Christ.

Footwashing reminds believers of the humility and humble servitude of Christ. In doing so, it binds the participants to his passion, calling them to follow the life of self-giving service. It also reminds participants that healing and cleansing grace is costly grace. When we submit to the waters of baptism we identify with Christ in his death and resurrection. As we submit to the waters of footwashing we are reminded that identifying with Christ is not a one-time event. Rather, it is a lifelong journey.

---

18. Harper, *Devotional Life in the Wesleyan Tradition*, p. 37.
19. Harper, *Devotional Life in the Wesleyan Tradition*, p. 37.
20. Harper, *Devotional Life in the Wesleyan Tradition*, p. 37.

The Grace of Community

Authentic Christian community is difficult. It is not easy to journey with others, sharing their burdens and allowing them to participate in our life. For this reason we are tempted to go it alone, especially if we have been hurt by others. Yet community offers us a dimension of grace not found in private faith.

Wesley believed in the power of community, so much so that he made it the heart of the Methodist movement. Convinced that there could be no spiritual maturity without discipline, he developed societies, classes, and bands designed to cultivate spiritual maturity. These groups developed practices designed to assist people in spiritual discipline.

Today people hunger for community, seeking it in small groups of every variety. Churches are rediscovering the power of small groups as a means of discipleship. Small groups give us accountability and provide opportunity for testimony. They create "free spaces" wherein people find assistance in living the Christian life.

Wesley designed his small groups as means of sanctifying grace. He did not view them as optional to Christian growth. Rather, they were necessary. After visiting Pembrokeshire, a place where the practice of small groups had been neglected, he wrote,

> I am more convinced than ever, that the preaching like an apostle, without the joining together those that are awakened, and training them up in the ways of God, is only begetting children for the murderer. How much preaching there has been for these twenty years all over Pembrokeshire! But no regular connection; and the consequence is, that nine in ten of the once-awakened are now faster asleep than ever.[21]

Today we need to return to this concept of connection. Penitents need a band for confession and restoration. Believers need friends who will hold them accountable and will help carry their burdens. Grace does its best work in the context of caring community!

Each church should work out how they will integrate small groups into their corporate life. There is a difference between a church that offers

21. "An Extract of the Rev. Mr. John Wesley's Journal," *Works*, 3:144.

small groups and a church composed of small groups. The difference is in the nature and function of small groups in the life of the church. The former sees groups as something offered as an option; the latter sees groups as vital to the church's life. Wesley would take the latter stance.

Prudential Means of Grace

While holiness is deeply personal it is also widely social. There is no holiness apart from social holiness, but likewise there is no social holiness that is separate from a deep personal piety.

Wesley wedded piety and mercy, holiness of heart and life. For the growth of these dimensions followed three principles: doing no harm, doing good, and attending upon all the ordinances of God.

Steve Harper points out that for Wesley true spirituality is never *made spiritual*. "Rather it is expressed through concrete acts of daily living."[22] First, there is the negative dimension, "doing no harm." We need to ask ourselves, "What do I need to be avoiding in my walk toward maturity in Christ?"[23] This is a question pointing to the heart of desire. It forces us to face our own hearts and to see how our desire is wounded and twisted. To avoid things in order to mature in Christ is to relinquish our own desires for that which God desires.

Second, there is the dimension of "doing good." For Wesley doing good involved caring for the whole created order. As agents of grace, believers can effect change upon human suffering. We are instruments of healing and join with God in the re-construction of life. Joined with God in healing the world, we, like Wesley, can say that the world is our parish.

Third, "attending to all the ordinances of God" reminds us to go back into the practices. Our social action is grounded in the ordinances which steady our feet, give us clear vision, and keep our heart pure. Social activism that fails to attend to all the ordinances of God results in shallow spirituality that collapses under pressure.

22. Harper, *Devotional Life in the Wesleyan Tradition*, p. 66.
23. Harper, *Devotional Life in the Wesleyan Tradition*, p. 66.

Healing Grace in Crisis[24]

While holiness grows in us by degrees, cultivated by the practices of prayer, fasting, attending to Scripture, and the sacraments, growth is not always steady and incremental. In fact, salvation is often initiated by crisis and the Christian journey is marked by crisis moments. Development takes place between the crisis moments. Wesleyans and Pentecostals are part of what is known as the "experiential wing" of the Christian world. In fact, we have been criticized for emotive, crisis-filled worship. While there has been much excess and over-emphasis upon experience, we should heed the words of Steven Land, who points out that these crisis events were "times when God did something decisive which made possible a personal or corporate development that, before that time, was not possible."[25]

In other words, crisis is good for us. It gives opportunity for God to shatter our comfortable world. Without crisis we are in danger of collapsing all grace into prevenient grace to the neglect of transforming grace. Crisis is messy and it is often profoundly painful. But it can yield the fruit of a greater passion for the Kingdom.

For the last half of the twentieth century the developmental paradigm in Christian discipleship was dominant. While this model helped us to see growth as organic and steady and assisted us in mapping the stages of life, it gave us an over-emphasis on "the human side of faith." The focus became the human person as the subject-in-relation to the world.

Mildred Bangs Wynkoop warned Wesleyans of the danger in substituting developmental psychology for the Wesleyan emphasis on both crisis and process. She posed the following question: "What are you doing with your Wesleyan commitment. . . . Are you letting your attractive new trends lead you out of the narrow way? Are you substituting developmental theories for the 'two-ness' of Wesleyan theology?"[26] She went on to note that the intersection of developmentalism with Wesleyan theology was appropriate under the condition that there could be maintained a view of a dy-

24. This section is condensed from Cheryl Bridges Johns, "From Strength to Strength: The Neglected Role of Crisis in Wesleyan and Pentecostal Discipleship," *Wesleyan Theological Journal* 39:1 (Spring 2004): 137-53.

25. Steven J. Land, *Pentecostal Spirituality: A Passion for the Kingdom*, JPT Supplement Series 1 (Sheffield: Sheffield Academic Press, 1993), p. 117.

26. Mildred Bangs Wynkoop, "Wesleyan Theology and Christian Development," *The Asbury Seminarian* 31 (April 1976): 36-41.

namic relationship with God and humanity. Furthermore, "so long as crisis and process are considered means to an end, no insurmountable problems are encountered. It is when crisis and process become ends in themselves that serious clashes begin between theological constructs and human nature."[27]

If we see crisis as a normative part of the Christian journey, we learn to embrace its wild and mysterious ways. God is in the crisis and works through crisis to deepen our relationship with him.

The work of James Loder is helpful in understanding the fearful domain of crisis. He attempts to uncover "the logic of the Spirit" in initiating and sustaining crisis events toward the transformation of persons into the image of Christ. Not afraid to go where others fear to tread, he plunges into the realm of what he calls "convictional knowing," those overpowering, life-changing moments that radically alter our ways of being in the world.[28]

Convictional experiences have a logic that Loder sees unfolding in a five-fold sequence: conflict, interlude for scanning, insight and release of mundane ecstasy, interpretation, and verification.[29] These steps govern all knowing events, but when carried into the dimension of "the holy" they have the capacity to transform the human subject from knower into one who is truly known. In other words, they have the capacity of bringing us into a relationship with God which results in our being radically changed.

At the core of conflict and crisis is the brokenness of creation that results in distortion of reality and misguided affections. Whenever conflict occurs there is a rupture in our existence, a dissonance between that which is and that which should be. In times like these we see our limited capacity to heal our world and to heal ourselves. This is a movement of human brokenness and our inability to fix things. Sometimes the conflict challenges the core of our affections and our ability to trust in the sufficiency of the grace of God.

The conflict initiates the scanning process. This period is a time of seeking solutions. It is an active time, one in which we seek solutions to our crisis. The search may involve fasting, prayer, participating in the com-

27. Wynkoop, "Wesleyan Theology and Christian Development."

28. James E. Loder, *The Transforming Moment*, 2d ed. (Colorado Springs: Helmers & Howard, 1989).

29. Loder, *The Transforming Moment*, pp. 2-4.

munity of faith, and attending to the Scriptures. While we are scanning for solutions the Holy Spirit comes alongside of us and attends to us as we journey into the conflict. We are not left alone during the time of crisis.

What is most difficult during this period is waiting, tarrying while in the conflict. There is the ever-present temptation to seek premature closure. Yet we must wait for the "fullness of time" to arrive. During our time of waiting we grow in grace. Herein is the mysterious synergy of convicting grace and sanctifying grace. It is grace that pushes us deeper into the arms of God.

After the period of scanning and waiting (which may seem like an eternity) we experience interruptive insight by transforming Presence. This experience reveals the intention and presence of God. It heals the rupture that has occurred in our known world and brings meaning to that which was previously chaos. This experience is a creative moment. We are transformed in our understanding of the world, self, and others. Hope and vision spring forth where there was once barrenness and despair.

The birth of newness brings about release and mundane ecstasy. Here is when we shout the victory and participate in the dance of the Triune God. The beauty of holiness is revealed and our hearts are realigned toward God as the object of our affections. This movement is characterized by testimony and witness and worship.

Finally, as we move forward in time we experience the verification of God's transforming power. We look backward and see afresh the hand of God. At the same time we anticipate the future with greater assurance and deeper love for God and others.

When crisis has done its perfect work in us we emerge stronger and wiser. We then take the lessons learned from the experience into the practices of prayer, fasting, Scripture reading, The practices bring about the verification of the crisis. They help us to pattern our new vision and renewed self into daily life. In addition, the community of faith walks with us through the crisis and helps us during the long scanning process. It is the role of Christian community to receive our testimony of transformation. In this way, crisis not only enriches our lives as individuals but it strengthens communities.

Conclusion

Personal holiness is possible in a world that is deeply and profoundly profaned by sin. Within the dialectic of crisis and development God's grace transforms us and enables us to overcome sin. The message of holiness is thus a message of great freedom, not bondage as some would suppose. In holiness we are freed from the tyranny of wounded desire. We are freed to love and desire the things of God.

In God's holiness we are made beautiful. This beauty is real and deep and reflects the divine image. God's "radical makeover" is not superficial. Rather, it cuts to the core of our very being, altering our affections and healing the deep scars of sin. There is beauty in a holy life and that beauty is rare today.

But because holiness is rare does not mean it is impossible. God is waiting on us to respond to his invitation to wholeness. His desire is toward us and his grace is extended.

CHAPTER 9

Social Holiness:
Journey, Exposures, Encounters

JONATHAN S. RAYMOND

Every faith community is faced from time to time with the challenge of re-thinking, reformulating, and rearticulating its core beliefs, values, and practices. This is not easy work, but it is essential for any faith community that desires that each generation respond effectively to new, contemporary circumstances, challenges, and opportunities. Wesleyan Holiness faith communities face this challenge now in passing an understanding and articulation of a doctrine to the next generation.

The present-day status of holiness is a far departure from our past. We are challenged because so many Christians today pay so little attention and interest to the idea of holiness anymore. Holiness is rarely taught, preached, or pursued. It is viewed by many Christians in a negative light. This may in part be due to its false identification with perfectionism, legalism, judgmentalism, privatism, and introspection. Holiness is seen as optional, a pursuit for a few saints; as restrictive and repressive, summarized by a long list of behavioral prohibitions; as individualistic and unattainable for most people, demanding superhuman striving. It is viewed by many as unimportant. Tragically, what many Christians consider important, by contrast, is "getting saved" (from sin), going to heaven, and in the meanwhile leading only a good, decent life. For a few, holiness is seen as a possible mountaintop experience attained at special spiritual retreats, but not as a way of life. Most see holiness as socially irrelevant and not necessary to a life of ministry and mission. The dwindling few who do embrace its importance remain divided in their understanding of its means of attainment. Some conceive of holiness as process (growth in grace) and others as crisis (a cleansing, second work of grace). For the majority, a great shroud of apathy cloaks and hides the idea of holiness as a viable, available, and necessary reality of the Christian faith journey.

The Idea of Holiness

Historically, the pursuit of holiness has been the centerpiece and orienting principle of Wesleyan Holiness faith communities. "Be holy as I am holy" echoes in our collective heart and mind as a people who, like Israel, are by our own choice "set apart" for God. The foundation of our understanding and vision of holiness remains scriptural. Holiness and related terms appear in Scripture over 1,000 times (800 in the Old Testament; 300 in the New Testament). In both the Old and New Testaments, holiness is the quality of God's character that the people of God are to evidence in their lives as they are one in spirit with God and being filled with the Holy Spirit. For this reason, our understanding of holiness does not place us on the fringe of Christian belief as obscure sects holding a strange idea. Rather, we are in the mainstream of Christian orthodoxy. At the very core of Scripture's portrayal of God and the church, we find the idea of holiness.

Holiness is not an option. We may like to think it is, and many live like it is. Many who treat holiness as an option may do so because they think it is an individual, private matter. They hope that the Lord might do a work of holiness in the other person, but otherwise leave them alone. They hope the Lord will do a work especially on those whose behaviors are found to be particularly bothersome, obnoxious, or disagreeable. However, in our theological orthodoxy, we know that holiness is for everyone, at all times, everywhere and as such it is not a private matter only. Holiness is very much a social matter. Its expressions are always worked out in the faithful fabric of social life in the community of believers and in the larger world.

In more traditional language, holiness is a major part of the *ordo salutis,* the way of salvation. Here we understand salvation to be a big idea. It is not restricted to merely that forensic point in time when we come to faith, accepting Jesus Christ into our hearts as Savior, repenting of our sins, and receiving God's forgiveness of our sins. Rather it is also that ongoing therapeutic work of God through his prevenient grace, by which we are being restored to the likeness of Jesus Christ. We sing about the *ordo salutis* when we sing "Jesus is mighty to save . . . from the uttermost to the uttermost." God commands us to "Be holy. . . ." It is our natural course of development in the presence of a holy God. We are predestined to holiness. It has always been and remains our destiny. It is a fulfilled destiny and identity to the extent that we are faithful to the words of Jesus Christ in John 15 when he repeatedly says, "Abide in me." In our Lord's great imagination, he created us in his image. Though the glory of his image in us was marred and stained through the Fall, still God's plan and intention is to restore us to that which he imagined from the very beginning — that we would be like Jesus through exposures to his grace, and to life-changing encounters by which we are filled with God's Holy Spirit.[1]

The Great Divide

The doctrine of holiness is historically the central doctrine of my own relatively young denomination, the Salvation Army. It is "the doctrine with which we most clearly identify ourselves as a people of God with something important to say to the wider Christian church."[2] In his address to the Christian Mission (the forerunner of the Salvation Army) in 1877, William Booth made this clear when he said, "Holiness to the Lord is to us a fundamental truth; it stands at the forefront of our doctrines."[3] Ever since, the Salvation Army has been an active participant and partner in the Holiness movement. Salvationists have long filled the pulpits of the movement and preached scriptural holiness. A legacy of literature has long existed written by Salvationist authors, including Samuel Logan Brengle, Freder-

1. After several years of reading, reflection, and writing it is difficult to say precisely who, what, and when were the primary and secondary sources of influence shaping my understanding of Wesleyan theology and holiness, but it is important that I acknowledge especially the writings of several authors in addition to the sermons and works of John Wesley, including, but not limited to, the following: Albert Outler, Kenneth Collins, Theodore Runyon, Howard Snyder, Richard Heitzenrater, Henry Rack, Henry Knight, and Randy Maddox.

2. This statement was made in the inaugural editorial written by Jonathan S. Raymond and Roger J. Green, the co-editors of the new journal *Word & Deed: A Journal of Salvation Army Theology and Ministry* 1:1 (Fall 1998): 12. The first two issues of the new journal were devoted to a discussion of the Salvation Army doctrine of holiness.

3. Jonathan S. Raymond and Roger J. Green, Editorial, *Word & Deed, A Journal of Salvation Army Theology and Ministry* 1:1 (Fall 1998): 12.

ick Coutts, Milton Agnew, and Edward Read.[4] More recently, contemporary Salvationist authors, including Donald Burke, David Rightmire, Wayne Pritchett, William Francis, Phil Needham, and Shaw Clifton, are paying scholarly attention to the topic of holiness.[5] While most Salvationist authors make reference in their writings to John Wesley, and some far more than others, there remains in Salvationist holiness literature a significant lack of accord on the nature of holiness. In large part we fall into three camps: first, the Brengle camp of holiness as crisis and second work of grace; second, the Coutts camp of holiness as growth in grace; and third, the camp of apathy, wherein holiness is not an issue. We will put this third and largest camp aside for the purpose of this discussion.

Brengle Holiness

Commissioner Samuel Logan Brengle understood, preached, and wrote of holiness as a special, distinct second work of grace whereby after God pardons, he then may purify. After saving, he may sanctify. His metaphor of salvation is that of a bridge with two great abutments — forgiveness of sins and purifying of the heart. Both are acts of grace by faith and not received through works. According to Brengle,

> Holiness, for you and for me, is not maturity, but purity: a clean heart in which the Holy Spirit dwells, filling it with pure, tender, and constant love to God and man.[6]

4. S. L. Brengle, *The Way of Holiness* (London: Salvationist Publishing & Supplies, Ltd., 1966); Frederick Coutts, *The Call to Holiness* (London: Salvationist Publishing & Supplies, Ltd., 1957); Milton S. Agnew, *Transformed Christians* (Kansas City: Beacon Hill Press, 1974) and *The Holy Spirit: Friend and Counselor* (Kansas City: Beacon Hill Press, 1980); Edward Read, *In the Hands of Another: Memoirs of Edward Read* (Toronto: Salvation Army Supplies and Purchasing, 2002).

5. These authors' writings on the topic of holiness may be found in the issues of *Word & Deed* from 1998 to 2004. In addition, see Shaw Clifton's discussion in *Who Are These Salvationists?* (Arlington, Va.: Crest Books, 1999), p. 120; the entirety of David Rightmire's work in his book *Sanctified Sanity* (Arlington, Va.: Crest Books, 2003); and Chick Yuill's book in its entirety, *We Need Saints: A Fresh Look At Christian Holiness* (London: Salvation Army International Headquarters, 1988).

6. S. L. Brengle, *Wait on the Lord: Selections from the Writings of S. L. Brengle*, ed. John Waldron (New York: Salvation Army, 1960), p. 24.

Brengle holiness, then, would embrace an understanding of holiness consistent with the Psalmist who wrote, "Create in me a pure heart, O God, and renew a right spirit within me." In Brengle holiness, entire sanctification is God's great gift given in response to complete, total consecration as a deliberate act of the will resulting in a cleansed heart fit to be a vessel for God's perfect love. As such it is a second blessing, the first being forgiveness of sins. A contemporary proponent of Brengle holiness may be found in Shaw Clifton as reflected in his book *Who Are These Salvationists?*[7] Here Clifton makes a clear separation of the two works of grace, calling justification by faith and forgiveness of sins "salvation" as distinct from a second work of "sanctification." A clear, concise, and thorough treatment of Brengle holiness may be found in the writings of David Rightmire.[8] The Salvation Army's former international leader, John Gowans, reflects the Army's emerging ambivalence with a Brengle holiness when he said that "God invented the Salvation Army to save souls, grow saints, and serve suffering humanity." While this reflects a distinct separation of a forensic salvation from holiness, his expression may move the Salvation Army away from identifying with a Brengle view of holiness toward a perspective more in line with Coutts holiness.

Coutts Holiness

The eighth general of the Salvation Army offers us a very different view of holiness. For Coutts, holiness is growth in Christ-likeness. Coutts kept a strong emphasis on the idea of the holy as grounded in the Jesus of the Gospels, not only in Christ's teachings, but especially in his example. Brengle's writings emphasize holiness as a crisis experience leading to a purity of heart. Coutts's holiness writings emphasize a progressive experience of maturity in Christ and to his likeness. In one of his books, *Call to Holiness,* Coutts intended to bring balance to Brengle's view of a second blessing/crisis of sanctification by giving an equal stress on the process of becoming more and more like Christ over time. In Coutts's thinking, then,

---

7. Clifton, *Who Are These Salvationists?* p. 120.

8. David Rightmire, *Sanctified Sanit: The Life and Teaching of Samuel Logan Brengle* (Arlington, Va.: Crest Books, 2003).

the holy life evidences over time the emergence of love, joy, peace, and other fruit of the Spirit that define Christ-likeness.[9]

While both Brengle and Coutts emphasized holiness as "Christ in you" and while both underscored the importance of experience and the role of the will, Coutts's distinctiveness lies in his emphasis on an ongoing, growing relationship, communion, and fellowship in Christ, and not just a single crisis experience.

Crisis or Process?

So which is it? Crisis or process? Who is more right? Brengle or Coutts? Which interpretation will guide the thinking and practice of the Salvation Army and other Wesleyan Holiness faith communities in the future? Is holiness a matter of purity or maturity?

The central criticism of Brengle holiness is that there are saints who do not testify to experiencing holiness as a crisis experience. There are legions of frustrated saints over time that do testify to seeking a crisis experience, but remaining frustrated. And there are those who do testify to a crisis experience, but not a lasting one. There are others, and I am one of them, that give witness to more than one encounter experience in holiness, and not necessarily always a crisis. The main criticism of Coutts holiness — although I believe it is an unfair one — is that it ignores the possibility that every believer may have a Damascus Road or Pentecost experience.

The portrayals and criticisms of Brengle's and Coutts's positions are often more extreme than warranted. There may be those among us who express their positions in the extreme and ignore that there is an appreciation in Brengle's writings for process and in Coutts's writings for crisis. Coutts, for example, very clearly espouses both a crisis and process perspective in his *Call to Holiness* when he says,

> In making holiness my aim on earth, a further truth has to be kept in mind. The question is sometimes debated whether the experience of holiness is gained instantly or gradually. The answer is that

9. Frederick Coutts, *The Splendor of Holiness* (London: Salvationist Publishing and Supplies Ltd., 1983).

the life of holiness is both a crisis and a process. . . . They are two sides of a coin. You cannot have one without the other.[10]

Coutts goes on to describe a developmental structure of the ongoing holiness experience:

First, there must be a beginning. There arises an awareness of personal need, which draws a man in to an act of full surrender. The forgiven soul awakes to the truth that forgiveness is not enough. . . . The life that is wholly forgiven must be wholly possessed. And to be fully possessed requires a full surrender. . . . I am bringing empty hands. I am bringing an empty life. God's answer is to grant me of his Spirit according to my capacity to receive. But the capacity grows with receiving. . . . A full surrender is the beginning of the life of holy living; the end of the experience I do not — I can not see. — The Experience can neither be explained nor lived without crisis and process.[11]

In many ways, Coutts's remarks parallel John Wesley's position at the end of his life, wherein he speaks more and more about the process of growing in grace and holiness than he does in earlier years. They also remind us of a story told by E. Stanley Jones in his book *The Word Become Flesh,* wherein he comments on pitcher plants in the South American *selva,* or jungle.[12] The plants have no root systems, yet as it rains, the plants face upward and fill up with rainwater, up to the brim. The rain they encounter and retain helps them to grow. The more rain they encounter, the more they grow. In the ecology of the rain forest, the rain comes down and fills the plants, and the plants continue to grow according to God's divine design. The plants represent a wonderful ecological and developmental metaphor for our understanding of holiness as God seeks to establish us in the Kingdom, and as we seek to find some resolution between Brengle and Coutts regarding crisis and process, purity and maturity.

10. Frederick Coutts, *The Call to Holiness* (London: Salvationist and Publishing Supplies Ltd., 1957).

11. Coutts, *The Splendor of Holiness.* For a more complete discussion of Frederick Coutts's writings on holiness, see Wayne Pritchett's article, "General Frederick Coutts and the Doctrine of Holiness," *Word & Deed* 1:1 (Fall 1998): 49-64.

12. E. Stanley Jones, *The Word Become Flesh* (New York: Abingdon Press, 1963).

The Ecology of Holiness

When the Apostle Paul says "Grow in grace," using the little word "in," we recognize that there is an ecology of grace and holiness. The little word "in" contextualizes holiness as ecological. Ecology is that branch of science that deals with the relationships between organisms and their environment. The key to thinking and speaking ecologically is to acknowledge that every living thing is immersed in a context or environment that has specific characteristics. Our first thoughts about ecology may be of a tadpole in a pristine stream, enriched by nutrients and free of toxins, in an ideal environment for growth, survival, and reproduction. There is such a stream high in the White Mountains of New Hampshire. When my children and I were younger, we backpacked together and swam there one afternoon. I have since wondered to what degree we changed the ecology of that stream with our dusty, sweaty bodies as we sought the water's cool comfort after hiking on that hot summer afternoon.

As there are biological ecologies, so there are social-spiritual ecologies wherein individuals are immersed in social-spiritual environments. It is not uncommon for us to be in and out of several ecologies in one day: for example, home, marriage, work, the supermarket, church, a Bible study, and a local community meeting. Among my favorite social ecologies are Christian summer camps. Like the pristine mountain stream teeming with tadpoles, the social-spiritual ecology of Christian summer camps can be nutrient-rich for young people, both campers and staff. Social ecologies are full of opportunities for growth and development, socially, physically, and spiritually.[13]

However, ecologies can also be toxic. When I was twenty years old, I served on a freighter on the Great Lakes. One evening the ship docked in Cleveland, about a half-mile up the Cuyahoga River. In 1969 it was a cesspool of industrial waste. Heavy industry along the river had for years belched the most disgusting and deadly substances into the water. So polluted was the river that one night a seaman from another ship threw a lit cigarette into the water, and the river caught fire. The fire spread so that a rather large area of the river was ablaze. The flames floated toward Lake

---

13. For a fundamental, classic understanding of social ecology and its relationship to human development, see Urie Bronfenbrenner's *The Ecology of Human Development: Experiements by Nature and Design* (Cambridge, Mass.: Harvard University Press, 1979).

Erie, destroying a railroad trestle and doing extensive damage along the way. Today the river is dramatically cleaned up. Gone are the toxins. A thriving economy of restaurants and tourist attractions exists along the banks of the Cuyahoga. Here is a marvelous example of ecological restoration.

Several years later, I traveled on business to Korea for the University of Hawaii. Our gracious Korean hosts took me to a wonderful restaurant in the Korean countryside. It was a famous establishment totally devoted to serving one particularly excellent variety of fish. The chefs strived to cook and serve the fish in wonderful ways. They also raised the fish in such a way as to maximize its flavor from the day they imported the carefully selected fish eggs from Israel. They established a fish farm, placing just the right kind of fish in a nutrient-enriched environment and thereby producing a high-quality, tasty fish for their restaurant. When Paul says, "Grow in grace," he is speaking ecologically. He means for us to mature as we immerse ourselves in nutrient-enriched (appropriate) environments of God's grace, in context of his lovingkindness, in his presence, and in our relationships with him and others.

O Boundless Salvation

The ecology of holiness may be seen in the celebration of God's love in the words of a song by William Booth, "O boundless salvation, deep ocean of love. . . ."[14] Booth uses an ecological metaphor of the ocean to speak of God's measureless love. It is powerful imagery that encompasses all the stages of the Christian life as it progresses from beginning to end. As we stand on the beach, the living waters of God's grace begin to wash up over our feet. We then are confronted with the decision whether to walk deeper into his love, accepting his justifying grace as Savior and Lord, or to retreat the other way. There is more to the Christian life than seeking to remain ankle-deep or even waist-deep. There is a boundless salvation and a deep ocean of God's love. There is wading deeper and deeper through reading

14. Commonly known as "the Founder's Song," "O Boundless Salvation" has become an anthem of sorts of the Salvation Army. For a more elaborate discussion of the relevance of the Founder's Song, see John D. Waldron's book *O Boundless Salvation* (Oakville, Ont.: Triumph Press, 1982), written to commemorate the centenary celebration of the Salvation Army in Canada.

and meditating upon his Word, by means of a devotional prayer life, and through fellowship with other believers. There is a commitment of the whole person as one plunges beneath the water, experiencing God's sanctifying grace as the fullness of God's Holy Spirit in one's life. And there is the joy of swimming, diving, snorkeling, windsurfing, and sailing in the deep ocean of God's love, experiencing his glorifying grace.

Booth's song gives us an image of God's love that is like an ocean available to be experienced by any and all believers. This helps us understand several things about the social ecology of holiness. First, God's intention is that we develop and progress. We move forward in our relationship with Christ and he does a deepening work. Often the work is done in a social and spiritual context where others are present and involved, and always it is done in the context of God's presence. Second, his love is always prevenient. At every stage and every level of our growth and development, his love goes before us. Wave upon wave in ever-flowing abundance, he helps us move toward what he has provided — a restoration to his image and likeness. Third, he provides for us a nutrient-enriched (appropriate) environment through "means of grace," his means of promoting our growth and well-being, often through others. The means of grace include good teaching, fellowship, breaking of bread, corporate worship, the sacraments, reading and hearing the Word, speaking and hearing testimonies of God's love, confession of sin, fasting, acts of mercy and service to others, artistic expressions, music, moral literature, all the wholesome activities of small group fellowship, and more. A setting that is nutrient-rich in means of grace is an ecology of grace and holiness. It is not difficult to see how the ecology of grace and holiness is social. Samuel Logan Brengle was often heard to echo John Wesley in saying that there is no holiness in the Christian life outside of social holiness. God uses others (home and family, church, work, etc.) to mediate his grace to us. It is the daily immersion in the means of grace that promotes this social ecology of holiness.

We use new language when we say "the social ecology of holiness," but it really is old imagery. In Jeremiah 13:1-11, God speaks through Jeremiah using an ecological metaphor. To paraphrase, God says to Jeremiah, "Go get a linen belt" — no doubt beautifully made and functional — "and put it around your waist and don't get it wet." Jeremiah is obedient. Then after some time God says, "Now take that linen waistband and place it down in the muddy bank of the Euphrates River and leave it there." Jeremiah is obedient. Then after more time God says to Jeremiah, "Now, remember that linen waistband? Go retrieve it from the river bank. See. It is marred, ru-ined, good for nothing. The people of Israel are like this ruined waistband. I intended and desired that, as the waistband clings around your waist, the people of Israel would cling closely to me. Instead they have followed other gods in the imagination of their minds. I intended them to be so close to me, in my presence, learning from me, growing in my grace so that they would become a people for me — a name, a praise, and a glory. But they would not listen!"

The imagery is relational and social-ecological. Israel was to be so close to God, in such proximity, that its people would benefit by being in those conditions and become a name (his name), a praise (bringing glory to him), and a people (clearly identified as his). Instead, as a people they placed themselves in the wrong context, under the worst of conditions, in an ecology that was toxic, destructive, and took them away from their des-tiny and identity. Like the waistband left in the muddy banks of the river for a long time, Israel fell apart immersed in ruinous conditions.

Our lives together represent the threads of a tapestry woven together to be both beautiful and functional for our Lord. We are to be a people who are a name, a praise, and a glory. The one way to be so is to intention-ally "grow in grace," to enter the living water of God's love, to draw near to God in response to his drawing near to us, and like Brother Lawrence to abide in his presence and to discover the God who is present. In the social ecology of holiness we are to help each other along the way to abide to-gether in Jesus Christ and to be immersed in the ecology of God's grace and holiness.

Social Holiness:
A Social-Ecological, Developmental Perspective

In the words of the Apostle Paul, we can explore "a more excellent way" to think about holiness beyond crisis or process, purity or maturity, and be-yond an individualistic understanding. Consider this proposition: an en-hanced understanding of holiness depends on how well we can hold to-gether and integrate an appreciation for three distinct aspects of holiness:

1. The ecological context in which holiness takes place;
2. The developmental process in which it unfolds; and

3. The events, which give holiness its distinct nature (Christ's character and likeness).

Regarding the ecological process — like the pitcher plant in the rain forest, life does not automatically unfold, nor is it experienced in a vacuum. There is no individual, personal holiness outside social holiness. Holiness must be grounded in the social context of our relationship with God and others. That is how we are created and re-created in God's image. God's very essence is social. It is Trinity in unity, in perfect, intimate communion. So our essence is designed to be social, relational, in unity and community. As we understand that there are "three distinct persons in the Godhead, the Father, the Son, and the Holy Spirit," so are we created in God's image as social beings seeking and enjoying relationships with the Trinity and with each other. Like God, we have distinct personalities, yet we are also created to give and receive from the social-ecological context of relationship with him and others, and more poignantly with God through others.

John Wesley acquired a good understanding of this last point. He appreciated that God influences, shapes, molds, and continues to do a work on us and in us through others. God employs human agency to continue his re-creation and restoration of us. He works to restore that which he originally intended from the beginning — that we be like him in holiness — in maturity and purity. Human agency is one of his most effective and preferred means of grace. The social context of holiness is our life together as the Body of Christ (communal life together, public prayer and Scripture reading, singing, testimonies, preaching, fellowship, service, music, theater, art, family devotional life, Bible study, etc.). It is life together in worship, in work, and in witness. God uses all these means, his means, to increase our awareness of his abiding presence, and to expand our understanding that he is who he is. God uses human agency to communicate his presence and his identity. This was true in Wesley's day in and through his class meetings, bands, and other forms of small, intimate social groups. It was true in the early church as well.[15]

We read in Acts 2:42 that the church grew as together they continually devoted themselves to participation in a social ecology of grace and holi-

15. For a full discussion of the role of the means of grace in the Christian life, see Henry H. Knight III, *The Presence of God in the Christian Life: John Wesley and the Means of Grace* (London: Scarecrow Press, 1992).

ness. This ecology of holiness is characterized by the means by which God may be experienced as present, and the means by which Jesus reveals himself for who he truly is. The four means of grace mentions in Acts 2:42 are

1. Good teaching,
2. Fellowship,
3. The breaking of bread, and
4. Prayer.

Wesley was clear to say that God uses an abundance of means by which to bring grace into our lives. Some means are personal and private, while many are public and social. Some are conventionally "sacred" and others found in more secular contexts. Some means of grace, like prayer, help us experience God's presence. Others, like preaching, teaching, public Scripture readings, and testimonies help increase our understanding of his identity — which it is that is present. Together, the mix of means of grace daily combines to form an ecology of grace and holiness. They work together to provide a context for maturity and purity. To the extent that we are receptive to God's use of us and others (human agency) in parting these means of grace, we may speak of a social ecology of holiness. There is no development of holiness outside of the social context of holiness.

Ecologically, the means of grace in the socially spiritual context of life together, in fellowship, worship, work, and witness together, are like the balanced nutrients of a mountain lake from which the fish, fowl, and other animals draw sustenance and life. When we read the words of the Apostle Paul to the Philippians, "My God shall supply all your needs according to his riches in Christ Jesus" (4:19), we know that he is speaking ecologically. All life exists in an ecology. God's provision is complete, all encompassing, and balanced. His promises are sure. His plan for our redemption and restoration is perfect. His follow-through is certain. Our Lord is faithful. As Psalm 85:10-11 states, "Love and faithfulness meet together; righteousness and peace kiss each other. Faithfulness springs forth from the earth, and righteousness looks down from heaven."

This brief passage communicates the interactive, dynamic relationship that characterizes our relationship with God in Christ Jesus and with each other as we participate in life with God together. It reflects an ongoing dynamic of both consecration and sanctification. In participating in the means of grace, we continually consecrate our lives, and our way of living together, to God, who in return continues to sanctify, bless, reveal, disclose, cleanse, illumine, edify, equip, deliver, transform, restore, make holy, and use us for his service. In short, in the social ecology of holiness, our Lord continues to restore and develop us in holiness and Christ-likeness. He continues to complete that which he intended from the beginning. We understand Paul's words to the Philippians (1:6) when he says, "May he who has begun a good work in you complete it . . ." and when he also admonishes them (2:12) with the words "continue to work out your salvation, with fear and trembling, for it is God who works in you to will and to do according to his good purpose." His good purpose is a salvation beyond redemption to a restoration to holiness and consecrated, sanctified usefulness. His means are social, ecological, and developmental.

Social Holiness — Shared Journeys, Exposures, and Encounters

When we speak of the means of grace, they are together the daily exposures that make up the Christian way of life, the way of holiness. As exposures to God's grace, the socially derived means of grace promote an awareness of God's presence and identity. These grace exposures provoke growth and give meaning to the journey. They are essential to the promotion of spiritual health and development of the saints along the way. They are fundamental to holiness as maturity in Christ. So far, however, we have only reviewed half the entities that give holiness its character of Christlikeness. In additions to exposures, there are encounters along the journey to holiness and usefulness. These encounters are Emmaus Road and Damascus Road experiences. They are Upper Room encounters.

Scripture is rife with this imagery of journeys and encounters. Abraham, David, Gideon, the disciples, Paul, and so many others' lives speak to the universality of encounters with the Lord in the midst of the journey. We need not come to the fork in the road and force ourselves to choose holiness as crisis or process. We do not have to choose between purity and maturity. When we come to the fork in the road, we may gain a more circumspect view from above. It is all the same journey and the Lord not only exposes us to his grace, but also encounters us each day and throughout the day. He stands at the heart's door and invites us out into his life to encounter us sometimes as crisis and deeper cleansing, sometimes as having our heart strangely warmed with deeper appreciation and thanksgiving.

Sometimes he encounters us in the hunger, poverty, and desperation of others and moves us to a holiness characterized by a deeper, Christ-like compassion. We then say with the Salvation Army poet and songwriter Albert Orsborn, "Unless I am moved with compassion, how dwelleth thy Spirit in me?"[16]

When we look at the lives and witnesses of other saints and reflect deeply on our own collective experiences with a kind of Wesleyan empiricism, we may come to view holiness as not a matter of either crisis or process. Rather, we see God's provision of opportunity for us to journey with him and others, and encounter him as together we abide and are immersed in his presence (John 15). It is in his presence that we immerse ourselves in a social ecology of grace and holiness and he promotes our growth and development. But herein God also does a work of cleansing, equipping, empowering, sensitizing, edifying, and so on. Together, we pursue the journey with Christ, through the ministry of the Holy Spirit as a community of believers. In the shared journey we come to know that we will encounter Christ many times, and in many ways, with many diverse and qualitatively different outcomes. And we come to realize that, in all of these varied encounters, Christ is forming us together into his likeness throughout our time on earth.

Social holiness, then, is both process and crisis facilitated by the Holy Sprit working within a social context of others (each other) who instrumentally bring God's grace to the believer. It is the shared process of an ongoing journey together as we walk and talk with Christ throughout each day. Along the way, we help each other encounter Christ in many and varied ways, with each encounter a crisis. Some encounters are more intense than others. Some call for the exercise of faith or the will. The greater the faithfulness to continue the journey with Christ each day, and the deeper the life we share together in Christ, the more frequent and more profound the encounters. This may be what the Apostle Paul refers to when he says that we go "from glory to glory" and "from strength to strength." As we journey together, we mature together, and at the same time become pure. The divine-human context is the ecological essence of holiness. God is holiest. As we are immersed in his presence, filled with his Spirit, and discover more intimately Christ's identity, the promise of the journey is that each day we become individually and collectively more and more like him.

16. Albert Orsborn, "The Saviour of Men," in *The Salvation Army Song Book* (New York: Salvation Army Supplies, Printing, and Publishing Dept., 1954), no. 478.

Social Holiness in Community

We do not journey alone. Our lives were never intended to be an existence in solitude. As God is a social being, so are we by his design. As people living together in obedience to God's commands, we progress together in the journey. His commands anticipate responses which are social in nature: love the Lord — a social, interactive act of the will; love your neighbor — a social, interactive act as well; make disciples — again, this requires social interaction; love mercy, do justly, and walk humbly with your God — all require social interaction with God and others in community.

The closest one comes in Salvation Army literature to a concept of social holiness may be found in the writing of Roger Green, who looks at the early Patristic writings and makes a distinction between personal holiness, institutional holiness, and relational holiness.[17] Relational holiness as a collective expression of personal holiness in the early faith communities comes close to the perspective presented here of a social-developmental ecology of holiness.

Phil Needham, in his article "Integrating Holiness and Community," critiques the status quo in regard to both the Salvation Army doctrine of holiness and its emerging thought about its ecclesiology.[18] One of the most central ideas he discusses is that of our need to move away from an orientation to holiness which is exclusively individualistic, to a strong sense of being a people, a church, part of the church universal, and in so doing to become a holy community. Needham calls us to integrate holiness and community, not so much by adding up the parts to become some holy whole, but rather to pursue the kind of community life together in which holiness as a people emerges. In his own words, he is making a plea for us to be a people immersed in the ecology of holiness such that we each bring ourselves and Christ in us to the social ecology of a collectively consecrated and sanctified community.

We may interpret Needham to mean that, in the social ecology of a sanctified community, we meet each other and discover that each of us en-

17. See Roger Green, "References To Holiness Teachings in The Patristic Writings," in *Heritage of Holiness: A Compilation of Papers on the Historical Background of Holiness Teaching* (New York: Salvation Army, 1977), pp. 19-31.

18. Phil Needham, "Integrating Holiness and Community: The Task of an Evolving Salvation Army," *Word & Deed: A Journal of Salvation Army Theology and Ministry* 3:1 (Fall 2000).

counters Christ and brings Christ with us on our journey. This requires a collective commitment to shift from living out a narcissistic theology of private, personal interests to a theology which celebrates (1) God's grace available to all; (2) the complementary gifts of the Spirit to every community member such that all people bring grace to the whole; (3) all members of the community belonging to Christ and therefore to each other; (4) a collective agenda of participating in and contributing to Christ's grand, divine project of restoring creation; and (5) the collective pursuit of *shalom* and human flourishing in the Kingdom of God.[19] Together as community in Christ, social holiness means we become a pilgrim people journeying together and encountering our Lord together in holiness.

Implications of Social Holiness

I chose to address the nature of social holiness before talking about its implications. To speak of the social implications of holiness is to risk the conversation remaining trapped in smaller, individualistic framing of an understanding of holiness and to miss the rich insights of a more social-ecological, developmental perspective. Within this perspective, it is possible to underscore several implications of social holiness, but it will suffice here to reflect on four: (1) fidelity to the Great Commission; (2) the inclusiveness of social holiness particularly with (not just for) people who are otherwise marginalized, stigmatized, and excluded from the benefits of community; (3) its implications for integrated mission and ministry with a preferential option with (not just for) the poor; and (4) finally the broad implications of social holiness for societal stability and the progress of nations.

Fidelity to the Great Commission

Social holiness faithfully fulfills the Great Commission. If social holiness involves the collective expression of the gifts God has provided throughout

---

19. Nicholas Wolterstorff, *Educating for Shalom: Essays on Christian Higher Education,* ed. Clarence W. Joldersma and Gloria Goris Stronks (Grand Rapids: Eerdmans, 2002), p. 142.

the faith community, their collective exposures to God's means of grace, their practicing God's presence, their daily learning more and more of the God who is present, and their growing in faith and identity in the likeness of Christ (maturity and purity), then they are further strengthened (empowered and equipped) to faithfully carry out the Great Commission. Fidelity to the Great Commission is realized when a faith community is continually committed to establishing all people in the faith and in the Kingdom. To be established is to go beyond the starting point (redemption) and journey well along the path of maturity and purity in Christ. The Lord's Great Commission was to "make disciples of all nations." This is all-inclusive, expansive, and compelling in its expectation that the faith community will be instrumental in the grand restoration work of the Kingdom, establishing well all peoples in the journey. It anticipates that the faith community will fully function toward the fulfillment of God's great forensic and therapeutic plan of salvation: redemption and restoration in holiness as a people to whom the Kingdom has already come.

Inclusiveness

The organizational psychologist Kurt Lewin is known for having said, "There is nothing as practical as good theory." A theological paraphrasing of Lewin would read, "There is nothing as practical as good theology." A practical Wesleyan theology would insist, then, that social holiness necessarily be integrated with ministry and mission so that its orthodoxy informs and is informed by its orthopraxis. In practice, then, social holiness by its very nature celebrates the inclusiveness of community. There is no room for a disposition of exclusion that says, for example, "Us four, no more." Social holiness would say that grace is for all and lived out with all. "For God so loved the world that whosoever. . . ." The inclusiveness of social holiness would resonate with a free and full salvation which emphasizes a holistic restoration of body, soul, and spirit carried out in the context of a consecrated, sanctified community and the potential for all, no matter how deeply immersed in sin and degradation, to progress in their faith journey with Christ and with each member of the faith community.

Integrated Mission

Social holiness is a collective reality characterizing the maturity and purity of an identifiable people. It is necessary to integrated mission, that is, to the integration of a multiply gifted community where each one, regardless of and possibly through personal history or life circumstances, brings gifts and contributions into the whole of a faith community's ministry and mission with (not just to) a needy, suffering world in Christ's name. Social holiness is made visible when the authentic love of Christ compels a consecrated, sanctified faith community into ministry, mission, and sacrificial service, and when their love is collectively expressed in what John Wesley called "the preferential option for the poor." It is made real when the faith community actively expresses Christ's love by actively reaching out to and actively identifying with the marginalized, dispossessed, oppressed, vulnerable, and powerless. Social holiness moves us to pursue options not so much for the poor as with the poor. It is completed in Christ when a people, in a working partnership with Christ, deliberately seek out, care for, and care with the lost and least of humanity.

John Stott, in his younger years, once wrote that the church may be divided into two groups: churches who proclaim and churches who identify. That is (1) those on the one hand who preach the gospel of Christ, but do nothing to serve the needy, suffering people of the world, whom Christ loves and for whom he died; and (2) those on the other hand who identify with and act on behalf of a suffering world to promote social justice, but never mercifully mention the love of Christ or the name of Christ to those on whose behalf they act.[20] In short, many churches have two faces with each one pursuing only half of the Kingdom mission. Stott's observation was a critique of the fragmented, less effectual state of the church of his day and a call for integrated mission. What he did not underscore at the time is that integrated mission necessarily derives from faith communities characterized by social holiness. Such faith communities succeed in the pursuit of the Great Commission to make disciples. Successful discipleship matures into faith communities whose members are compelled by the love of Christ into effective ministry and mission beyond the boundaries of a particular faith community in ways that are inclusive and appropriate to

---

20. John R. W. Stott, *Our Guilty Silence: The Church, the Gospel, and the World* (Grand Rapids: Eerdmans, 1967), pp. 64-65.

the time, and to their multicultural, complex societal context. The goal of social holiness is achievement by a faith community of a balanced, integrated mission and of ministries wherein evangelism and social justice are a seamless whole.

Societal Stability and Progress

Rarely do social contexts of holiness spontaneously generate. Social holiness is not inclined to spring forth unaided by intentional human agency although its impact upon society may not have been intended and foreseen. Social contexts must be intentionally designed, established, and cared for. Someone pays attention to them and provides the structure which carries the social processes resulting in the intended outcomes. It is the responsibility and stewardship of leaders to occasion opportunities for the emergence of social holiness among a people. This is what leaders do. They create the social-ecological-developmental contexts for people to grow, mature, and be cleansed in personal and social holiness. This was the case with John Wesley and the implications of the social holiness seen in the many types of small groups (class meetings, bands, penitent groups, etc.) that comprised the Methodist societies of his day. The thousands of small group expressions of social holiness resulted in an enormous ethical impact and, some might say, a spiritual transformation at best and political stability at least of British society during and after the lifetime of John Wesley. This is especially poignant in contrast to the violence of the French Revolution during the same period.

The same has been said for the impact of the Salvation Army upon British society in the late nineteenth and early twentieth centuries in contrast to the rise of communism elsewhere. The extensive work of the Salvation Army among the poor and working class of England in the early twentieth century are credited with a social stability that precluded a British embrace of communism.[21] A similar observation may be made for the impact upon Canadian society made by "prairie social reform" movements provoked by Spirit-led Christian leaders from prairie provinces in the early twentieth century. Their faith convictions about Canadian soci-

21. Personal communication with Professor Raymond Everett Cattell, University of Hawaii, 1983.

185

ety were acted upon through their election to Parliament and the propagation of provincial and national legislation (social policy) that have transformed Canadian society and values to the present day.

Finally, further reflection on the implications of social holiness may be made in two areas of inquiry: (1) the universality of social holiness within and across time and cultures, and (2) the role of social holiness in workings of the Kingdom of God now and in the future. In the former, the core idea of social holiness may be juxtaposed with the ideas of such culture-focused writers as H. Richard Niebuhr[22] and T. S. Eliot.[23] On the latter, a new look at the writing of E. Stanley Jones may serve to illumine how social holiness functions in the perfusion of Kingdom living.[24]

Finding the Words

Every generation must find their own words to communicate the life of holiness to which we are called as individuals and as members of faith communities. Each generation must find the appropriate paradigms and frameworks with which to appreciate what Christ continues to do among his people. And each generation must work out the implications of social holiness in the context of the issues and challenges of their particular time. This generation is no exception. It must discover the wondrous things about which Joshua spoke when he said, "consecrate yourselves, for tomorrow God will do amazing things among you" (Josh. 3:5).

Brengle, Coutts, and many other Nazarene, Methodist, Wesleyan, Free Methodist, and Salvationist authors, along with other branches of the Wesleyan Holiness movement, have given us a rich tradition of writing and thinking on matters of holiness. The Wesleyan Holiness Study Project helped us to reflect on their contributions, to hopefully extend their thinking, to open ourselves to the Spirit's further guidance, and to engage in enriching dialogue which transforms us as integrated faith communities of

22. H. Richard Niebuhr, *Christ and Culture* (New York: Harper and Row, 1951).
23. T. S. Eliot, *Christianity and Culture* (London: Harcourt, 1948).
24. E. Stanley Jones, *The Unshakable Kingdom and the Unchanging Person* (Nashville: Abingdon, 1972). The word "perfusion" is deliberately used here as a medical metaphor as in the life-giving exchange of oxygen into blood in physiological inspiration through the lungs' alveoli. Herein, the functioning of social holiness similarly achieves a perfusion of the Holy Spirit into the life of the Body of Christ, the many who make up the Kingdom of God.

social holiness. As we continue to take steps in the journey, I pray that our increasingly frequent and deep encounters with the living Christ, through the ministry of the Holy Spirit, will continue to transform and restore us as a people to the marvelous idea of Christ's which he has held from the very beginning. I pray we may always sing together the song "To be like Jesus, this hope possesses me. In every word and deed, this is my aim, my plea. . . ." As a holiness community on a journey of exposures and encounters, may it be so!

CHAPTER 10

Holiness in the City

GEORGE McKINNEY

> To be holy is to belong to God;
> To be holy is to come under God's authority;
> To be holy is to conform to God's will and plan for one's life.
>
> (SEE LUKE 19:41, 42)

The city represents people, power, and holy potential. People can be the glory or the shame of the universe. They reflect the glory of God when they practice compassion, righteousness, and justice. They reflect Satan's damnable influence as they live in selfishness, greed, and unbelief. Biblically and historically, the city has been a visible expression of people's rejection of God's authority, power, and sovereignty, and their attempt to find security, power, purpose, and meaning apart from God.

Yet the city dweller is not exempt from God's demand for holiness. The wicked cities of Sodom and Gomorrah were destroyed because there could not be found ten holy, righteous citizens there (Gen. 18:16-33). The prophet Jonah was sent by God to the wicked city of Nineveh with a message of "repent or perish" (see Jon. 3:1-5). God's judgment and wrath were cancelled when the king of Nineveh and the people turned from sin to righteousness, from ungodliness to holiness (Jon. 3:6-10).

In Luke 9:41, we are told that Jesus wept over the wicked city of Jerusalem. Jesus' heart was broken because of the pain, suffering, and death resulting from the rejection of God's offer of salvation and holiness for all the people. Jesus wept as he considered the spiritual, social, and economic conditions then present in Jerusalem. As Jesus "came near and saw the city, he wept over it, saying, 'If you, even you, had only recognized on this day the things that make for peace! But now they are hidden from your eyes'" (NRSV). God's plan and provisions were for a holy and just city under his authority. In addressing the wickedness of Jerusalem, Jesus directed his attention first to the religious leaders, the rulers in the Temple. He denounced the corruption in their spiritual leadership, and he drove out the moneychangers they had permitted to set up shop there. Jesus said, "My house shall be a house of prayer" (Luke 19:46). Thus he declared that the Temple is holy, that is, that it belonged to God. Furthermore, during his final week in Jerusalem before his arrest and crucifixion, Jesus offered that the people in Jerusalem and all people who had gone astray really belonged to God — that is, we all are called to holiness.

The good news of the gospel is that God has made a way for whoever will believe to return to the family of God and experience the blessedness of holiness. This good news extends even to those in cities, despite their corruption and poverty and despite their magnificence and wealth.

Urban Crises

The urban crises that demand attention from the church and from faith-based agencies are essentially spiritual problems that require spiritual solutions. While each of the problems may be analyzed from the social, political, and economic perspective, the desired changes will only occur when there is an application of spiritual truth. Take, for example, the problem of fatherlessness. The absent father is a manifestation of the fact that human beings have rejected God's plan for families to be led by mothers and fathers. For more than sixty years in the United States there was a welfare system that promoted fatherlessness, and the church was generally silent. When fathers are absent, mothers and children suffer. The church cannot ignore its responsibility to train boys to become men who are willing to accept the responsibility of becoming a father. Nor can the church ignore its responsibility to train girls to become women who are willing to accept the responsibility of becoming a mother. The church's ministries also must encourage and equip men to fulfill their roles as fathers and husbands, and to encourage and equip women to fulfill their roles as mothers and wives.

By addressing the problem of fatherlessness, among other problems, the church will at the same time address the problem of violence, especially gang violence. Gangs and violent activities are manifestations both of the absence of the strong family connection, resulting from fatherlessness, and the frustration caused by unfulfilled needs. Certainly the urban crisis related to fatherlessness, violence, and especially gang violence is complex, requiring extended study and multiple means of resolution. However, churches must become actively involved both for ministering to those in need and for advocating personal, social, and institutional changes necessary for addressing the complexity of the problems.

Another crisis we cannot afford to ignore is the growing culture of death through abortion and euthanasia. The truth must be told that abortions are brutal and immoral, and that late-term abortions, in particular, are barbaric. To be sure, the issues related to abortion as well as to euthanasia are as complex as other urban crises. We must always be careful in the public arena to share ideas humbly, yet persuasively. Christians need not fear participating in public debate and policymaking simply because they are Christians and integrate their beliefs, values, and practices into what they say. All participants in public debate and policymaking have presuppositions, assumptions, and axioms, regardless of whether they are based on faith. Christian voices also need to be heard in ways that are informed, interdisciplinary, and persuasive. Such voices need to be heard because of the seriousness and multifaceted nature of the problems involved. Abortion, for example, is a blatant denial of the sacredness of life. The church and those who represent it must be clear in their message that human life is sacred, and that the lives of the unborn are precious in God's sight.

The education of our children must also be high on our agenda. The church, home, and school must work together in the re-establishment and maintenance of quality education. Ignorance and simplistic ways of viewing things should not hamstring people, especially children, who live in urban settings. The promotion of quality education helps to remedy a variety of related urban crises, just as failure to promote it helps to exacerbate them. The failing urban schools, for example, have been correlated to the growing prison population. Such ought not to be the case, and the promotion of education for our children should endeavor to address the multiplicity of problems associated with urban life.

What is the fundamental nature of the human predicament? A traditional Christian response is the problem of sin. Perhaps this response, more than any other, encapsulates biblical teaching about that which troubles people in the present and damns them in the afterlife. Although the problem of sin may represent the fundamental predicament people encounter, there are other things that exacerbate problems in their lives. People also struggle with their finitude — their limitations as creatures, restricted by space and time. Foremost among their limitations is their ignorance of so much about themselves, the world in which they live, and, of course, God. People are also limited, to varying degrees, by the misery they experience due to challenges of various natures: physical, mental, emotional, relational, political, economic, and so on. Such challenges, too, prevent people from flourishing with the goodness, holiness, and happiness God intends for people.

Finally, people find themselves subject to various forms of bondage. Biblically and historically, such bondage was thought of in terms of demonic oppression or possession. However, it might also occur as physiological or psychological bondage to drugs, alcohol, sex, pornography, violence, and so on. Such forms of bondage may be just as detrimental to living lives pleasing to God and being in a right relationship with God as a clear demonic oppression.

Cities seem to be detrimental to people in terms of living lives pleasing to God and being in a right relationship with God. No doubt there are various reasons for this. However, living in a city seems to increase seriously the problems people face. Some of this, no doubt, has to do with the increased number of people living in close quarters. The problems people experience seem to compound when they occur in proximity with a large number of other people. The problems also seem to compound qualitatively. The net result is that city life poses a unique challenge to being a Christian and a church, especially as cities grow in size, complexity, and thus incomprehensibility. The sum of the problems seems to be greater than the mere sum of individual problems, concerns, and difficulties. Truly the crises cities face seem to increase, rather than decrease, with the passage of time, the growth in the number of large cities, and their overall size.

The Role of Churches

There are many things that can be said about the role of churches in cities. It goes beyond the scope of this chapter to present an exhaustive assessment and prospect for churches and church ministries. Let me begin, then, with special interests that I have in ministering to cities.

In every urban community, churches would do well to consider establishing interdenominational educational networks that would establish Christian schools and after-school learning centers. These educational activities should draw from the wealth of retired and active teachers, parents, and other resources so that those students that have been written off as incapable of being educated may be reached. Wherever possible, these efforts should include interaction with the public school system. When the public schools are resigned to the failure of students, the churches and the parents must shoulder the responsibility to save the education of children.

Churches need to be creative and flexible as well as faithful to their core beliefs, values, and practices. This is especially true in cities and the variety of urban settings they represent. Churches must be advocates of the young, the uneducated, the misunderstood, the misdirected, and others who are impoverished socially and politically as well as economically. As Jesus said, "The Spirit of the Lord is upon me, because he has anointed me to bring good news to the poor. He has sent me to proclaim release to the captives and recovery of sight to the blind, to let the oppressed go free, to proclaim the year of the Lord's favor" (Luke 4:18-19, alluding to Isa. 61:1-2).

Christians and churches need to follow this example of Jesus Christ. Yes, they are to preach. Christians and churches are called to proclaim the good news — the gospel, the evangel *(euangelion)* — of Jesus and of salvation. To whom are they primarily to preach? The poor, or "Christ's poor," which is how Albert Outler described John Wesley's self-chosen constituency — those who are impoverished in so many ways.[1] This preferential option for the poor seems to be a common theme in Scripture. It does not neglect the needs of others — those who were not poor at the time of Jesus, and those who are not poor today. However, Jesus seems to emphasize over and over again how Christians are to place primacy upon ministering to those who are impoverished in one way or another. People are spiritually impoverished, and churches need to address their spiritual needs. People are impoverished in other ways as well, and churches need to be advo-

1. Albert Outler, Introductory Comment to Sermon 50, "The Use of Money," in *The Works of John Wesley,* vol. 2, *Sermons II, 34-70,* ed. Albert C. Outler (Nashville: Abingdon, 1985), p. 263.

cates on their behalf just as much as they need to fulfill compassionate ministries for the poor.

What does holiness demand of Christians? What does holiness demand of churches, especially those in cities? Certainly it includes that they be set apart, which is stated over and over again in Scripture (e.g., Lev. 11:44; Rom. 12:1-2; 1 Peter 1:16). It includes that they be compassionate toward those in need, physically as well as spiritually. However, holiness also demands that Christians and churches be concerned about the righteousness of God, be concerned about that which is good and to withstand that which is sinful, evil, and unjust. If Christians and churches are to be truly loving and compassionate toward their neighbors, then they need to become increasingly concerned about, informed of, and proactive about dealing with the causes of injustice as well as caring for the victims of injustice. Causes of sin, evil, and injustice — of course — can be the result of individuals who have gone astray. However, they can also be due to societal problems over which individuals have little or no control. Such problems can be due to institutional sin, evil, and injustice, which are not easily recognized, but which can be just as pervasive and detrimental to people. Reinhold Niebuhr, in *Moral Man and Immoral Society,* first made Christians aware of the systemic nature of immorality, pervading the lives of people, societies, and cities far beyond the simple notion of personal sin.[2] If Christians want to minister holistically, especially to people in cities, then they need to be as "wise as serpents" in withstanding sin, evil, and injustice in its many manifestations (Matt. 10:16). We must get to the roots of people's problems and not just minister to their symptoms. We must become more aware of the various ways people become impoverished physically and spiritually, and then we must become proactive in dealing with every dimension of their impoverishment.

There are few places in which more impoverished people are found than in cities today. Moreover, it seems that their problems are increasing numerically as well as in complexity, so churches cannot afford to shy away from their responsibilities for emulating the beliefs, values, and practices of Jesus. Just as Jesus proclaimed good news to the poor, he also wanted to proclaim release to the captives, recovery of sight to the blind, and freedom to those who are oppressed. These are very real, concrete problems for which Jesus was concerned. They are problems that Christians too often

2. See Reinhold Niebuhr, *Moral Man and Immoral Society* (New York: Scribner's, 1948).

overlook as incurable or unimportant, particularly as compared to the loftier spiritual goals reminiscent of the Great Commission: "Go therefore and make disciples of all nations, baptizing them in the name of the Father and of the Son and of the Holy Spirit, and teaching them to obey everything that I have commanded you" (Matt. 28:19-20). Certainly the Great Commission represents a great priority Jesus left the disciples, but it does not take away from the holistic approach to ministry that he emulated in his life as well as his preaching, teaching, and advocacy for the poor. Such advocacy is especially needed on behalf of the urban crises facing people — Christian and non-Christian — in cities today. Jesus did not just minister to the spiritual needs of people. He also ministered on behalf of what held them captive — socially, politically, economically, ethnically, linguistically, and in other physical ways as well as spiritually and, perhaps, demonically. Jesus ministered so that people who are blind — one way or another — might see, and he ministered so that people who are oppressed — one way or another — might be free.

These ministries of Jesus are not just holistic. They reflect the holiness of God and the holiness to which God calls people. Cities are not generally thought of as places conducive to the cultivation or flourishing of God's holiness, much less as places conducive to wholeness, health, and the kind of flourishing God intends for everyone. However, hindrances that cities pose to the salvation, holiness, wholeness, health, and flourishing that God intends should not prevent Christians — individually and collectively — from ministering, advocating, and hoping for those ends. By the grace of God, which Christians believe is always present, there are always reasons to hope. Such hope is not unwarranted for cities. On the contrary, God promises greater grace where the needs are greatest. There is no lack of spiritual empowerment for those who minister in cities, and they will need it, given the extensive needs of people who live there.

Historic Precedents

There is no lack of historical precedents for Christians and churches who wish to minister effectively to cities. In the Bible, most ministries took place in the large urban centers of the ancient world: Jerusalem, Antioch, Corinth, Ephesus, and Rome. Certainly first-century Christians were aware of the special needs of city dwellers. Subsequent developments in church history continued to occur in and around urban centers. Never have Christians been unaware of the neediness of people living in cities. As the church developed, there were times when the mission of the church included missionary and other ministries that reached out to smaller communities and countries that were less developed. However, seldom were such outreaches far from nearby urban centers. On the contrary, the mission of the church throughout human history has been inextricably bound up with urban settings one way or another.

Sometimes Christians and churches understood God's call to holiness to be a call to oppose the world — to oppose or withdraw from the cultural influences as well as the sins, evils, and injustices of the world. H. Richard Niebuhr documents such views in his book *Christ and Culture*.[3] Yet Niebuhr also documents the views of Christians and churches that take more active roles in engaging the world, in engaging culture and its many challenges to God and God's holy will. Some try to find a synthesis between the beliefs, values, and practices of Christianity with those of the world and of culture, in its various manifestations. Other Christians and churches engage it paradoxically, recognizing the tension between the two; still others seek to transform it. Christians and churches, of course, are not always consistent in terms of how they engage the world and culture. However, engagement for the sake of holiness is needed more than withdrawal. If Christians and churches want to minister effectively to cities for God, then they need to develop rationales, theologies, or some type of praxis that supports their proactive engagement with the world in all its sin, evil, and injustice, as well as in the good that remains in it because of the residue of God's image in the lives of people, individually and collectively.

From time to time, special outreaches to urban settings occurred in church history. Notable contemporary examples include the founding of the Salvation Army by William and Catherine Booth, which advocated for special care for the salvation and promotion of holy living among the poorest and neediest people of society, usually found in the neglected urban centers of the world. The Booths, in fact, found the concept of holiness to be quite compatible with actively reaching out to the poorest, hungriest, often homeless people so often found in cities. Holiness to them demanded as much concern for the physical well-being of people as for their spiritual well-being.

3. See H. Richard Niebuhr, *Christ and Culture* (New York: Harper & Row, 1956).

Yet there are other examples: Walter Rauschenbusch advocated the "social gospel" on behalf of the poorest of people in the biggest of cities, maintaining that Jesus came to meet people's physical as well as spiritual needs.[4] Liberation theology arose in order to minister to and to advocate on behalf of people who suffered injustice or were neglected on account of their social, economic, or political status, or on account of their ethnicity, gender, and so on. It has sought to alleviate the impoverishment, marginalization, oppression, and persecution — sometimes violent or even deadly persecution — of such people. One may consider Martin Luther King Jr., a forerunner of liberation theologies, since he sought in the Civil Rights Movement to liberate people from bondage to the injustices of racism, segregation, and persecution as well as from the bondage of sin and evil.[5]

We could name other examples of Christians and churches that have sought to go beyond compassionate ministries that meet the symptoms of impoverishment. They also advocated for the poor — in whatever forms it appeared — in order to challenge the causes of their impoverishment. Today we may not always agree with particular historical attempts to follow the life and teachings of Jesus on behalf of the poor. Indeed, there always remains the need to be wise, critical thinkers with respect to the ways in which we promote Jesus' beliefs, values, and practices. However, the fact remains that Christians and churches can neglect neither the holistic approach to ministry that Jesus embodied, nor that both Christians and churches need to be obedient in balancing the various physical and spiritual needs of people — needs that are especially evident in cities today. If Jesus actually promoted special care for the poor of the world, then there is no better place for Christians and churches to be at work than in urban settings. Nowhere else are the needs greater, and nowhere else can Christians and churches better fulfill Jesus' calling to salvation, holiness, and health than in cities.

4. See Walter Rauschenbusch, *A Theology for the Social Gospel* (New York: Macmillan, 1917; repr. Louisville: Westminster John Knox Press, 1997).

5. More explicit examples of liberation theologies include the Latin American liberation theology of Gustavo Gutiérrez, *A Theology of Liberation: History, Politics, and Salvation* (Maryknoll, N.Y.: Orbis Books, 1973); the black theology of James Cone, *Black Theology and Black Power* (New York: Seabury, 1969); and the feminist theology of Mary Daly, *The Church and the Second Sex* (New York: Harper & Row, 1968) and Rosemary Radford Ruether, *Sexism and God-Talk: Toward a Feminist Theology* (Boston: Beacon, 1983).

The Holiness Manifesto captures the necessity of ministering holistically to the needs of people. It invites all Christians to embrace God's call to practice compassionate ministries; it invites solidarity with the poor; and it invites advocacy for equality, justice, reconciliation, and peace. Are these goals idealistic? They certainly are holy ideals, and this is why Christians need to preach the transforming message of holiness, teach the principles of Christ-like love and forgiveness, embody lives that reflect Jesus Christ, lead in engaging with the cultures of the world, and partner with others to multiply its effect for the reconciliation of all things.[6]

Conclusion

Certainly the city represents people with holy potential as well as with power, both of which can function for the shame of the universe as well as for the glory of God. Cities and the people who live in them can reflect the glory of God when they practice compassion, righteousness, and justice. However, if they live in selfishness, greed, and unbelief, then they live for themselves. They are lacking in love and are characterized by lawlessness and injustice; they are susceptible to various forms of personal, social, and demonic bondage that enslave every aspect of their lives, individually and collectively. Too often cities have accentuated the plight of humanity, literally and symbolically, as visible expressions of people's rejection of God's authority, power, and sovereignty.

However, the good news of the gospel is that God has neither neglected humanity nor cities. God has provided ways for whoever will believe to return to the family of God — the church — and experience the blessedness of holiness, individually and collectively. This good news extends to cities as well as to individuals, and Christians and churches need to work with the presence and power of God's Holy Spirit for the sake of those in need, especially those in cities. It is no accident that heaven is visualized as a heavenly city — "the holy city, the new Jerusalem" (Rev. 21:2).

The fullness of God's Kingdom will occur in the future; however, God's Kingdom is already present. It is present in individual Christians; it is present collectively in churches; it is present in various ministries on be-

---

6. "The Holiness Manifesto," Wesleyan Holiness Consortium, available in this volume and online at http://holinessandunity.org/fs/index.php?id=796.

half of the physical as well as the spiritual needs of people; and it is present in cities, though not yet perfectly. Far from being perfect, cities seem at times impregnable bastions, resistant to the ministrations of God, of churches, and of Christians. It is easy to become discouraged, complacent, or neglectful of the needs of urban centers. Yet God loves people in cities. Indeed, since God has special care for those who are impoverished — and there are so many levels of impoverishment in cities — God has special care for those in cities. Christians and churches must diligently work on behalf of those in cities, ministering to their social, political, economic, ethnic, and other needs as well as their spiritual needs. As we minister thus, we demonstrate our love toward the unique needs of those who live in cities, and we reflect the holistic and holy ministry Jesus embodied and promoted. By the grace of God and the obedience of Christians and churches to the role model of Jesus, great things will happen for the sake of God's Kingdom, which will extend to cities as well as to the uttermost parts of the world.

CHAPTER 11

Local Church Impact

JIM ADAMS AND C. STEVENS SCHELL

Does Wesley's vision for a church transformed and empowered through the holiness of God still hold meaning for evangelicals in a postmodern world? Postmodernism provides both a troubling context and encouraging challenge for local church pastors and leaders. The Wesleyan Holiness movement historically embraced a "shoe leather theology" that adapts to current culture while retaining Scripture as paramount for faith and practice in the local church.

When I was a kid, my father would string up Christmas lights on our house each December. These were not the glittering icicles or intricate designs of today, but just a simple string of colored bulbs outlining the eaves. A boy down the street, the local hoodlum, discovered that the removal of a single bulb from each house would bring down the entire system, immediately darkening the festive look of the neighborhood. Practically the entire street went dark as the vandal pulled a bulb from each string. My dad came up with a creative solution. As a machinist, he had access to metallic bluing, a compound used to mark and dye metal aircraft parts. He knew that this substance was impossible to remove from skin, requiring a week or two to "wear off." Sure enough, after a careful application of the stuff to our bulbs, he caught the culprit "blue-handed," so to speak. The evidence was compelling, and the kid and his parents spent a weekend visiting each home with an apology and a returned bulb.

My father's solution to the problem he faced was elegant and simple. Using the right tool to solve a problem came naturally to him. Likewise, pastors often find themselves searching for the right tools to fix the often complex and daunting problems surfacing in the church in this so-called postmodern age. These thorny issues include the following:

- *Building Community* — while dealing with people who lack relational skills, possess a casual mentality toward the church, are excessively influenced by mass media, believe lying is normal, are expected by employers to carry out dishonest business practices, and sometimes live in rebellion against authority.
- *Building Families* — in the midst of rampant divorce rates, domestic and sexual abuse, a growing lack of parenting skills, and the neglect of children and spouses.
- *Building the Person* — while confronted with alcohol/substance abusers, and those who are addicted to pornography, steeped in materialism, and lack a moral compass.
- *Building Spirituality* — while experiencing an increase of apparent demonic manifestations or activity, an ongoing barrage of cultic and occult messages, and congregations distracted from spiritual life.

These categories are not mutually exclusive and do overlap extensively. Moreover, seeking vision and achieving meaningful praxis for the local church in the twenty-first century confronts us with an ever-changing dynamic of decision-making. While scriptural approaches and models remain consistent, culture does not. Today's church leaders often wonder if their congregations are best served by confronting postmodernism or adapting to it. This struggle is important because the decisions church leaders make concerning culture and adaptation will shape the future of the church.

Ministry in a Postmodern World

Briefly, *postmodernism* is an oft-used term describing the perceptions and unique characteristics of our culture since the decade of the 1950s. Postmodernists reject the Age of Enlightenment–inspired notion (typically known as modernism) that rationality and reason alone will lead to a meaningful understanding of the world around us. Postmodernists hold a complex view that sometimes inspires ethical relativism, a troubling concept for many evangelicals. Yet regardless of whether postmodernists are misguided, the movement has certainly taken our culture by storm.

What happens when your theology won't transfer to a postmodern culture? The church has always coexisted with a culture hostile to its calling and purposes. Some examples include the paganism of ancient Rome; the superstition and lack of biblical literacy among the laypeople of the Middle Ages; and the sexual revolution of the twentieth century. In reality, postmoderns don't challenge the church in any greater or lesser degree than it has been challenged by other socio-cultural constructs throughout its history. Pastors and church leaders have been struggling, knowingly or not, with the question of postmodernism for several decades. According to George Barna,[1] most pastors believe "a large majority of their congregants deem their faith in God to be the highest priority in their life." At the same time, this research reveals, "in contrast to the upbeat pastoral view of people's faith . . . only one out of every seven (churched) adults placed their faith in God at the top of their priority list." Why the disconnect here? Barna concludes:

> There has never been a time when American society was in more dire need of the Christian church to provide a pathway to a better future. Given the voluminous stream of moral challenges, and the rampant spiritual hunger that defines our culture today, this should be the heyday for biblical ministry. As things stand now, we have become content with placating sinners and filling auditoriums as the marks of spiritual health.[2]

It appears that many modernist[3] churches are failing in their well-intentioned attempts to provide such pathways. This failure may be occurring because leaders are not accurately assessing the spiritual lives of their people, nor do they clearly understand postmodern socio-cultural needs. Modernist churches are progressive, and sometimes strive to eliminate historicity and tradition in their search for relevance. Contemporary methods for church growth (the seeker-sensitive, Gen-X, team-centered, new

---

1. See The Barna Group, "The Barna Update," January 9, 2006, available online at http://www.barna.org/.

2. Barna Group, "The Barna Update," January 9, 2006.

3. The term "modern" here describes churches that practice ministry based on the traditions of Age of Enlightenment thinking.

paradigm, and purpose-driven models) have experienced limited success, but do not seem to have reversed the erosion of influential Christian thought in culture.

Recently, the *emerging church* model is attempting to address postmodern culture through an increased sensitivity to local needs and global perspectives. The emerging church model hearkens back to a time when the Christian faith seemed more simple and accessible. It recognizes the reality of postmodernism, and seeks to adapt to it through promoting the positive elements of the primitive church while recognizing the uniqueness of this present culture. The emerging church model seeks the successes of simple, relevant, and meaningful Christianity. According to Gibbs and Bolger, emerging churches "remove modern practices of Christianity, not the faith itself."[4] The authors suggest that the mission of the emerging church employs an approach recognizing the uniqueness of the world today.

> The new paradigm, purpose driven, seeker, and Gen-X churches are not postmodern in this sense. These movements venerate the large gatherings and the heart as primary spiritual domains. They do not challenge the many dualisms of modernity but rather continue the divisions between natural and supernatural, individual and community, mind and body, public and private, belief and action, and they leave controlling power structures in place. In these movements, religion and spiritual practices are activities one does apart from the culture, and spirituality is still very much at the margins. In contrast, the clarion call of the emerging church is Psalm 24:1: "The earth is the Lord's, and everything in it." For emerging churches, there are no longer any bad places, bad people, or bad times. All can be made holy. All can be given to God in worship. All modern dualisms can be overcome.[5]

The emerging church movement, while not necessarily the only (or best) answer to the challenges of ministry today, does nonetheless provide important insights to making the local church effective and transforma-

---

4. Eddie Gibbs and Ryan K. Bolger, *Emerging Churches: Creating Christian Community in Postmodern Cultures* (Grand Rapids: Baker Academic, 2005), p. 29.

5. Gibbs and Bolger, *Emerging Churches*, p. 67.

tional in its mission. In fact, this missional approach tightly links with scriptural injunctions for the role of the church.[6]

The Bible is the story of God that transcends culture. It is the telling of how God establishes and imparts holiness as a transferable self-characteristic. While many of God's attributes are unique (i.e. omnipotence, omniscience, omnipresence), the characteristic of holiness can be conveyed and become part of our nature. God commands us to "be holy as I am holy" (1 Peter 1:16).[7] At the same time, God is our source for holiness: "but now he has reconciled you by Christ's physical body through death to present you holy in his sight, without blemish and free from accusation — if you continue in your faith, established and firm, not moved from the hope held out in the gospel" (Col. 1:22-23a). Focusing on God's relationship to people through the agency of holiness is fundamental to understanding the function of the local church in the twenty-first century. To this end, Howard Snyder asks a vital question, ". . . times and cultures change . . . is the holiness message still relevant in a so-called postmodern age?"[8]

> I believe it is. Paradoxically however, the relevance of the holiness message for today becomes clearest when we first go back and look anew at what the Bible says about the holiness message, examining it in light of the questions and challenges of today. The church has always been the most prophetic when it has rediscovered the relevance of the "eternal gospel" (Rev. 14:6) for a new age. My thesis here is that the biblical message of holiness is pointedly and powerfully relevant to the world in which we live. . . . The need for biblical comprehensiveness is especially important when it comes to the subject of holiness. Holiness should mean wholeness, the integrity of heart and life. Therefore, we should pay close attention to the full scope of God's call upon our lives, upon the church.[9]

Snyder's assertion that the holiness message is relevant today provides a launching pad for exploring the means by which the church can function

6. See Ephesians 4:11-13.

7. Unless otherwise indicated, all biblical quotations in this essay are from the New International Version (NIV).

8. Howard A. Snyder, "Holiness and the Five Calls of God," lecture, Asbury Theological Seminary, Wilmore, Kentucky, November 11, 2004. The essay is also available in this volume, pp. 129-51.

9. Snyder, "Holiness and the Five Calls of God."

in an ever-changing landscape of relativism and globalization. The good news for pastors and church leaders is that effective ministry and outreach transcends culture, and that the Bible provides the reference points and instructions for engaging vital, relevant, and powerful ministry today.

Wesley's Vision

John Wesley was particularly intrigued with the notion of connecting scriptural holiness with practical Christianity by creating refreshing methods of ministry within his stodgy eighteenth-century church. Wesley did not desire to break away or form a new denomination, though this did occur after his death. Rather, he sought to bring revival to the turgid Anglicanism of the day. Likewise, we have much to learn from Wesley in making such connections between the local church and contemporary society.

Wesley's personal experiences and dedication to biblical Christianity inspired his vision for the church. His outlook for the people of God embraced five characteristics: (1) promoting Spirit-empowered prayer, (2) working effectively within the established church, (3) encouraging small group ministry, (4) living out a "deeply felt and actively expressed" faith,[10] and (5) recognizing holiness as requisite to the Christian life.

Promoting Spirit-Empowered Prayer

Spontaneous and personally expressive prayer was unusual or nonexistent in the institutional church of the eighteenth century. Yet Wesley recognized, possibly through his association with the Moravians, that Scripture models and speaks to the need for personal, heartfelt prayer. According to Wesley, we are exposed and alone without Spirit-empowering prayer, and the community of believers offers the opportunities needed to share in such prayers.

> If you remain in me and my words remain in you, ask whatever you wish, and it will be given you. This is to my Father's glory,

10. Chris Armstrong, "How John Wesley Changed America," *Christian History Newsletter,* June 20, 2003. Available online at http://www.christianitytoday.com/history/features/archive.html.

that you bear much fruit, showing yourselves to be my disciples. (John 15:7-8)

Interceding for one another is a community activity of the church. At the same time, intercession finds its basis in "remain(ing)" or staying connected with Christ while his words bond with our own heart and spirit. Note the outcome — a connected community of believers who will bring glory to God, demonstrate fruitfulness, and be marked as God's followers. As in Wesley's ministry, the releasing of God's people to passionate prayer is an urgent and compelling element of what it means to be Kingdom people. Moreover, the effective building of the Kingdom will only occur when leaders release God's people to pray.

Working Effectively within the Established Church

Wesley was somehow able to navigate the precarious tightrope of a radical evangelical faith within a staid and bureaucratic church. Although Methodism did eventually emerge as a separate and international movement, Wesley's belief was that one could work from the inside to bring renewal and refreshing. The revival fires of Wesleyanism thus touched thousands of card-carrying Anglicans who never left their churches. Without a doubt, Wesley was an intrapreneur.[11] He worked from within the tradition of Anglicanism and never strove to harm the existing institution or begin a new religion or denomination. For example, Wesley's meetings occurred on days and times other than those prescribed for Anglican worship. Wesley never relinquished his ordination as an Anglican priest. As a result, he was able to encourage a deepening and passionate faith without separating his movement from the mainstream.

Encouraging Small Group Ministry

Wesley practiced building upon the spiritual community of the local church with smaller-group building blocks. His renowned "societies,

11. An intrapreneur is a creative leader who encourages change and develops new thinking within an existing organizational structure. See G. Pinchot and R. Pellman, *Intrapreneuring in Action: A Handbook for Business Innovation* (San Francisco: Berret-Koehler, 1999).

classes, and bands" reached out to thousands of spiritually hungry people who were able to mature and deepen in their faith through these small groupings. According to Tracy,[12] the "society" was a sort of local congregation within the traditional church that gave opportunity for a Sunday evening service in a chapel, hall, or home, and provided other interactive and relational meetings for believers. The next subdivision, known as the "class meeting," was a group meeting of about twelve persons. Members of a society attended these on a weekly basis. "Bands" were same-sex groupings of about five people for the purpose of deep sharing and mutual support toward personal holiness. Less known, but clear from Wesley's writings, was the practice of pairing "twin souls." These smallest of groups were intended for one-on-one peer mentoring and open, unencumbered sharing.[13] Observing these structures for spiritual formation at different levels truly reveals Wesley's genius for encouraging holiness through building community.

Living Out a "Deeply Felt and Actively Expressed" Faith[14]

Though sometimes accused by his detractors of promoting "enthusiasm" (the eighteenth-century term for overt superstition and religious fanaticism), Wesley encouraged a moderate and balanced view of faith, reason, and experience. His convictions for healthy *church* life included a desire that people experience a meaningful and growing *spiritual* life. He valued and encouraged personal experience in God, but not at the cost of reasonableness.

> Beware you do not fall into (this kind) of enthusiasm . . . fancying you have those gifts from God which you have not. Trust not in visions or dreams; in sudden impressions, or strong impulses of any kind. Remember, it is not by these you are to know what is the will of God on any particular occasion, but by applying the plain Scripture rule, with the help of experience and reason, and the ordinary assistance of the Spirit of God. Do not lightly take the name of God

12. Wesley D. Tracy, "Spiritual Direction in the Wesleyan-Holiness Movement," *Journal of Psychology and Theology* (Winter 2002).

13. Tracy, "Spiritual Direction in the Wesleyan-Holiness Movement."

14. Tracy, "Spiritual Direction in the Wesleyan-Holiness Movement."

in your mouth; do not talk of the will of God on every trifling occasion: but let your words, as well as your actions, be all tempered with reverence and godly fear.[15]

Recognizing Holiness as Requisite to the Christian Life

Perhaps the most enduring legacy of Wesley's life was his promotion of the theme of holiness throughout the church. To Wesley, holiness was essential. A holy God provides the means by which people might themselves become holy. Moreover, holiness not only cleanses "flesh and spirit," but also has the "consequence [of] being endued with those virtues which were in Christ Jesus; the being so 'renewed in the image of our mind,' as to be 'perfect as our Father in heaven is perfect.'"[16] Unlike some of God's attributes, holiness is a transferable and obtainable resource rich in both effect and transformation. When we partake of God's holiness through faith in the Savior, we are receiving from him the essential means by which we can become separate from sin and evil, while at the same time embracing all that is good, righteous, and of value for our lives in Christ. Wesley was no "pie-in-the-sky" theologian. He ardently preached that God's holiness was available by faith to any willing Christian. The overarching love of God overpowers problems of the human condition, including personal sin, social injustice, and societal weaknesses.

Just as in the institutional church of Wesley's day, leaders today struggle against a sort of spiritual fatalism that supports the notion that sin is inevitable. Many operate from the false assumption that substantive change is impossible, and hope for freedom from sin's grasp must be deferred until the hereafter. Wesley rejected this sense of despair, and believed that true hope for change existed because holiness can break through into the world now. While many Christian leaders today despair of winning the battle against unrighteousness and sin, this circuit-riding preacher from long ago still inspires us in his contention that God's pure love and holiness leads to the most profound transformation of heart, mind, spirit, and relationships.

---

15. John Wesley, Sermon 37, "The Nature of Enthusiasm," in *The Works of John Wesley*, 3d ed., ed. Thomas Jackson, 14 vols. (Grand Rapids: Baker, 1978), vol. 5, p. 478.

16. Wesley, "A Plain Account of Christian Perfection," in *The Works of John Wesley*, vol. 11, p. 366.

These five themes of Wesley's ministry form an interdependent approach to building healthy and vibrant communities of believers. Likewise, these characteristics of the historic Wesleyan Holiness movement still speak to the church in the twenty-first century. A community forms through ongoing, interactive, and persistent relationships. In a healthy community, people spend time together in order to both contribute to and benefit by that relationship.

The Biblical Community

If, as some believe, postmodernism is all about going back to basics, then perhaps the church can benefit from revisiting the concept of the people of God as community. Our English word *community* finds its roots in the Latin terms denoting a body of fellowship or common citizenship.[17] The Old Testament speaks to the meaning of community in a number of its books with the first mention in Genesis 28. In this passage, Isaac's blessing of Jacob marks the first use of the term *community* in the Bible.

> Go at once to Paddan Aram, to the house of your mother's father Bethuel. Take a wife for yourself there, from among the daughters of Laban, your mother's brother. May God Almighty bless you and make you fruitful and increase your numbers until you become a *community* of peoples. May he give you and your descendants the blessing given to Abraham, so that you may take possession of the land where you now live as an alien, the land God gave to Abraham. (vv. 2-4)

It is clear that Isaac's blessing of Jacob will lead to the establishing of community — as "you . . . increase your numbers." In one sense, a community is indeed a number of people who live, work, and raise their families in a common locale. In a larger sense, a community exists when any group shares the same legal system, possesses common interests, or holds common ownership, participation, identity or likeness.[18] By necessity,

---

17. "Community," in *Oxford English Dictionary*, 2d CD-ROM ed. (New York: Oxford University Press, 2005).

18. "Community," in *Oxford English Dictionary*.

community includes commonality of purpose and shared citizenship; this is sometimes referred to in the New Testament as the Kingdom of God.

The book of Acts speaks to this sense of community without necessarily employing the same language as the Old Testament. However, the meaning is clear — the church is a community because it is of the Kingdom of God, and Kingdom people share a common heritage — faith in Christ Jesus. God marks the community of Christ with the possibility of holiness because God is holy.[19] In Acts 4 we see the results of the church under attack. First, Satan attacks externally — through arrests, jailing, and fear. He is a devouring lion (1 Peter 5:8). Next, he tries a more subtle approach — going on the offensive as a deceiving spirit (2 Cor. 11:3, 13-14) internally to attack the community of believers. Clearly, Satan is alarmed and concerned about the power of community and is willing to deploy any resources he can to sabotage or mitigate the building of community among believers.

In an Acts account of prayer-laden spiritual warfare, Peter and John report their struggle with the chief priests and elders to the community of believers. The resulting communal prayer results in a release of spiritual boldness to overcome the attack against the people of God. The Acts believers were thus "filled with the Holy Spirit," "spoke the word of God boldly," and were "of one heart and one mind."[20] These three components compellingly illumine how faithfully stewarding God's plan for the church can make a difference. The Holy Spirit's infilling indeed empowers the community to engage in connecting humankind with God's holy will, while speaking the word boldly provides his people the means to communicate their faith. Being of one heart and mind provides the context for an authentic and holy community that walks together in the faith journey. These are indispensable spiritual resources given by God to build the Kingdom as an effectual and vibrant redemptive community.

Howard Snyder points out how Henry Fish described community. Fish used the term *communion,* making the case that it is "expressly warranted" by Scripture.[21] These activities cannot occur in a vacuum, neither can they exist in full measure without giving opportunities for people to assemble for the purposes of

---

19. See Acts 2:44, 45; 4:27-32, 34-37; 5:1-10.

20. Acts 4:23-31.

21. List adapted from Henry Fish, "Manual for Class Leaders," in *The Radical Wesley,* ed. Howard Snyder (Eugene, Ore.: Wipf & Stock, 1980), pp. 20-21.

Fellowship;

The breaking of bread;

Exhorting one another daily;

Comforting and edifying one another;

Provoking one another to love and good works;

Confessing faults to one another;

Praying for one another;

Teaching and admonishing one another in psalms, hymns, and spiritual songs;

Bearing one another's burdens;

Weeping with those who weep;

Rejoicing with those who rejoice.

How, then, is it possible to structure the church to meet these scriptural mandates? It is difficult if not impossible for a local church to provide holistic ministry in a single, large public gathering alone. Sitting in rows and directing attention to a single focal point (i.e., the platform or pulpit) is hardly conducive to releasing many of these scriptural activities for building community. Only through providing organic groupings of appropriate and varying sizes can the church hope to build an atmosphere of acceptance and spiritual engagement. Studies consistently demonstrate that the larger the group, the more a participant will tend to fade to the background and avoid interaction.[22] Wesley's "methodism" of creating various welcoming, supportive, enabling, and empowering groups that retain the standards of the Bible is still germane to local church impact. Holiness is as vital in the twenty-first century as it was in the first century. While postmodernism provides new contexts for applying the principles of Wesley and his beloved Scriptures, the underlying principles remain true today.

James 5 in the Twenty-First Century

James, the quintessential "just do it" book of the New Testament, is intended to give instructions for believers regarding how to live out their

22. Kenwyn K. Smith and David N. Berg, *Paradoxes of Group Life: Understanding Conflict, Paralysis, and Movement in Group Dynamics* (San Francisco: Jossey-Bass, 1997).

lives; James speaks to living life as a Christian, not how to become one. In his frank and straightforward manner, James issues simple commands for community life.

> Is any one of you in trouble? He should pray. Is anyone happy? Let him sing songs of praise. Is any one of you sick? He should call the elders of the church to pray over him and anoint him with oil in the name of the Lord. And the prayer offered in faith will make the sick person well; the Lord will raise him up. If he has sinned, he will be forgiven. Therefore confess your sins to each other and pray for each other so that you may be healed. The prayer of a righteous man is powerful and effective. (5:13-16)

Here we find the pattern for creating and cultivating a community of healing and confession. People in this postmodern world no longer find solace in the belief that humankind is progressing, and that we'll eventually figure it all out. The James 5 pattern flies in the face of such fatalism by explaining the typical way in which the community should conduct spiritual business. It is especially interesting how James connects sin and healing with confession.

While science continues to search for the connections between mind and body, James helps leaders understand the preeminent role of one's spirit in the sin-confession-healing cycle. In reason-laden modernism, many people, even people of faith, hoped for and believed in an eventual solution to the problem of sickness. However, the church today must understand that many of its members and attendees do not hold to such a belief anymore. The James 5 paradigm therefore comes alive again when people realize its relevance in twenty-first century ministry.

Transformation Now

Building an atmosphere of grace as opposed to judgmentalism is no easy task for church leaders in this postmodern age. The Bible writers demonstrate how God, in his perfect love, transcends culture, but allows — and sometimes encourages — his people to adapt to culture without becoming controlled by it. Grace, holiness, and the standards of Scripture are held in tension, and yet are complementary to one another. Grace without holiness is weak and non-transforming, while holiness without grace is legalism. Grace and holiness together provide the context for forgiveness, spiritual growth, and joyful living. The struggle to teach and promote righteousness has always existed in juxtaposition with grace. In *Organic Church: Growing Faith Where Life Happens,* Neil Cole speaks to this issue:

> How can we possibly expect lost people without Christ to make righteous decisions and live moral lives? That is like expecting a lone sheep to fend off a pack of vicious wolves using its nonexistent strategic cunning and ferocious growl. So I suggest we not expect moral wisdom and righteous actions from lost people. We need to stop judging them and start feeling compassion for them, as Jesus did.[23]

Without the transforming grace and holiness of God, people will not change. Cole points out the need for compassion, and without compassion there can be no impact from the church to the world around it. Compassion transcends postmodernism. Throughout human history we have experienced loss, emptiness, personal pain, loneliness, spiritual devastation, and the sting of death. No cultural wave or societal context will ever change the reality and foundations of the human condition. Sociological considerations and philosophical convictions do not alter Adam's sin and Christ's redemptive work. While postmodernists tend to believe the human condition is unchangeable, it is through the compassion and intervention of God's people that hope can arise in the hearts of the spiritually disconnected. The patterns of Scripture as interpreted and expounded through the teachings of Wesley give us powerful tools as fresh and useful today as ever before.

Let us revisit Wesley's vision for the church as summarized in the five characteristics detailed above, and examine how each can influence the church of the twenty-first century.

First, *promoting Spirit-empowered prayer* can and should occur as an expected and consistent component of a healthy church. Prayer is vital at all levels: congregational, in small groups, one-on-one, and in private. The Scripture recognizes and models multiple modes, including congregational, intercession, meditative, and conversational prayer.

---

23. Neil Cole, *Organic Church: Growing Faith Where Life Happens* (San Francisco: Jossey-Bass, 2005), pp. 148-49.

Postmoderns also recognize the value of tradition. Many youth groups have abandoned spotlights, Power Point presentations, and electric guitars (not that they're not cool, too) in favor of candlelight, contemplative music or pure silence, and ancient spiritual disciplines such as lectio divina, Ignatian prayer, and Taizé-style worship. Postmodernism encourages us to explore worship as an experiential and participatory act. It takes seriously Jesus' words in Matthew 18:20: "For where two or three are gathered in my name, I am there among them."[24]

Pastors and leaders can create environments for prayer through several means. Examples of methods to involve the entire community in prayer at various levels include the following:

Modeling prayer in public, private, and small group settings;

Teaching specific biblical models of prayer;

Offering frequent small group or one-on-one opportunities for prayer;

Encouraging believers to share stories about their own transformational prayer experiences;

Promoting creative opportunities that differ from the recent church traditions or look back to ancient church traditions;

Employing technology to disseminate prayer requests and answered prayer (technologies such as *ePrayerConnect*[25] offer churches the opportunity to share prayer needs with congregants through a daily e-mail).

Second, *working effectively within the established church* was a constant challenge throughout Wesley's life, and it continues to be so for today's

24. Matt Kelley, "An Introduction to Postmodernism (and Why It's Not a Bad Word)," *Youth Worker* (November-December 2003): 22.

25. *ePrayerConnect* states that it is "a Web-based tool that makes creating and sending attractive, dynamic e-mails easy and economical. More than an e-mail communication tool, ePrayerConnect builds relationships. You can use it to encourage your church in daily prayer, involve more people in outreach ministries, and provide daily news and event updates to your congregation." Its simple-to-use website claims to "take . . . all the hassles out of staying connected . . . with . . . (an) easy-to-use set-up wizard (that) will have you ready to send your first e-mail in little more than one hour." See *ePrayerConnect*, accessed August 1, 2006, http://www.eprayerconnect.org.

leaders. The decision to adapt ministry to meet the needs of postmoderns is daunting, especially in light of the real possibility of working at cross-purposes with the established structures of one's local church or denomination. Confronted with the calling to create radical change, ministers and leaders must depend on prayer, conscience, and wisdom when deciding to work from within or outside the existing organization. The table below illustrates the differences of each in ministry.

ENTREPRENEURIAL MINISTRY	INTRAPRENEURIAL MINISTRY
Strengths:	**Strengths:**
• Greater freedom for decision-making • No encumbrance from preexisting systems • Ability to create new mission • Ability to make "snap" decisions or respond quickly to needs	• Accountability • May have access to greater resources • Ability to make use of existing structures • Can piggyback on existing infrastructure (clerical help, lines of communication, technology, etc.) • Have existing relationships to build upon • May have the advantage of being accepted as non-rebellious by power structure
Threats:	**Threats:**
• Lack of accountability • Lack of resources • No existent structures or support • Time required to build relationships • Risks being construed by the existent power structure as "rebellious"	• Difficulty in working with preexisting mission • Lack of freedom in decision-making • Potential inability to make "snap" decisions or respond quickly to needs • Stagnant or rigid power structures
Working outside the established church to build community through creative and biblical ministry *Example: Aimee Semple McPherson*	*Working within the established church to build community through creative and biblical ministry* *Example: John and Charles Wesley*

One may act as an agent of change in the church through either entrepreneurial or intrapreneurial efforts. Wesley's choice to remain within the existing system worked well at times during his life, but ultimately led to the formation of a new denomination.

Third, *encouraging small group ministry* is a pervasive priority in the early twenty-first century, and it has its roots in Wesley's vision for the church. However, the church of the twenty-first century must not only emphasize small groups, but understand them as the basic building blocks of community. Discussing churches that change lives in the twenty-first century, Gibbs and Bolger observe that

> because of the highly relational, continual, and missional aspects of community, emerging churches tend to be either small groups or networks of small groups. Their ways of life together are as varied as the people who make up the communities. The groups take a variety of forms and may meet in response to a range of objectives expressing both presence and connectedness.
>
> Emerging churches have no desire to grow big. Their missional commitment in their desire to reproduce when they begin to stretch relational aspects too far.
>
> Whenever the issue of small groups is raised, the debate rages as to whether they represent "birds of a feather flocking together" or whether diversity brings greater creativity and personal growth. (Pastor) Jason Evans (Matthew's House, Vista, California) prefers diverse house groups rather than grouping people according to their generation or interests. He believes the segmenting of the church is the biggest thing wrong with church as a whole.[26]

This draws our attention to the issue of unity and diversity in local church ministry. Obviously, a larger traditional public service usually offers greater opportunities for worship and teaching in a context of diversity, although some stagnant churches encompass less diversity. The large size of public worship often precludes intimate and consistent community building. Pastors must carefully explore the best ways for addressing this problem. Some important questions include the following:

- Should our church offer groups that focus on common interests or affinity (e.g., men, women, professionals, recovering addicts, couples, youth, children, etc.)? What are the pros and cons of this approach?
- Should our church focus on groups that encourage diversity by providing cross-generational opportunities for worship, fellowship, and prayer? What are the pros and cons of this approach?
- Alternatively, should we avoid focusing on a single emphasis (i.e., affinity groupings, diverse groupings) and provide multiple small group opportunities to engage our community? If so, how frequent and how many?

26. Gibbs and Bolger, *Emerging Churches*, p. 29.

The intimacy and relational aspects of small groups no doubt are attractive and meaningful to postmoderns. Some recent thinking in the church has emphasized very small groups of two or three persons as the basic building blocks for foundational community building. A growing number of churches seek to meet this need through Life Transformation Groups (LTGs). These smallest of groups are promulgated by Neil Cole, a leading author and leader in the movement.

> An LTG is made up of two to three people, all of the same gender, who meet weekly for personal accountability in the areas of their spiritual growth and development. A group should not grow beyond three, but multiply into two groups of two rather than a single group of four. If a fourth person is added to the group it is recommended that the group consider itself pregnant and ready to give birth to a second group. Once the fourth person has demonstrated sufficient faithfulness (2-3 weeks) then the group should multiply into two groups of two.
>
> There is no curriculum or training needed in an LTG. A simple bookmark which stays in the participants' Bible is all that is needed. The LTG accountability consists of three essential disciplines for personal spiritual growth — a steady diet of Scripture, confession of sin, and prayer for others who need Christ.[27]

LTGs resonate with postmoderns seeking authentic relationships and a deep sense of community. They offer the chance for a safe haven to confess sin, while growing in faith through reading Scripture and prayer.

Fourth, *living out a deeply felt and actively expressed faith* was a foundational aspect of the Christian life. While rejecting the excesses of what was known at the time as "enthusiasm," Wesley nevertheless promoted a sense that believers could and should experience their faith in tangible ways. Postmoderns are people in search of truth, but who avoid treating truth as holding inviolable meaning for everyone. In other words, one person's truth may not be another's. Therefore, personally experiencing truth and fulfillment are important in this culture. Deeply felt faith works today, just as it did in biblical times. "Feeling" one's faith does not mean that faith only comes through feeling alone. Indeed, feelings must always be subjugated to the teachings of God's word. Nevertheless, God never seems to

27. Neil Cole, *Cultivating a Life for God* (Carol Stream, Ill.: ChurchSmart, 1999), p. 63.

prohibit a personal sense of his presence or work in one's life in either the Old or New Testaments.

Allowing the active expression of one's faith is also crucial. The Pentecostal/Charismatic movement has provided examples for engaging people in heartfelt and expressive forms of worship and prayer. Pastors and leaders from all evangelical traditions can learn important lessons from certain aspects of the Pentecostal/Charismatic movement. These include joyous worship styles, active outpourings of faith-filled prayer, and recognizing that emotion is not, de facto, a bad thing in the Christian's life and ministry. Likewise, Pentecostals and Charismatics can benefit by reexamining the role of liturgies and ancient church traditions in creating and building spiritual community. In addition, pastors themselves must experience the reality of a worship-filled faith in order to model it to the church community. Accordingly, Jack Hayford exhorts pastors to understand the work of the Spirit of God in this regard.

> Worshipful song often leads to the beautiful exercise of Holy Spirit-assisted praise that, whether sung or spoken, is surely appropriate for my agenda as a shepherd in the Lord's presence as the day begins. Paul's frequent references to singing are probably telling us something about the apostle's secret to spiritual joy, notwithstanding the incredible burdens, trials, and pressures he faced. Paul said, "I will pray with the spirit, and I will also pray with the understanding. I will sing with the spirit, and I will also sing with the understanding" (1 Cor. 14:15). His stated action of the will deserves to be noted: "I *will* sing with the spirit. . . . I *will* sing with the understanding!"[28]

Fifth, *recognizing holiness as requisite to the Christian life* is the final characteristic in Wesley's vision for the church. The word "holiness" does not hold much currency or meaning for postmoderns, despite the fact that they need it desperately. Whatever word or words leaders may use to describe it, the function and meaning of holiness provides a key to unlocking meaning and fulfillment in the twenty-first-century church. If postmoderns use the term — and they rarely do — it is generally associated with fundamentalism, intolerance, and the religiously narrow-minded. Nevertheless, authentic holiness is a positive message. It is the message of

---

28. Jack Hayford, *Pastors of Promise* (Ventura, Calif.: Regal), p. 178.

redeeming love, the ability to overcome sin, and a means by which we separate from a cruel and despairing world without becoming insensitive to the needs or the people of that world.

Consequently, finding methods to disseminate the holiness message in a seemingly hostile cultural environment is a great challenge for pastors. Withdrawing from culture as an act of holiness is not the answer. Confronting the need for holiness while at the same time acknowledging the realities of culture is paramount, and does not mean we have surrendered or compromised our faith. Cultural and institutional barriers often frustrated Wesley's vision for the church, but he either adapted or found creative ways to overcome such barriers. Moreover, he did not compromise the call to holiness, but actually engaged it to bring change. While postmoderns may not fully grasp the meaning of holiness, they do understand many of the crucial concepts that relate to it. Accountability, being a change agent, personal responsibility, ethical living, love, and compassion are all part of the process of living life in a productive way. Likewise, leaders in the church today can illustrate and fill out the meaning of these ideas. This will in turn teach holiness in a context understandable to and adaptable by postmoderns.

Conclusion

The call to holiness is a call to change in the church. The question of how holiness works has confronted every generation of church leadership. Its application today is fundamental to building community. John Wesley's life and ministry provide timeless themes by which we can better understand how to build community in our socio-cultural context. His work continues to inspire pastors and church leaders to adapt these themes to meet the needs of the present. While postmodernism presents both challenges and opportunities, the message of holiness is a fresh word that brings life, wholeness, and healing. The works and structures may change, but the call "to be holy as I am holy"[29] is a standing invitation from God. And the local church is the best and most visible place for that message to find expression in the twenty-first century.

29. 1 Peter 1:16.

CHAPTER 12

Preaching as Charisma

JAMES EARL MASSEY

The way of a preacher with a sermon is marked out for him or her by two basic influences: nature and grace. The influence of nature is seen in the preacher's intellect, temperament, gifts, and training. The influence of grace is seen in how these natural factors are enlisted and enhanced by the touch of God. Sermons become charismatic when natural factors and spiritual conditioning together determine them, when they issue from one upon whom mercy and grace have been bestowed, granting humanity a set of special benefits through "the participant presence of God."[1] It was to this that Dietrich Bonhoeffer was pointing when he told his seminary students at Finkenwalde that "a sermon is only relevant when God is there. He is the One who makes its message concrete."[2]

Implicit in these two basic dimensions of preaching is the duality of the grand theme of holiness: nature and function. Holiness is both the essence of God's very nature and a description of his activity or function in salvation. In like manner, the preacher embodies this holiness as the ser-

1. See Wayne E. Oates, *Christ and Selfhood* (New York: Association Press, 1961), ch. V.

2. Dietrich Bonhoeffer, *No Rusty Sword: Letters, Lectures, and Notes 1928-1936*, ed. Edwin H. Robertson, trans. Edwin H. Robertson and John Bowden (New York: Harper and Row, 1965), p. 20. See also Eberhard Bethge, *Dietrich Bonhoeffer: Theologian, Christian, Contemporary*, ed. Edwin H. Robertson, trans. E. Mosbacher et al. (London: Collins, 1970), esp. pp. 361-63; Clyde E. Fant, *Bonhoeffer: Worldly Preaching* (Nashville: Thomas Nelson, 1975), p. 140.

mon is both an extension of his or her transformed nature as well as an activity of his or her surrendered function.

The charismatic nature of the preaching task is seen again and again in Scripture. This charismatic nature is a result of the preacher's proximity to God and his holiness, as well as the outflowing of the Holy Spirit effecting a divine grace through anointing. The New Testament explains the power and dignity of preaching under that apt phrase "anointed to preach" (Luke 4:18; Acts 10:38), linking together in vital fashion the service of preaching with the fact of prior selection by God to do so. Luke's interest in this theme is well-known,[3] and it is he who has preserved for us our Lord's own description of his direction and authority: "The Spirit of the Lord is upon me, because be has anointed me to preach . . ." (Luke 4:18). This characterization, quoted by Jesus from Isaiah 61:1-2, stands as something more than a comprehensive statement about his messianic uniqueness. It points out a requisite for the task of preaching. It reminds us that those who are sent to preach are first accredited for this service by the Holy Spirit. Peter understood this and referred once to "those who preached the good news to you through the Holy Spirit sent from heaven . . ." (1 Peter 1:12). This requisite of being "anointed to preach" is highlighted throughout the Acts of the Apostles, where we see a succession of witnesses at work spreading the Christian message, all of them qualified because they were possessed and anointed by God's Spirit. As for the book of Acts, F. F. Bruce has stated, "In all the book there is nothing which is unrelated to the Holy Spirit."[4] Christian sermons have no independent integrity or power; they find life and effectiveness only under the creative touch of God. The preacher and his or her sermon are the synergy of divine integration of condition and ability in the preacher — transformed by God's holiness. The New Testament sums up this fundamental, inclusive, and compelling gift in the descriptive words "charisma" and "charism."[5]

The concept of charismatic or anointed service reflects at least six distinct features which we experience through grace: (1) a sense of assertiveness by which to act; (2) a sense of being identified with divine will; (3) a perceived intensity because what is done relates to the highest frame of ref-

---

3. See C. K. Barrett, *The Holy Spirit and the Gospel Tradition* (London: S.P.C.K., 1954).

4. F. F. Bruce, *The Acts of the Apostles: The Greek Text with Introduction and Commentary* (Grand Rapids: Eerdmans, 1952), p. 30.

5. See *charisma*, by Hans Conzeman, and *chrisma*, by Walter Grundmann, in *Theological Dictionary of the New Testament*, ed. Gerhard Friedrich, trans. Geoffrey W. Bromiley (Grand Rapids: Eerdmans, 1974), vol. IX, pp. 402, and 572, respectively.

erence; (4) a sense of self-transcendence; (5) a kind of instinct for what is done; and (6) a knowledge that the deed is avowedly moral and religious in nature and reason, which is to say that the deed is traceable to God's prompting and power, and that it happens for his own reasons.

The word "charisma" is in common and widespread use in our time and it is even being used in quite secular references and connections. Students of sociology are familiar with the way Max Weber (1864-1920) analyzed and applied the concept of charisma in relation to sociopolitical causes and structures.[6] As one of the pioneers in advancing the subject and concerns of the sociology of religion, Weber worked seriously to trace the effects of religious beliefs within the wider social order. Weber commented extensively about the "charismatic figure" and his or her relation to the secular and spiritual order and institutions, seeing such a person as an agent in the process of breakthrough and morally ordered change. According to Weber's definition, "The term 'charisma' will be applied to a certain quality of an individual personality by virtue of which he is set apart from ordinary men and treated as endowed with supernatural, superhuman, or at least specifically exceptional powers or qualities."[7] The wideness of his definition enabled Weber to deal with the enlarged sphere of social life, but the distinctively religious connotations of his use of the term cannot be missed. Max Weber wrote as a specialist in religious studies and not merely from the secular perspective of a sociologist. Although Weber kept the religious notion clearly focused as he did his work, some who followed him did not; and in widening the term to apply to heroism, populism, social movements, and behavioral control techniques, they secularized its meaning and identified it with the notion of special leadership per se. A clear example of this kind of application appeared some years ago in a Daedalus Library book entitled *Philosophers and Kings: Studies in Leadership.*[8] Too, recently John Howard Schutz has discussed the problem of how that originally religious term has been secularized and its meaning widened to the point of abuses.[9]

6. See *Max Weber on Charisma and Institution Building,* ed. S. N. Eisenstadt (Chicago: University of Chicago Press, 1968). See also Max Weber, *The Sociology of Religion,* ed. and trans. Ephraim Fischoff (Boston: Beacon Press, 1963), esp. pp. 2-3, 46-47.

7. *Max Weber on Charisma and Institution Building,* p. 48.

8. *Philosophers and Kings: Studies in Leadership,* ed. Dankwart A. Rustow (New York: George Braziller, 1970), esp. pp. 1-32 and 69-94.

9. See John Howard Schutz, "Charisma and Social Reality in Primitive Christianity," *The Journal of Religion* 54:1 (January 1974).

The fact is that the concept of charisma relates us centrally to the moral and spiritual order. Although there are some features that are common to both religious and social leadership roles — projection, interplay between self and group, rapport, courageous action, aggressiveness, and authority, to name but a few, there are vast differences between the two. There are differences of values, goals, source and use of power, and the spirit of the persons involved. There is a vast difference between being an instrumental agent due to social demand and being an instrumental agent due to sacred anointing.

Our emphasis here is on the sermon as a charismatic instrument in the will of God. We are dealing with a guided and girded action called preaching, a happening in which nature and grace make claim upon each other to effect an end through speech that neither rhetorical nor sociological theory can fully explain. Anointing is integral to the very purpose of the sermon. In significant fashion the holy nature of God is finding expression in the transformed nature of the preacher and their resulting natural abilities being marshaled to a holy purpose.

Understood as a way of orienting hearers to an experience with God through truth, the sermon must open to the hearer's perception that which is on a transcendent level. The sermon must be anointed to bear the needed noetic quality, bestow authoritative knowledge, generate an awareness of awe, and help the hearer to perceive the religious dimension as an immediately real order.[10]

Paul was so mindful of this decisive mission of preaching that he wrote exultingly about the grace given to him to preach. Paul declared that he was called "to make all men see . . ." (Eph. 3:9a). In using the Greek word *phōtisai* here, Paul reveals something beyond the ordinary, meaning that in preaching he was concerned to go beyond mere informing or announcing. Paul preached to illuminate his listeners, heighten their level of consciousness, and grant contact with the transcendent. Such results demand the participating presence of God through his Spirit.[11]

It must be said, then, that charisma in preaching has to do with the

10. For further insight into these categories, see Ralph W. Hood Jr., "Religious Orientation and Experience of the Transcendent," *Journal for the Scientific Study of Religion* 12:4 (December 1973): 441-48.

11. S. F. D. Salmond has commented, "The verb φωτίσαι is more than διδάξαι or κερύξαι. It means to illuminate." *The Expositor's Greek Testament*, ed. W. Robertson Nicoll (Grand Rapids: Eerdmans, 1897), vol. III, p. 307.

God-given ability to project an awareness of God in connection with the presentation of biblical truth. Anointed preaching can effect a situation of "discernment-commitment," to use Ian T. Ramsey's phrase.[12] The sermon is an agency for "entailment." Entailment is the right word for what happens under anointed preaching because the fundamental end of the sermon is to guide the hearer in matching and fitting the Word of God to his or her life, indeed to ready him or her for living on God's terms.[13] The anointed preacher is an agent of mediated meaning, on the one hand, and mediated presence, on the other. It is this that makes the sermon more than mere speech.

1. *Anointed preaching therefore carries the hearer beyond the limited benefits of the preacher's personality and rhetorical abilities.* Anointing from God makes the preacher an agent of grace, a person furnished to point beyond self and to allow the holiness of God to break through with immediacy and authority in his or her words. One aspect of that holiness is God's otherness and the real awe of being confronted. It is an awe that is fear, but more than fear. It is a fascination, yet more than that.[14] It is an awareness of being before God, challenged, called to account — claimed. It is a sense of *kairos*, a special moment that is unique and individual.

2. *Such preaching also involves something more than enthusiasm, as popularly understood.* "Enthusiasm" has meant many things to many people, and the term has been used in connection with both worthy and unworthy experiences. It has been linked with celestial inspiration, poetic fervor, fancied inspiration, ardent feeling, ill-regulated feeling, irrational agitation and movement, ardent zeal, emotionalism, and so forth,[15] some of these states being too passionate to be rational and too individual to be trusted. Charisma in preaching has nothing to do with what is dark and ambiguous, however passionate and lively. Charisma has to do with mediated meaning and mediated presence, with both affective and intellectual levels

---

12. See Ian T. Ramsey, *Religious Language* (New York: Macmillan, 1963), esp. pp. 11-54.

13. I have borrowed the term "entailment" from J. L. Austin, who used it to explain the refinement we give to words in expanding their meanings, in adjusting them to fit new and different objects. See Mats Furberg, *Saying and Meaning: A Main Theme in J. L. Austin's Philosophy* (Totowa, N.J.: Rowman and Littlefield, 1971), esp. pp. 70-71, 166-67.

14. On this, see Rudolf Otto, *The Idea of the Holy,* ed. and trans. John W. Harvey, 2d ed. (London: Oxford University Press, 1950), esp. pp. 8-40.

15. On the varied history it has had as a word, see Susie I. Tucker, *Enthusiasm: A Study in Semantic Change* (Cambridge: Cambridge University Press, 1972).

of life being addressed. Preaching involves speech, and speech must convey and bestow meaning. Preaching is not divorced from feelings or emotions, but it is not directed primarily to them. Preaching at its best will have aliveness, interest, and excitement, but the "plus" element that makes it creative and convicting comes through neither the preacher's personal intensity nor the listener's rapt involvement but through the participant presence of God. It is true for the preacher today as for Zerubbabel of old, to whom the words were first directed, "Not by might, nor by power, but by my Spirit, says the LORD of hosts" (Zech. 4:6b).

3. *Nor should charisma be confused with communalism, which is but a sense of contagious engagement between preacher and people.* Hailing as I do from the Black Church tradition, in which a sense of community has helped to shape "black preaching," as it is called, I understand quite well the rich benefits for worship when preacher and congregation have achieved a sense of basic togetherness. This sense of communalism is a must particularly for the pastoral preaching task. But charisma in preaching carries the total group beyond mere social unity generated by common concern under the guidance of a common leader. Charisma conditions pastoral judgment and sharpens prophetic thrust. Charisma heightens the awareness level to a sense of participation with God, thus deepening the drama of worship. The essence of holiness is being like Jesus. Participation with God draws the hearer to Christ-likeness in fulfilling that message. Here again we see meaning and presence working together. It must always be so, because as Jesus explained it, "God is spirit, and those who worship him must worship in spirit and truth" (John 4:24). Spirit and word — presence and meaning: it is to these that charisma keeps both preacher and people linked.

Dr. Henry H. Mitchell has called attention recently to the relation in the Black Church tradition between the biblical concept of anointing and the common notion from ancient Africa of being possessed by deity."[16] In both traditions of belief there is a kind of claiming that is perceived. The claimed person is aware of a heightened purpose in what he does, while the people observe and acknowledge what happens to and through him. This tradition of possession carries the notion of being under divine influence, overwhelmed perhaps, but definitely being used by a higher order of meaning.

---

16. Henry H. Mitchell, *Black Belief: Folk Beliefs of Blacks in America and West Africa* (New York: Harper and Row, 1975), esp. pp. 136-52.

Black Church tradition carries the concern for possession by deity one step further in expecting the claim upon the preacher to become a claim upon those who hear and accept the message. In Black Church life, then, the preacher becomes the agent of contact with divine will and holiness. The preacher is understood to be a charismatic figure, and so is followed. It is this aspect of the Black Church tradition that accounts for the preacher's authority in the midst of the people, and that authoritative leadership is never greater than when the black preacher is guiding his or her people in a worship setting and speaking the Word from God. And since blacks consider worship to be the most fundamental experience and expression of the self and the community, the preacher is free in the sermon to deal with any and every aspect of life (birth, death, politics, economics, social relations, etc.) because he or she is expected to bring "a word from the Lord" about the living of life. The radicalism of black preaching is rooted in this freedom, and this freedom is grounded on the authority of the preacher as a possessed and claimed person.

Given this tradition of belief within which to live and work, a tradition almost parallel to that of the biblical prophetic order, the black preacher has usually given himself or herself to the preaching task with such abandon that a heritage of freedom and involvement continues to characterize Black Church worship. This worship freedom is not purely Christian in origin, related as it is to an ancient African belief in being possessed by the deity, but it does carry us right to the heart of why the spoken word is so vital in Black Church worship. It also explains why certain forms of body action are allowed and sometimes encouraged in that worship setting. The charisma needed for preaching relates to all this, but sometimes it is also required as a prophetic check on excesses. Anointing is needed not only by preachers who seek freedom to speak effectively in settings that are more formal and sometimes closed to spontaneity; it is needed as well to provide balance in settings that are otherwise open and free. In all instances of preaching there is the perennial need for anointing from God. Whatever the setting, whatever the worship style, whatever the background and prevailing concepts within the respective group, there is need for mediated meaning and mediated presence. The meaning does not always diminish or dim our background and concepts, but the presence helps us to sift them, understand them, accept and adapt them, and use them fruitfully without prejudice or pride. This means that ultimately we will not unwisely associate God with only one worship style, nor will we mistakenly associate him with only one people.

This next word is about the obvious — but it must be said: charisma fulfills itself only in relation to persons. Anointing is to benefit community, just as holiness is not a private matter. It is fulfilled and seen at its effective best in relation to persons. Paul was underscoring this when he commented, "To each is given the manifestation of the Spirit for the common good" (1 Cor. 12:7). Sermons must be prepared and preached with hearers in mind, and to be an effective agent of meaning and presence each sermon must bear the form and flavor of the personal.

The form and flavor of the personal is certainly evident when the preacher is known to be a person identified with God, a committed believer and faithful servant of the Word. Charisma attends those who have identified themselves with God and his will. Persons identified with the will of God are not afraid to be themselves or to use their gifts in God's honor. Their experience of charisma enables them to be active, assured, individuated, and assertive.

Long ago Thomas Carlyle argued eloquently for "an original man; not a secondhand, borrowing or begging man." He continued his comment, advising, "Let us stand on our own basis, at any rate! On such shoes as we ourselves can get. On frost and mud, if you will, but honestly on that; — on the reality and substance which Nature gives us, not on the semblance, on the thing she has given another than us!"[17]

Charismatic agents have always been able to stand on their own, use their own gifts, assert themselves with high warrant in a cause greater than their own lives. Willing to risk themselves under the influence of a great meaning, they become creative persons of social importance and characters of spiritual persuasion. They become integrative figures, leaders around whom people rally. Although a strong self-image and the ability to project oneself can be natural factors in the lives of some persons, charisma performs its indispensable ministry and accredits their identity in a still higher manner. Those who live unto God, fully committed, experience this, and those whom they serve can bear witness to it.

Respect for charisma has generated in some church circles an almost instinctive concern to preserve the good name and honor of the charis-

17. Thomas Carlyle, *On Heroes, Hero-Worship, and the Heroic in History,* ed. Archibald MacMechan (Boston: Ginn and Co., 1901), p. 206.

matic leader against even common criticisms. There are those anointed persons whose lives make others feel guilty of a kind of treason when their story is tampered with, or their faults isolated. Such individuated people, divinely gifted and committed, carry an atmosphere and become legendary. Carlyle once referred to "a few Poets who are accounted perfect; whom it were a kind of treason to find fault with."[18] Preachers with charisma are often "accounted perfect," but charisma must never be associated with faultlessness. Anointing from God is granted for specific services; it is not given to create legends or to build a person beyond his or her true size.

Every preacher must watch the contagion that he or she generates and must watch the basis on which that contagion grows. She must remain alert and forever separate and distinguish between self and service, and most especially between her opinions and God's Word.

There are some obvious dangers to church life when a charismatic person does not keep these distinctions in view. For one thing, the opinions of the preacher can sometimes become mandates by the sheer forcefulness of his personal presence and the flavor of his personal appeal. Church history is filled with instances when people became enamored of the power of charisma, and the end result was that the personal form and flavor were distorted and the effects of their service misapplied. Charismatic figures can distort and thwart what is personal when their opinions bind and constrict beyond the guidance of the Word. As for their opinions, charisma cannot make them more than they are, namely beliefs held and voiced with confidence but not yet tested nor positively proved. Church life is always endangered when opinions associated with charismatic leaders are accepted as final and binding. Pursuing the call to Christ-likeness, which is the essential element of the injunction to be holy, will mitigate this danger.

Sermons demand a surer foundation than personal opinion. The conclusions they voice must be biblically based. The applications they urge must be demonstrable in the light of the wisdom of Scripture. Sermons must be grounded on more than personal preference and must be free from personal prejudices. They must go beyond the collective opinion of the group one serves. The forces at work in a given group can be even more dangerous and erroneous than those at work in a single mind and heart. The Christian pulpit must not capitulate to popular notions of morals and

18. Carlyle, *On Heroes, Hero-Worship, and the Heroic*, p. 93.

ethics, nor must it yield to stereotyped views on race and social relations. To yield a prophetic word in favor of acceptable and popular prejudices is but to allow a configuration of chaos. Personal opinion — even of the charismatic leader — is not always right, and public opinion — even of the church in a given era — is not always wise.[19] Not only is charisma fulfilled in relation to persons, it is to be checked against biblical principles. This keeps the charismatic agent right, relevant, and regulated.

The responsible preacher will have opinions, as will anyone who thinks, but they should be checked against the Word before uttering them in a worship setting. The preacher will hear opinions, as will anyone who listens long to others, but they must be assessed in the light of the Word. The preacher will influence opinion, as will anyone in the social arena, but he or she should use the informing Word as the work is carried out. In this way the preacher can seek to guarantee that their appeal and authority serve more than the end of self-expression. She can thereby serve a purpose higher than herself — and larger than the group which looks to her as leader.

Given the purpose of anointing from God, namely to make the preacher an agent of mediated meaning and presence, it must be clearly understood that the charismatic thrust of the sermon is first evident in the sermon idea or insight. Preaching mediates meaning from the Word of God. Sermon charisma is granted to serve biblical meanings applied to human needs.

The chief end of a sermon is to make an informed, aroused, and God-committed person. Central to this end is the hearer's awareness of God in connection with a basic biblical insight addressed to his or her listening level and state of life. The shaping of such a sermon constitutes the preacher's undertaking, but the spirit and substance of that sermon must be rooted in God if understanding and insight are to be effected. Insight is the crucial concern in planning the sermon, for as Bernard J. F. Lonergan has well stated, "Once one has understood, one has crossed a divide."[20] This is true for both preacher and hearer. Once the preacher has gained insight into the textual meaning and its application, he or she has crossed the

---

19. See Martin E. Marty, *The Improper Opinion: Mass Media and the Christian Faith* (Philadelphia: Westminster Press, 1961), esp. pp. 65ff.

20. Bernard J. F. Lonergan, *Insight: A Study of Human Understanding* (New York: Philosophical Library, 1956), p. 6.

divide and can use the text for a sermon; once the hearer has heard and seen the holy insight addressed to him or her, he or she has crossed the divide and is responsible to its claim on the heart.

It is sometimes overlooked that preaching is essentially oral for reasons of greater impact through insight. True hearing is meant to allow (and force) a kind of seeing. The very word *idea* — whether from the Greek *eidon,* or "idea," or from the Latin *video* — has to do with seeing, perceiving, or experiencing something.[21] Intent on communicating, the God-anointed preacher will work wisely with words in seeking to mediate the insight from God's Word. Granting hearers an image of God's holiness as best seen in Christ-likeness is the best and central purpose of the preacher.

It is a well-known fact that we all tend to see more clearly when something is shown to us through striking speech, especially when the words heard are pictorial in suggestion. The sound itself becomes an inward event, and the meaning stands as part of the hearer's experience. The very act of preaching brings truth within the range of a hearer in order that he or she may see, understand, be aroused, and act. The words of the sermon must be planned to express and share biblical insight. Rooted as it is in God's Word, the insight will bear the signature of divine presence. It will also effect a definite psychic "How?" within the hearer that is spiritual in origin and purpose.

This kind of result is due, in part, to the very psychology of language itself. Quite beyond the meanings that words suggest and convey, language affects consciousness itself. Preaching relates speaker and hearer in a lively context where concepts, consciousness, and claim all go together. We all hear words that carry meanings which move us from the state of mere awareness to attitudes out of which action of some kind follows. Consciousness and meaning follow from hearing, but there is a deeper demand on us when a sense of claim is realized upon our being addressed. It is at this point that the effects of charisma in preaching become imperative. The self needs more than meanings to be fully aroused; the self also needs a sense of divine presence and longs for wholeness. The charisma that attends preaching not only declares meaning, it illuminates and conveys a

---

21. On the Greek terms, see Wilhelm Michaelis's article in *Theological Dictionary of the New Testament,* ed. Gerhard Friedrich, trans. Geoffrey W. Bromiley (Grand Rapids: Eerdmans, 1967), vol. V, pp. 315-43.

sense of claim. This aspect of preaching is a direct result of the participating presence of God through his Spirit. The Holy Spirit blesses the hearing occasion with effects far beyond the normal range of the psychology of language. Anointed preaching is always more than mere speech. It bears a realization of engagement with God.

It is important that preaching be anointed because the sermons we create are always less than the texts we use. The preparation and delivery of sermons always involve an inherent difficulty: how to break through the limitations of what is only human. That difficulty is overcome by appeal to a higher order. The answer is charisma, anointing from God. In the delivery of a sermon we must deal with the problem that what is being heard — and what is yet to be heard — is not there all at once; attention and patient listening are demanded. There must be something more at work than just a sense of logical flow to encourage interest in continued listening. With the delivery of every sermon we must deal with the "biology of time."[22] The sermon is never a whole thing as we are giving it; we give only a part at a time. This means that the hearing moment is so precarious that something more is needed for preaching besides words. Charisma solves this problem by granting a sense of presence and by quickening within the hearer a sense of promise of mediated meaning from the whole. The whole is important because the spoken sermon is only part of the process. It is not a complete thing by itself; it is an agency of meaning and presence.

Both listener and preacher undergo the experience of the sermon: the preacher as shaper of the words and style, the listener as the one alerted by its signals of meaning. Both preacher and listener share in the meaning and the presence. Both share in the vision of truth, and when both respect its message and accept its thrust, the time of hearing is experienced as reliable, qualitative, revelational, and integral.

Here is the secret of power in Christian witness, for preacher and people: Jesus, "that great Personality," continues with us in word and presence. He companions, leads, and speaks to us, always evoking emotion that spills over in praise and proclamation. True preaching is the sharing of his words and the mediation of his presence, through the anointing of his indwelling Spirit that hearers are aroused to respond to the call to be like him in holiness.

---

22. This expression has been used with reference to hearing music. See David Burrows, "Music and the Biology of Time," *Perspectives of New Music* (Fall-Winter 1972): 241-49.

APPENDIXES:
DESCRIPTIONS OF HOLINESS

What Is Holiness?

ROGER GREEN

I was a member of the Salvation Army's International Spiritual Life Commission that met in London in the late 1990s for five meetings of one week duration each. We were given the charge to look at every aspect of the Army's spiritual life, and, of course, gave a great deal of attention to holiness, our central doctrine. Regarding the doctrine of holiness, the commission first affirmed the teaching of holiness, and also sent out a challenge around the Army world. The affirmation read as follows:

> We affirm that God continues to desire and to command that his people be holy. For this Christ died, for this Christ rose again, for this the Spirit was given. We therefore determine to claim as God's gracious gift that holiness which is ours in Christ. We confess that at times we have failed to realize the practical consequences of the call to holiness within our relationships, within our communities and within our movement. We resolve to make every effort to embrace holiness of life, knowing that this is only possible by means of the power of the Holy Spirit producing his fruit in us.

The call read as follows:

> We call Salvationists worldwide to restate and live out the doctrine of holiness in all its dimensions — personal, relational, social and political — in the context of our cultures and in the idioms of our

day while allowing for and indeed prizing such diversity of experience and expression as is in accord with the Scriptures.

Allowing for various definitions of holiness that are rooted in the biblical text, I continue to find strength in a definition of holiness as a life of obedience, rooted in love, to the Great Commandment of our Lord — to love God and love our neighbor supremely. Samuel Logan Brengle in his work entitled *The Way of Holiness* wrote that "sanctification is to have our sinful tempers cleansed, and the heart filled with love to God and man." Obedience is the natural outcome of that love for God, and so we are compelled to love our neighbor also. Because holiness is corporate as well as personal, such obedience is to be manifested by the church as well as by individual believers.

Holiness as Praxis

Lisa L. Dorsey

The church is living in the midst of an age in which holiness is spoken of in a negative sense inasmuch as it encroaches on the rights of individuals. The church is subtly drawn into an individualistic morality that mirrors the world system, substituting true holiness for relative morality and causing a cheapening of God's grace. Hence this paper calls for holiness as praxis, which assumes an origin apart from the world system, a nature distinct from the cultures of the world, and a character that is pervasive with the power to draw nations unto the Lord. The Word becomes manifest in the character of the believer and it is this living Word in the believer that is read by men and women, drawing them to faith in God. This theme is an essential message throughout the Old and New Testaments.

In articulating a definition of holiness it is essential to dialogue about the biblical, theological, and historical constructs of holiness. This includes the origin, nature, and character of holiness; the work of Christ on the cross; the work of the Holy Spirit in the church and the missiological imperatives of holiness; and finally the eschatological hope of the consummation of all things. Historical and theological constructs must be articulated in light of their ultimate purpose in the life of the believer, in the Church as a whole.

In examining the origin, nature, and character of holiness it is essential to commence with the *imago Dei*. I posit that there are two natures of holiness, divine and human, and both are essential to the holiness journey. This duality is demonstrated throughout Scripture and is the basis for the tensions that existed in the early church as articulated in Pauline theology. The terminology "holiness journey" is helpful in articulating the progressive nature of holiness, which becomes perfected at Christ's appearance. God's people are to reflect a lifestyle that is distinctively different than that of the world. Although perfection, in the sense of God's perfection, is not obtained until Christ's return, there is a level of perfection that is obtainable to those who have been sanctified by the work of Christ on the cross and who are receiving the fullness of God's Spirit for this church era. The process of this continuing perfection is ignited by one's love for Christ and desire of someday seeing him face to face. The work of Christ on the cross is critical because it is there that God's holiness is revealed and made available to the believer. It is the internal work of Christ in the believer that allows him or her to become holy. One is able to discern the outward demonstration of this holiness (the outward manifestation of an inward work) through one's lifestyle, demeanor, and character (the work of the Holy Spirit in the believer manifested outwardly as the fruit of the Spirit), which can only be obtained through a true relationship with God. It is a way of life (in a most ontological sense) that the church has been called to live to bring others into the light.

The church is called to be the light and salt of the world. There is to be a distinct difference between the two (the church and the world) which entails the submitting of individual will and rights to the will and work of God. As the church perfects holiness and comes into the fullness of Christ, the Kingdom of God is advanced. To further explain this viewpoint it is necessary to revisit key biblical and theological themes surrounding the terms "holiness," "sanctification," "regeneration," "perfection," "ethical faith," and "God's love."

Based on a synthesis of the above constructs, the definition of holiness must be ontological in nature and practical in application, emulating the work of Christ in the believer for the purpose of expanding the Kingdom of God. Hence, holiness is an outward manifestation of the inward work of Christ in the believer for his sovereign purposes.

A Quick "Definition" of Holiness

CRAIG KEEN

"Holiness" means, in the first place, what is peculiar to God. It is God's separateness, difference, from the world. Insofar as it is a true otherness it is to be understood as God's qualitative distinction from all that God is not. However, at the same time this otherness is "defined" by the narratives of Scripture and the liturgy that constitutes the church.

The Old Testament accounts of the holy God fall into four broad literary groupings: priestly, prophetic, wisdom, and apocalyptic. All of these texts clarify the way God is holy by speaking at once of God's discontinuity from the world and of God's gathering inherently unholy creatures into God's holiness — particularly by God's making them enter into the manifestation of God's holiness in the world, i.e., they are glorified in the event of God's act of glorification in the world. One finds metaphors of "purity" (in complex ways setting certain things in the world apart from other things — stressing difference) and "justice" (clarifying the manner in which God's holiness is made manifest — i.e., glorified — in the world, viz., by caring for the weak, the stranger, the poor) and "personal adjustment" to God (marked by a kind of wisdom and faithfulness to God, steadfastness especially in suffering) and expectancy of a coming future revolution (God's inbreaking to make the world radically new).

In the New Testament these themes are radicalized — not in total discontinuity with the Old Testament, but in taking Old Testament themes to extreme excesses. Thus God's holiness is made manifest — glorified — in Jesus' suffering, death, damnation, i.e., where the old order had maintained that God could not be glorified. Thus God's holiness is a freedom for what is far gone from holiness. This is an apocalyptic vision which is oriented to the inbreaking of a radical other and the outpouring in that event of God's own life, it connects particularly with prophetic themes which call for a peculiar justice/righteousness, it is reminiscent of wisdom literature's call to faithfulness especially despite apparently conflicting evidence, and it looks to a God who is separate and calls for separateness — but all of this is taken way over the top, to the extent that one adhering to the old order would be profoundly tempted to offense.

The way of Jesus is the hallowing of life that is separated to a God who is love — and in loving the world calls upon the separate to be separated with God to the world. Thus the liturgy of the church is constantly moving Eucharistically from the world to the exalted crucified Jesus and from this Jesus to the world. All of time is understood thereby to be redeemed as witness is borne to the manifestation of God's holiness in Jesus. And "witness" was understood to be as bodily as Christ's declaration of the coming of God's reign. Thus martyrdom emerges — and is practiced in the early church in expectation of the day in which the believer would be called to bear witness to Christ in actual death (e.g., before Roman spectators) — and is practiced as a dimension of Eucharistic liturgy.

APPENDIX 4

Holiness

THOMAS A. NOBLE

For *Christians* the meaning of "holiness" is determined by the *Christian* God. This is the Lord whose story, told in *Holy* Scripture, is summed up in his name, "the Father, the Son, and the Holy Spirit." This God of grace liberated his people Israel from slavery and freely bound himself to them by covenant in order that through them he might liberate and *sanctify* all humankind and all creation. Yet he was the *Holy* One, "separate" from sin and sinners, and so had elected Israel to be a *holy* community, reflecting his *holiness.* He therefore spelled out for them in Torah the obligations of his covenant, instructing them how they must live, and appointed priests to offer sacrifices of atonement for them. Because of their perpetual sin and idolatry and social injustice, corporate and personal, they were eventually exiled from the land he had given them, but the Lord remained faithful to them in steadfast covenant love, and brought them back. He thus prepared the way to become one of them in Jesus of Nazareth, the *embodiment* of the *new* covenant, through which their inner hearts would be *purified.*

When the Word or Son of God was made flesh, united to all humankind as Jesus, he *sanctified* our human nature in his incarnation. He continued to *sanctify* human living by his obedience in the power of the *Holy* Spirit. The inner secret of his *holy* life was his loving relationship with his Father in the Spirit. In the Father's heart, then, revealed in Jesus, we see that the eternal *holiness* of God is not just to be seen negatively as "separation," but positively as *love.* "God is love," a tri-personal *koinonia* of interpersonal perfect love. *Holiness is pure and perfect love.* The self-sacrificing,

239

holy life of Jesus led all the way to the cross, where the old, dying, Adamic humanity, having been *sanctified* in his selfless and sinless life, was finally crucified, thus triumphing over the powers of evil. In his resurrection by the power of the *Holy* Spirit, he was vindicated by the Father, and he *perfected* in his own resurrection body the prototype of the new humanity, resplendent and glorious in *holiness*. Having ascended, he poured out at Pentecost upon the community of his followers that same Spirit by whose power he himself had first walked by faith along the Way of *Holiness*, the Way of the cross, so making it possible for us to follow him.

Our *sanctification* as members of Christ takes place within the community of the "new Israel," which is the church, his body. Although still in a fallen world and in fallen "flesh," and *not yet* in the resurrection body, by the Spirit we are *already* united to Christ in such a way as to share in his loving relationship with the Father. We are adopted into the loving *koinonia* which *is* the Triune God, Father, Son, and Holy Spirit. Christians, then, are those who are "born again" into the family of God, a new birth celebrated in the sacrament of baptism. They share in his vindication: they are justified through faith. They are given to share in his *perfected, holy* humanity within the *koinonia* of the church, celebrated and enacted in the sacrament of *Holy Communion*. For only within his *holy* church can *perfect love* be nurtured and flow outward to the world in mission and service. The initial *sanctification* of believers in regeneration produces an immediate effect on their thinking and willing and behavior, so that they no longer deliberately disobey him in outward act. By the poured-out Spirit, they have increasing victory in their thought-life over the remaining habitual pull to self-centered living and so, through testing, they develop in *holy* character. They engage in mission, *embodying* the message of the love of Christ.

As they grow in maturity and self-understanding and *holy* character, and as they are nurtured within the fellowship of the church, the community of *perfect love*, so they come to the point where they trust God to fill their hearts with his Spirit of love. From then on, as long as they continue to walk in the light, they are no longer divided in heart between love of God and love of the world and self, but serve him single-mindedly as the "pure in heart" with "perfect" (that is, wholehearted) love. But although *already* they no longer have the "*mindset* of the flesh," they are *not yet* in the resurrection body of the age to come, but in the cracked "clay jars" of the mortal body. They still live as fallen creatures sharing in the natural, mortal, fallen flesh of a fallen world. Correspondingly, they still face temptation, they are still very conscious of how far they fall short, and they still must seek daily forgiveness for their failures and failings. But they look for the day of his coming, when, in the power of the Spirit, Christ will offer up the Kingdom to the Father and God will be all in all. They look expectantly for the resurrection of the body, when they will be like him. They await the final *perfecting* of the *holiness* of the people of God as all creation is redeemed and *sanctified*. Then indeed, in the new creation, the community of Christ will reflect fully the *holiness* of God, namely, the perfect interpersonal love of the *holy* community of the Triune Lord.

What Is Holiness?

Lynn Thrush

We derive the meaning of holiness, rather than describe an independent object. The word begins to be defined when we know the source from which it springs, or the entity with which it is identified. Holiness is properly identified with God: "I will show my greatness and my holiness" (Ezek. 38:23). Holiness is connected to the very positive terms, such as "majestic" and "splendor" (Ps. 29:2). Holiness is contrasted to that which is profaned (Ezek. 36:22-23) and to that which is unclean (Lev. 11:44).

Holiness as a noun is best understood as a gerund, that is, as a noun derived from a verb. Holiness is a description of God or a person or thing because of action done, or as the result of a prior action (2 Cor. 7:1; Eph. 4:24). Thus, as a description related to activity, action, or behavior, holiness is not static; it resists being defined as a state of being or attainment. Holiness, then, is comprehended in the life, behavior, and thinking of the disciple.

The opposite of holiness is that which is adulterous or mixed. Holiness is unmixed. God is love, and there is no admixture of anything other than love within him. God is other-oriented, and there is no admixture of selfish behavior in him. Jesus everywhere saw an adulterous generation, a culture of mixed loyalties. Jesus wants no admixture of loyalties in his disciples.

Holiness should not fundamentally be described by that which ought not to be present, namely, sin. Such a negative, passive and reactionary inversion of holiness assures that holiness is taught in terms of what ought not to be. Rather, holiness is the good character of God unmixed by any shadow of darkness. The love of God and the fruit of the Spirit depicted in unmixed intention and action go a long way in describing holiness. The relational dimensions of Romans 12:1-2 and Ephesians 3:19 call all persons to transformation of life and fullness of God, holiness working out in the disciple's life as an ongoing journey of yielding to God and growing in grace.

Acknowledgments

The idea that any book could be written without a great deal of help from many people is a myth. To say that this particular book is the result of great collaboration and support from many is an understatement. This volume owes its very existence to dozens of highly competent and deeply committed leaders.

From the outset of the effort, the leaders of ten denominations saw the possibilities for partnership in a fresh articulation of this transforming message. They committed themselves, their churches, and their best leaders to the task. Without the following denominational leaders, the very source for the content of this book would not be possible:

The Salvation Army — Tod Bassett & Israel Gaither
Brethren in Christ — Warren Hoffman
Church of God, Anderson — Ron Duncan
Free Methodist Church — Roger Haskins & David Kendall
Church of the Nazarene — Jesse Middendorf
Shield of Faith — Henry Alexander
International Church of the Foursquare Gospel — Jack Hayford
Church of God in Christ — George McKinney
Christian & Missionary Alliance, Canada — Franklin Pyles
International Pentecostal Holiness — James Leggett

Each of these denominations designated up to three scholar-leaders to meet together over a four-year period. At each event those 30-40 people discussed and reflected thoughtfully and prayerfully on the papers presented there. The synergy of spirit and common commitment that emerged gave rise to the chapters of this book, which began as presentations to the total group. Many of the participants' names appear here. Others were equally involved in the usual give-and-take that accompanies this kind of group effort. All of these participants have shared their wisdom, time, and talent to give us a powerful book that reflects Christ well and will impact the minds of leaders for decades to come.

A great debt of gratitude is owed to America's Christian Credit Union. From the earliest days ACCU and especially its president, Mendell Thompson, has affirmed the message and the ongoing vision of the Wesleyan Holiness Consortium. Because of their consistent support, this book as one of the outcomes is now a reality. Although one might first wonder what interest a credit union may have in such happenings, you don't have to talk to any of the board or officers long before their interest in holiness becomes very apparent. ACCU has been a consistent and unflagging blessing, especially in the form of staff member Fawn Imboden, whose administrative help over the last four years has allowed the Consortium to grow and this book to be published.

Of course, a lot of thinking and writing would be of little use unless someone saw the dream and ventured in faith to put it into book form. Eerdmans has captured that passion and we are deeply grateful for the faith they express in this message and in those who will read and be influenced by it to the glory of God. From the beginning, Bill Eerdmans affirmed the work as being consistent with his own commitment to theological clarity, unity in the church, and church leaders finding their voice for a new day.

I am thankful for all of these people, and mostly for the gracious nudges of the Holy Spirit along the way. Without a doubt this is an effort that is traceable back to God alone. To God's glory and for Kingdom purposes we have worked and now commend this effort to you.

Kevin W. Mannoia
February 2008

Contributors

Editors

Kevin W. Mannoia

Kevin W. Mannoia is chair of the Wesleyan Holiness Consortium. He is also professor of ministry and serves as chaplain at Azusa Pacific University. He has served as dean of the School of Theology at APU, president of the National Association of Evangelicals, bishop of the Free Methodist Church of North America, and superintendent in two regional districts of his denomination. He is a graduate of Roberts Wesleyan College (B.A.), Trinity Evangelical Divinity School (M.Div.), and the University of North Texas (Ph.D.). He has authored six books, including *15 Characteristics of Effective Pastors, Church 2K — Leading Forward,* and *The Integrity Factor,* as well as many articles. He and his family make their home in Southern California. He maintains a web site at http://www.kevinmannoia.com

Don Thorsen

Don Thorsen is professor of theology and chair of advanced studies in the Graduate School of Theology at Azusa Pacific University. He has numerous publications, including the following books: *The Wesleyan Quadrilateral: Scripture, Tradition, Reason, and Experience as a Model of Evangelical Theology, An Exploration of Christian Theology,* and *Theological Resources*

246

for Ministry. He has served in editorial positions with *Christianity Today, Christian Scholar's Review,* and *Light and Life.* He is a graduate of Stanford University (B.A.), Asbury Seminary (M.Div.), Princeton Seminary (Th.M.), and Drew University (Ph.D.). His scholarly and ecumenical involvements include the Faith and Order Commission, Word Made Fresh, and the Wesleyan Theological Society.

Contributing Authors

Jim Adams earned the Ed.D. in higher education leadership from the University of Southern California. He is the executive director of the Center for Global Learning and Engagement at Azusa Pacific University. He has served in various ministerial capacities in the Foursquare Church.

Cheryl Bridges Johns earned the Ph.D. from Southern Baptist Theological Seminary. She is currently professor of Christian formation and discipleship at the Church of God Theological Seminary in Cleveland, Tennessee. She is a leading Pentecostal ecumenist and has served on the executive committee of the Association of Theological Schools.

Barry Callen holds the D.Rel. from Chicago Theological Seminary in Christian social ethics and the Ed.D. from Indiana University in educational administration. He is an editor for Anderson University Press and the *Wesleyan Theological Journal,* and is currently special assistant to the general director of Church of God Ministries. He is the author of over thirty books, and a leader of a large ministry to AIDS orphans in southern Africa.

Lisa L. Dorsey holds a doctorate in public administration from the University of La Verne. She is currently pursuing a Ph.D. in practical and systematic theology from Fuller Theological Seminary. She is the co-founder and co-pastor of Lifeline Fellowship Christian Center and the Lifeline Community Services and Economic Development Corporation. Lisa is also the cofounder and dean of Lifeline Academy, which is a part of her church ministry.

Roger Green earned the Ph.D. from Boston College in theology. He is professor and chair of biblical and theological studies at Gordon College in Wenham, Massachusetts, and also Terrelle B. Crum Chair of Humanities there. Since he is a representative of the Salvation Army, his published works are primarily on the history and theology of the Salvation Army.

Craig Keen earned the Ph.D. degree in philosophy of religion and theology from Claremont Graduate University. He is professor of systematic theology at Azusa Pacific University. He is the author of the forthcoming *After Crucifixion: The Promise of Theology,* an introduction to the discipline of embodied theological discourse.

Jon Huntzinger holds the Ph.D. in biblical studies from Fuller Theological Seminary. He is professor of Bible and chair of pneumatology at the King's College and Seminary in Van Nuys, California. He serves the Foursquare denomination through teaching and is New Testament editor for the *Spirit-Filled Life New Study Bible.*

David W. Kendall earned the Ph.D. in biblical studies with an emphasis in New Testament from Union Theological Seminary in Virginia. Currently he is lead bishop of the Free Methodist Church of North America. He is author of *God's Call to Be Like Jesus.*

William Kostlevy earned the Ph.D. in history at Notre Dame University. He is associate professor of history and political science at Tabor College. He also served as editor of the *Historical Dictionary Holiness Movement.*

Diane Leclerc earned the Ph.D. from Drew University. She is currently professor of historical theology and homiletics at Northwest Nazarene University and is president of the Wesleyan Theological Society. As a minister in the Church of the Nazarene, her areas of writing and presentations include the nineteenth-century Holiness movement.

George McKinney holds the Ph.D. from California Graduate School and degrees from Oberlin School of Theology. He serves as bishop of the Church of God in Christ in the Southern California jurisdiction. His several books focus upon religion and community service, and he served as senior editor of the *African American Devotional Bible.*

James Earl Massey holds degrees from Oberlin Graduate School of Theology and Asbury Theological Seminary. He has served as dean of the chapel and university professor of religion at Tuskegee University. He has written in the fields of preaching and New Testament and has filled distinguished pulpits around the world. As a minister in the Church of God, he has served Anderson University as campus pastor, professor of New Testament and preaching, and dean of the School of Theology.

Thomas A. Noble holds degrees in modern history and politics and in Christian dogmatics and holds the Ph.D. from New College in Edinburgh in the Greek Fathers. He is professor of theology at Nazarene Theological Seminary in Kansas City and supervisor of research at Nazarene Theological College in Manchester.

Jonathan S. Raymond earned the Ph.D. in cross-cultural social psychology from the University of Kentucky. Currently he serves as president of Trinity Western University in Langley, British Columbia.

C. Stevens Schell earned the D.Min. from Fuller Theological Seminary. He is pastor of Northwest Foursquare Church in Federal Way, Washington, and serves as chair of the Foursquare Commission on Doctrine and Licensing. He has served as a church planter and as a teacher at LIFE Bible College in the area of biblical studies.

Howard A. Snyder earned the Ph.D. at the University of Notre Dame in historical theology. As a Free Methodist minister, he has been a pastor, a missionary, and a professor at Asbury Seminary. Currently he is professor of Wesley studies at Tyndale Seminary in Toronto. His many books focus upon missiology, church renewal, and church history.

Lynn Thrush earned the D.Min. from Gordon-Conwell Theological Seminary. He is senior pastor of the Gateway Community Church in Chino, California, and an adjunct professor at Azusa Pacific University. In his service within the Brethren in Christ Church he serves on the denominational Equipping for Ministry Task Force and was one of three writers of the Brethren in Christ Articles of Faith and Doctrine.

Kenneth L. Waters Sr. earned the Ph.D. in New Testament from Fuller Theological Seminary. Currently he is professor of New Testament at Azusa Pacific University. He is an ordained elder and former pastor in the California-Pacific Conference of the United Methodist Church, and has 29 years of pastoral experience.